PRAISE FOR *BREAK*

It is rare to read such great insights on the future of banking, written in plain English, from a lifetime banking practitioner. Joseph, as co-founder and joint leader of Judo Bank, will deliver considerable opportunities for clients in the huge and unsatisfied small to mid-sized banking market.

JOHN DAHLSEN, FORMER ANZ DIRECTOR

This book makes a powerful argument for professionalism in banking and a reminder that banking needs to always focus on long-term outcomes for customers, the bank and the economy.

CHRIS WHITEHEAD, CEO AT FINSIA

This is a very worthwhile, well-informed book, by an experienced banker.

PROFESSOR ALLAN FELS AO
FORMER CHAIR, AUSTRALIAN COMPETITION AND CONSUMER COMMISSION

Healy brings decades of experience in senior roles in the UK, New Zealand and Australian banks. He asks fundamental questions that demand answers, and places responsibility squarely where it belongs: with bank senior management and boards of directors. Breaking the Banks focuses on the fundamental fissures in Australian banking and how to reconceive and rebuild the banks to fulfil their original purpose.

PROFESSOR THOMAS CLARKE, UTS BUSINESS

Joseph Healy is a well-seasoned banker, academic and entrepreneur but, most importantly, a thinker. Credentials that make this book very timely and a key contribution to the current and ongoing debate on the evolving financial system.

JOHN FRASER, FORMER SECRETARY TO THE TREASURY

Joseph Healy has written a blueprint for building a sustainable future for ethical banking in Australia. His unique mix of experience and expertise has resulted in a compelling book that should be a 'must-read' for anyone with an interest in Australian banking.

ANTHONY THOMSON, FOUNDER, METRO BANK, ATOM BANK AND 86400

It is great to read a book on banking and the failures of this essential part of our economy that is knowledgeable, fact-based and courageous. The book is a well-written mix of history, research, and personal experience at very senior levels of the industry. This is an essential read for all people interested in what went wrong with the banks and what has to change.

KATE CARNELL AO, AUSTRALIAN SMALL BUSINESS OMBUDSMAN

Healy brings refreshing moral clarity to the question of what's gone wrong with Australian banks. His insights lay the foundations for customers and citizens to demand real change.

DR LESLIE CANNOLD, ETHICIST

Joseph Healy's depth of experience reveals the skills and judgement required for the banking system to work well for customers and professionals. No amount of regulation will replace the need for a good banker to run a bank.

DAVID MURRAY AO

Courageous, ambitious, practical and hugely insightful. Joseph Healy combines his three decades of experience as a seasoned banker with academic rigour to cut straight to the heart of the most difficult issues. It is a must-read for all bankers, industry leaders, company directors, regulators and – especially – concerned citizens. The important insights contained in this book will reverberate beyond antipodean shores.

MARK LAWRENCE, FORMER CHIEF RISK OFFICER, ANZ BANKING GROUP

WHAT WENT WRONG *with* AUSTRALIAN BANKING?

BREAKING *the* BANKS

JOSEPH HEALY
CO-FOUNDER *of* JUDO BANK

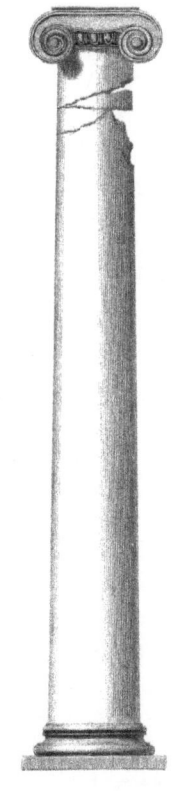

IMPACT PRESS

BREAKING THE BANKS
WHAT WENT WRONG WITH AUSTRALIAN BANKING?

JOSEPH HEALY

First published in 2019 by Impact Press
an imprint of Ventura Press
PO Box 780, Edgecliff NSW 2027 Australia
www.venturapress.com.au

10 9 8 7 6 5 4 3 2 1

Copyright © Joseph Healy 2019

All rights reserved. No part of this book may be reproduced or transmitted in any form or by any means, electronic or mechanical, including photocopying, recording or by any other information storage retrieval system, without prior permission in writing from the publisher.

ISBN: 978-1-920727-95-6 (paperback)
ISBN: 978-1-920727-94-9 (ebook)

A catalogue record for this book is available from the National Library of Australia

Cover and internal design by Deborah Parry

Printed and bound in Australia by Griffin Press of Ovato Book Printing

The paper in this book is FSC® certified. FSC® promotes environmentally responsible, socially beneficial and economically viable management of the world's forests.

TO MY FAMILY

CONTENTS

ABOUT THE AUTHOR *ix*

LIST OF FIGURES AND TABLES *xi*

LIST OF ACRONYMS AND ABBREVIATIONS *xii*

PREFACE: WHY I WROTE THIS BOOK *xvii*

INTRODUCTION *1*

1 THE BANKING SYSTEM *57*

2 SOCIAL LICENCE AND PURPOSE *107*

3 THE DECLINE OF PROFESSIONALISM IN BANKING *135*

4 THE DEMISE OF THE CRAFT IN SME BANKING *159*

5 THE DEMISE OF RISK MANAGEMENT IN BANKING *187*

6 THE ROLE OF LEADERSHIP AND CULTURE *221*

7 THE ROLE OF THE BOARD OF DIRECTORS *249*

8 MOVING FORWARD AND LOOKING BACK *287*

EPILOGUE *315*

ACKNOWLEDGEMENTS *321*

APPENDIX I –
WHAT DO BANKS DO? *323*

APPENDIX II –
BANKER RISK ASSESSMENT TEST *324*

APPENDIX III –
PRINCIPLES OF CREDIT RISK MANAGEMENT *335*

APPENDIX IV –
THE THREE LINES OF DEFENCE FRAMEWORK *340*

APPENDIX V –
ROLE SPECIFICATION FOR A BANK DIRECTOR *343*

APPENDIX VI –
THE ESSENTIALS OF GOOD BANKING *346*

BIBLIOGRAPHY *347*

INDEX *353*

ABOUT THE AUTHOR

JOSEPH HEALY is a 35-year career international banker who has worked for six banks across several markets. He is a co-founder and co-CEO of Judo Bank, a challenger bank focused on the SME market.

Joseph was a director of Football Federation Australia (FFA) from 2010–18 and he is an Adjunct Professor at the University of Queensland Business School. He is the author of two books: *Corporate governance and wealth creation* (2003) and *Chinese firms going global – can they succeed?* (2018). Joseph is also a member of the advisory council of World Vision Australia and a member of the Australian Institute of Company Directors.

He holds an MA in Contemporary Chinese Studies, an MBA, an MSc in Finance, an MSc in International Management in China, and a Master's in Banking. As part of his commitment to lifelong learning, Joseph is completing an MSc in Psychology and Neuroscience of Mental Health at the Institute of Psychiatry, Psychology & Neuroscience (IoPPN), Kings College, London.

He is a member of the Chartered Institute of Bankers in Scotland, a Fellow of FINSIA, and holds five international football caps for Scotland at youth level.

LIST OF FIGURES AND TABLES

FIGURES

CHAPTER 1
    Figure 1: Bank ROE comparisons
    Figure 2: Trust deficit
    Figure 3: Banking trust index

CHAPTER 2
    Figure 4: Bank lending – household and business
    Figure 5: Major bank risk weights summary
    Figure 6: Australian banks addicted to property
    Figure 7: Global household debt
    Figure 8: Australian banks loan losses
    Figure 9: Credit risk appetite discipline
    Figure 10: Ratio of household debt to bank profits in Australia
    Figure 11: New lending landscape

CHAPTER 4
    Figure 12: SME bank trust index
    Figure 13: Primary business advisor
    Figure 14: Reasons to not choose a banker
    Figure 15: Barriers to accessing credit
    Figure 16: Bank similarity perception
    Figure 17: Survey results of SME finance enquiries

TABLES

CHAPTER 1
Table 1: Australia number one for bank profits
Table 2: Enforceable undertakings (2013–18)

CHAPTER 2
Table 3: Bank market share
Table 4: Standardised credit risk weightings
Table 5: Household debt levels – international benchmarks

CHAPTER 4
Table 6: Framework for evaluating Four C's – Transactional model
Table 7: Framework for evaluating Four C's – Relationship model

CHAPTER 8
Table 8: Example framework for evaluating directors and boards

LIST OF ACRONYMS AND ABBREVIATIONS

ABA	Australian Bankers Association
ABS	Australian Bureau of Statistics
ACCC	Australian Competition and Consumer Commission
ADI	authorised deposit-taking institution
AFC	Australian financial crisis
AI	artificial intelligence
AICC	Australia-Israel Chamber of Commerce
AIG	American International Group
ANZ	Australia and New Zealand Banking Group
APRA	Australian Prudential Regulatory Authority
ASIC	Australian Securities and Investment Commission
BDD	bad and doubtful debts
BB	business bank
BBA	British Bankers Association
BBSW	bank bill swap rate
BCBS	Basel Committee of Bank Supervisors
BCG	Boston Consulting Group
BEAR	Banking Executive Accountability Regime
BFO	Banking and Finance Oath

BIS	Bank for International Settlements
BOQ	Bank of Queensland
bps	basis points
CAPM	Capital Asset Pricing Model
CBA	Commonwealth Bank of Australia
CBD	central business district
CCRC	credit card repayment cover
CDO	collateral debt obligation
CDS	credit default swaps
CEO	Chief Executive Officer
CFMP	Customer First Management Process
CFO	Chief Financial Officer
CIB	Corporate and Institutional Banking
CIS	Customer-led Innovation Strategy
Citi	Citibank
CRO	Chief Risk Officer
CSR	corporate social responsibility
C-suite	Senior executives reporting to the CEO
CSV	Citicorp Scrimgeour Vickers
CV	curriculum vitae
EAD	Exposure at default
EBITDA	earnings before interest, tax, depreciation and amortisation
ELP	Enterprise Leadership Program
ERM	enterprise risk management
ESG	environmental, social and governance
EVA	economic value added
EY	Ernst & Young
FCA	Financial Conduct Authority (UK)
Fed	Federal Reserve (US central bank)
FINSIA	Financial Services Institute of Australasia

LIST OF ACRONYMS AND ABBREVIATIONS

Four C's	character (reputation and track record), capacity (cash flow), capital (equity) and collateral (security)
FSA	Financial Services Authority (UK)
FSB	Financial Stability Board
GDP	gross domestic product
GE	General Electric
GFC	global financial crisis
GP	general practitioners
HBOS	Halifax Bank of Scotland
HEM	household expenditure measure
HR	human resources
HSBC	Hongkong and Shanghai Banking Corporation
ICI	Imperial Chemical Industries
IMF	International Monetary Fund
LBS	London Business School
LGD	loss given default
LIBOR	London Interbank Offered Rate
LMI	lender mortgage insurance
LTV	loan-to-value ratio (same as LVR)
LVR	loan-to-value Ratio
M&A	mergers and acquisitions
MBA	Master of Business Administration
MBS	mortgage backed securities
MIT	Massachusetts Institute of Technology
NAB	National Australia Bank
NED	non-executive director
NPAT	net profit after tax
O&M	Organisation & Methods
OECD	Organisation for Economic Co-operation and Development

OWD	originate-warehouse-distribute
PD	probability of default
PEF	Performance Evaluation Framework
PPI	Payment Protection Insurance
PR	public relations
PRA	Prudential Regulation Authority
PwC	PricewaterhouseCoopers
QC	Queen's Counsel
RAS	risk appetite statement
RBA	Reserve Bank of Australia
RBNZ	Reserve Bank of New Zealand
RBS	Royal Bank of Scotland
ROE	return on equity
RWA	risk-weighted asset
SDA	Scottish Development Agency
SEC	Securities and Exchange Commission (US)
SME	small-to-medium-sized enterprise
SMSF	self-managed superannuation fund
TSR	Total Shareholder Return
UNSW	University of New South Wales
VAR	value-at-risk

PREFACE: WHY I WROTE THIS BOOK

THIS is a book about banks and banking in Australia, with relevance also to New Zealand given the strong similarities between the two banking markets – the Australian banks lend nine out of every ten dollars borrowed in New Zealand. The primary audience I have in mind is the general reader interested in the role of banks in society. The book will appeal to those with knowledge of and interest in banking, at a practitioner, governance and policy level. Students interested in banking will find this useful supplementary reading both at undergraduate and postgraduate level. This book will also be of value to future generations of bankers.

I have sparingly sprinkled the book with academic references where I think they might be helpful in providing insights and reflection points, but this is not a book for those in search of scholarly rigour. It is a book that will provide readers with a framework for thinking about the banking industry we have and the one we deserve. The book does not assume any expertise or knowledge of economics, finance or banking. I have tried to keep jargon to a minimum and where it is unavoidable, then it is explained. Banking is an industry that has done a masterful job in creating its own jargon-built language barrier, which can feel quite impenetrable to outsiders.

This is a book that I have been thinking about writing for some time. It has genuinely not been motivated by any event such as the much-publicised Royal Commission into misconduct in the banking, superannuation and financial services industry (2019) (the Royal Commission) or the Productivity Commission inquiry report, *Competition in the Australian financial system* (2018) (the Productivity Commission), though both have been a rich source of material. In this book, I also refer to the APRA, Prudential Inquiry into the Commonwealth Bank of Australia (2018), which highlights governance and cultural problems faced by that bank, and to the Financial Systems Inquiry (2014), chaired by David Murray (the Murray Inquiry).

My motivation in writing this book has more to do with the issues and trends that I have seen in the industry over time, which unsurprisingly have mirrored some of the factors that caused much of the disappointing revelations from the Royal Commission and the Productivity Commission reports (and the APRA report). At its core, these issues and trends have seen the banking industry progressively develop a culture and behave in a manner which is inconsistent with the *social licence* that should govern its activities and incompatible with the professional standards that society should reasonably expect. These outcomes are not because of natural evolutionary forces – though there have been evolutionary forces at play such as computerisation (and digitalisation), globalisation and industrialisation – but largely as a result of a series of *miscalculations* at public policy, regulatory and corporate governance levels specific to the banking industry. I explore these miscalculations throughout this book.[1]

---

1   I use the term *miscalculation* throughout this book to mean a calculated error of judgement, instead of a *mistake*, which can often be due to inexperience. In my mind the difference is more than semantics.

This book goes well beyond the scope of the Royal Commission and the Productivity Commission reports. In a holistic way, it considers the factors that drove the changes in the banking industry, the cause and effect, and in doing so maps out the change agenda essential to restore confidence and trust. An ambitious but worthy goal.

The APRA inquiry into the Commonwealth Bank of Australia (CBA) highlighted issues that are evident, to a greater or lesser extent, in some if not all the other major banks and reflects a high level of 'sameness' among these so-called 'four pillar' institutions. CBA presents a useful case study but as it will become apparent throughout this book and particularly in the case of NAB, it would be unfair to suggest that they are an outlier; banking in Australia (and in New Zealand) is an industry where the banks like to operate in a pack, true to the oligopoly nature of the industry. CBA and NAB get many more citations in this book than the other banks. There is no bias intended, it simply reflects the fact that they have both tended to create significantly more headlines and have presented much more material and insights into the public domain.

Although much has been made of the Royal Commission, it is important to remember that it was an inquiry narrow in its scope and operated within a constraining time frame, at the request of the major banks.[2] It was never intended to be a comprehensive root and branch review of the banking industry. It inevitably concentrated on what was wrong. It tended to read critically with a bias in its focus on Retail/Personal Banking and Wealth Management. In my analysis, I have sought to be balanced and to keep opinions to a minimum, using extensive reference to reported events to support interpretation, insights and conclusions. It is as

---

2   Long S., 'This letter from the big banks helped shape the royal commission', *ABC News*, 5 February 2019, <https://www.abc.net.au/news/2019-02-05/big-banks-ask-government-to-call-short-royal-commission-letter/10778928>.

easy, as it is mischievous, to fall into the trap of sensationalising matters and creating a sense of a utopian world of right and wrong; of black and white, of good and bad. Harsh judgement on bank conduct, though not to be excused, should equally not be thought of as binary. The reality often is that cause and effect are multidimensional, multilayered and complex. To tarnish all, equally vigorously, with the same brush is unfair. This is particularly true of the thousands of hardworking bank employees who earn a fair wage with a very modest (if any) bonus, and do their best, often in challenging conditions, in an industry where job security is not what it once was. The issues within the banking industry are fundamentally leadership ones – senior management and boards of directors. The Royal Commission was, at the very least, the distressed sound of the 'canary in the coalmine'.

In weaving this book together, there are four threads or themes that are central to its thesis. The themes are Path Dependency, Financialisation, Market Failure and Social Licence. *Path Dependency* is based on the premise that the future of the major banks is shaped by their history and that their future is a continuation of their historical and current trajectory. Left to their own devices, given deep-rooted institutional inertia, there will be no meaningful change; they simply cannot change. The cultural concrete has set.

Financialisation denotes a situation where the financial economy becomes disconnected from the real economy in motivation, size and influence. It is a term sometimes used to describe the growth in financial capitalism, loosely connected to activity in the real economy. It also characterises the 'sales' culture that has come to plague the industry. As the financial economy grows, it exerts undue influence on the real economy – the tail wags the dog. In fairness, the scale of financialisation that occurred in the United Kingdom (UK) and the United States (US) markets is not reflected in the Australian market to the same degree. While I would characterise the major change in the Australian market as the *retailisation* or *productisation* of the banking industry, I am going to stay with the descriptor of financialisation as the issues are the same.[3]

Market Failure is a concept I use many times in this book. It is an important concept that describes a situation in which the allocation of capital in a free market is not efficient and can lead to a net loss to the economy and society. That market failures can and do happen is central to the thesis in this book.

Social Licence is another central theme. By social licence I mean the level of acceptance by a community of an organisation's activities and conduct. Different organisations can have specific social licences and the importance of a social licence can vary among industries; in domestic banking it is a central idea, critical to the legitimacy of the banks given the unique privileges they enjoy.

SOME CONTEXT

I set the context for the book by walking through my own 35-year career, not because of some desire to feed an ego in need of nourishment but rather by using my journey to describe and illustrate how the industry has evolved, to provide important contrast and to highlight where the industry has, in my opinion, miscalculated, often in quite serious ways. The purpose in taking this approach will become clear and hopefully helpful to readers as progress is made through the book. I should make it clear that the views in this book are strictly personal and should not necessarily be read to represent the views of my employer, Judo Bank.

History tells us that banking is *not* an industry that learns much from its past miscalculations; bank management and boards are

---

3   Financialisation is not an ideology in the way that capitalism is; it is more a phenomenon in the same way that globalisation is. It can be controlled and channelled.

good at convincing themselves that 'this time is different' and there is evidence of this miscalculation today. The truth is that it rarely ever is different when it comes to banking and economics. This amnesia risk is exaggerated in Australia because it has been a very long time since there has been a major economic correction, and therefore the collective industry memory lacks the knowledge and experience of what can go wrong.

In this book, I frequently draw parallels between the Australian and British banking systems. Having worked in and knowing both well, there are uncanny similarities, though the scale of the miscalculations made by British banks such as RBS, HBOS and Barclays have no parallel in Australia (at least that can be said at the time of writing).

PRE-BIG BANG

I began my career at Lloyds Bank in London in 1983. My first two years were spent in the Organisation & Methods (O&M), which looked at workflows, controls and operational risks and efficiency. I remember being attracted into O&M for two reasons: first I would get to understand how the bank worked from 'A to Z', and second, a corporate hero at that time was Sir John Harvey-Jones who was the chairman of Imperial Chemical Industries (ICI) (1982–87), then an iconic British firm. Sir John was a legend in British industry, and he had started his career in O&M. If it was good enough for Sir John, then it was more than good enough for me. I did realise a big lesson then however that I have seen played out so many times: cost cutting is easy but it rarely answers any core business model questions over time. You do not need much talent to cut costs, but you do need a lot of talent to grow sustainable risk-adjusted revenues in banking.

Lloyds Bank at that time was chaired by Sir Jeremy Morse, one of the most influential bankers of his generation. Sir Jeremy was then succeeded by Sir Brian Pitman, the first banker I came to know who grasped the importance and real meaning of shareholder value, not in the crude, narrow and sometimes corrupting sense as it is so disappointingly framed today, but more a *shared value* view of wealth creation, as has been popularised by Harvard's Michael Porter and Mark Kramer (2011). Both Sir Jeremy and Sir Brian were bankers of the highest standing, oozing integrity and role models to all who would aspire to build a career in banking. Individuals of great virtue.

Given an interest in economics and business, banking was a natural career. As a proud Scot, I knew that my heritage *had* some credibility in the field. The Scots had developed a reputation for financial acumen, defined by traditional values such as caution and financial prudence; they were renowned for being canny and cautious with other people's money. Two of Scotland's institutions, the Bank of Scotland (which was to become HBOS) and the Royal Bank of Scotland (RBS), had histories that dated back to 1695 and 1727 respectively. Both banks were built on the Presbyterian values of hard work, modest behaviour and loyalty. HSBC, one of the world's true global banks, has a strong Scottish heritage. The founder of HSBC, Thomas Sutherland, wanted a bank that operated on 'sound Scottish banking principles' and Scottish Chief Executive Officers such as Sir William Purvis were to carry on that tradition (there was a joke in Scotland in the 1980s that HSBC stood for 'Home for Scottish Bank Clerks' as so many Scots had joined that bank). I had an offer to join HSBC in 1985. To add to its banking and economic heritage, the founder of the Bank of England in 1694, Sir William Paterson, was a Scot, and the founder of *The Economist* in 1843, James Wilson, was also a Scot. The founding of the Bank of England marked the beginning of monetary macro-economics and the political economy as we know them today. Of course, the intellectual father of modern economics and capitalism, Adam Smith, was a great Scot who wrote *The theory of moral sentiments* (1759) and *The wealth of nations* (1776). Smith is famous for his metaphor of 'the invisible hand' and readers will note that I reference Smith's work in several places in this book. This is done for good reason, particularly in discussing the challenges that banking and capitalism face. Capitalism generally, and banks in particular, more now than ever must rediscover the compassionate, social conscious and ethical philosophy of Adam Smith. More on this in Chapter 3.

For a country of less than five million people, the Scots punched well above their weight. Alas, the Scots also produced one of the world's worst 'bankers' in Fred Goodwin, who at one time was touted as a future NAB Chief Executive Officer (CEO) and was responsible for destroying RBS – although I will argue later, as others have, that Goodwin was *not* a banker. He was, as I describe later, part of a trend in CEO appointments that has cost many banking institutions and their investors dearly.

In the 1980s, banking was an honourable profession that served with strong purpose in developing local, national and international economies. It was a profession like no other in that it offered a 'helicopter view' of how the economy worked and, at that time, bankers were held in high regard by the community; they were particularly critical to the success of small-to-medium-sized enterprises (SMEs), just as they were in Adam Smith's day when dealing with the butcher, the baker and the candlestick maker. Banks had a strong sense of *purpose* and *social licence*, even though those terms were never explicitly used back then. To be a career oriented banker there were professional qualifications that you had to meet; becoming a member of the Chartered Institute of Bankers in Scotland was a prerequisite to career development. The Institute is the oldest professional banking institute in the world having been established in 1875; the qualification was then equivalent to university undergraduate degree level. I discuss the role of professional standards in banking in Chapter 4 and the need to reinstitute a degree-level qualification as a hallmark of a professional banker.

In 1985, I moved to Citibank (Citi) in its retail banking business as a business analyst, then as chief of staff to the Head of the Retail Bank. A year later, I moved into the City of London, where salaries were double that of retail banking and in 1986 there was much excitement following the financial deregulation known as the 'Big Bang'. Citi had acquired the UK stockbroker Scrimgeour Vickers and the bank was looking to move some analytical staff into the business to help with financial control, compliance and risk management. This was a hugely exciting world, an era where the then Prime Minister Margaret Thatcher and her accomplice in the US, former President Ronald Regan, had embraced the free market economics of the Chicago School of Milton Friedman and others such as Friedrich Hayek.

BIG BANG (1987–2007)

I started out in the financial control team at Citicorp Scrimgeour Vickers (CSV), analysing where the firm made and lost money, and the economics of how it employed its capital. A year later, I moved into risk management and a year later became Head of Risk Management in the Market Making Division. The Market Making Division was the part of the firm where most of the risk was taken and most capital was at stake, and the truth was that back then there were few from the banking world who knew how to develop the science of risk management in a global equities market setting. The merging of agency execution and proprietary trading was also new and created huge behavioural complexities.

I got to know Professors Dick Brealey, Elroy Dimson and Paul Marsh from the London Business School (LBS) who were pioneering studies into capital markets risk and reward. I later went on to do an MSc in Finance at LBS. A highlight of my time there was the industry economics classes given by a fellow Scot, Professor John Kay, who is now a mix of academic economist, *Financial Times* columnist and author, whose works include the excellent *Other people's money* (2015), *Obliquity* (2010) and *The truth about markets* (2003) to mention only three of his influential books. John Kay is an authority on banking in the UK and has led post global financial crisis (GFC) industry thinking on the concept of 'Narrow Banking' and the 'Twin Peaks' debate over the structure of regulation, and in particular the role of the central bank (the Reserve Bank). In this book, I occasionally refer to his work.

At CSV, I reported to another Scot, John McFarlane, who was to become an important person in my career. John was parachuted in as the CEO of CSV from Citicorp Investment Bank at a challenging time for the firm post the 1987 stock market crash. He went on to become CEO at ANZ and arguably the best CEO in Australian banking in modern times (though I would say that David Murray might also have a claim to that crown and prior to David, Bob Joss at Westpac. Don Argus certainly had. Don was CEO at NAB from 1991–99 and his reputation within NAB only grew in stature over the years that I was there, which postdated Don). John McFarlane went on to become the chairman at Barclays.

Citi in the early 1990s was a hotbed of global talent. I worked closely with Mervyn Davies (now Lord Davies), who would become CEO and then chairman at Standard Chartered Bank and then later a UK government minister for Trade, Investment and Small Business in Gordon Brown's cabinet. The executive suite in London also included Eric Daniels who went on to become CEO at Lloyds Bank, Ian Cormack, CEO at AIG Europe, and Shaukat Aziz, who went to become the Prime Minister of Pakistan. Numerous 'Citibankers' went on to play big roles in banking, central banking and politics globally from around that time, in the same way it appears that Goldman Sachs and JP Morgan bankers tend to do today. The focus on talent, or human capital as I like to think of it, was something that struck me as being critical and I was to see it again at ANZ under the leadership of John McFarlane.

With the de-emphasising of stockbroking at Citi in the late 1980s, I moved into a senior risk management role within the debt capital markets business at Citicorp Investment Bank in London covering all European markets, working closely with colleagues in Tokyo and New York. I got to know debt capital markets well, building on the knowledge I had acquired of the equity capital markets. Markets risk management combines the complexity of market volatility, product complexity, counterparty risk management and systemic risk in a truly global setting. Being in risk management early in my career, in what were challenging markets with very strong personalities and in a complex organisation, taught me great respect for risk management. I see risk management skills as the defining core competency of a banker. I believe today, just as I did in the 1980s, that you cannot be a 'banker' in a professional sense unless you are first a risk manager acting as a first line of defence. I come back to this important theme in Chapters 4, 5 and 6.

My introduction to Australia came in 1991–92, when I joined John McFarlane on a project under the sponsorship of Citi's then chairman and CEO, John Reed. Citi had lost a lot of money in Australia and elsewhere. Reed wanted to know if there were systemic issues, evident in Australia, on how the Citi decentralised global model worked. At that time, Citi was led in Australia by two highly regarded executives, John Thom and Michael Cannon-Brookes Snr. It was a huge lesson in managing a banking business and understanding how individual bank strategies can lead to excessive risk when placed in the context of the industry and the domestic economy. It made me reflect on how bank CEOs often worry what the economy might do to bank profitability, without ever asking what banking might do to the economy, in a similar vein to when former US President John F. Kennedy said, 'Ask not what your country can do for you – ask what you can do for your country.'

Of course, the Australian banking industry back then was still in the early stages of adjusting to the Hawke-Keating deregulation of the sector, and miscalculations were bound to be made. For Citi, as seems to have been a feature of its modern history, these miscalculations were magnified – Citi back then did not do things by half measures. That induction to Australia introduced me by reputation to two standout bankers of that era, Rob Ferguson who ran Bankers Trust and Allan Moss who went on to run Macquarie Bank for 15 years until 2008.

Following my time on the 'Australian Project', I then spent a year working with former Goldman Sachs training executive and Harvard PhD, Peter Mathias, hired by Reed to introduce a global customer and business planning framework called the Customer First Management Process (CFMP). The symbolism of this approach was hugely important. Banking should be first and foremost about understanding customers.

In preparation for a move into relationship management, I went back into a four-week credit risk management training program. Using a Harvard Business School case study after case study approach to learning, with experienced risk executives leading the classes, it was a demanding but rewarding learning experience, the lessons from which are deeply ingrained. It struck me then that Citi, at least in its commercial banking business, placed a career premium on risk management and much of that was down to Massachusetts Institute of Technology (MIT) trained John Reed.

Readers will find that I make several references to John Reed throughout this book. He was a banker and CEO endowed with what the Romans called *virtus* (virtue): moral courage, intellect, integrity, values, measured and a deeply held vision of global banking, not in a financialisation sense, but in the sense of meeting the needs of a growing globally integrated real economy. When the Citi board decided that the co-CEO model was not for them and they chose Sandy Weill over John Reed in 2000, they made a serious miscalculation. The likely course of Citi's history since then would have been very different. Its shareholders might have enjoyed a different experience just as those at JP Morgan Chase & Co. have, thanks to the stewardship of Jamie Dimon, who Sandy Weill sacked from Citi in 1999.[4] The appointment of Weill over Reed was the first time I reflected on how defining CEO appointments can be.

In 1993, for family reasons I transferred to New Zealand with Citibank. I spent the period from 1993–96 as a relationship banker focused on large and mid-sized corporates and then two years in financial institutions banking. In 1996, I left Citi and moved back to London, partly as I wanted to further my academic interest in finance at LBS.

Post-LBS, I spent two years as an 'Executive Director' in the European client coverage team at Canadian bank, CIBC Wood Oppenheimer (now called CIBC World Markets), specialising in leisure, hospitality and the health sectors (if it is possible to 'specialise' so broadly). CIBC were rebuilding their European operations after the shocks of the losses in the early 1990s, when they had been heavily exposed to the Reichmann family investments at Canary Wharf in London. The bank was hiring extensively from places such as Citi, Credit Suisse, Deutsche Bank, BZW, Bankers Trust and Drexel Burnham Lambert, which had imploded under the leadership of the 'junk bond king', Michael Milken. What a mix of cultures that was.

In 1999, I went back to New Zealand to take up a Head of Corporate Finance role at ANZ Investment Bank, a role that then morphed into establishing an in-house private equity business

---

4   Carney, J., 'Sandy Weill: I fired Jamie Dimon because he wanted to be CEO', *Business Insider*, 5 January 2010.

focusing on the bank's SME customers. ANZ had a great SME franchise, with many customers in need of capital solutions beyond senior debt, but who had a real challenge in accessing equity and quasi-equity capital. Indeed, it remains so today; in fact, the problems SMEs face in accessing the right kind of capital are more severe today than they were some 20 years ago – hence the raison d'etre for Judo Bank.

In 2000, I moved to Sydney to establish that same business in Australia and an SME-focused strategy we called 'Wall St to Main St'. This was a strategy of bringing capital solutions, not just senior debt, to the SME and mid-corporate market. At that time, I became a strong advocate of economic value added (EVA) and worked closely with Joel Stern at Stern Stewart & Co. I became convinced that firms had to earn a return at least equal to their risk-adjusted cost of capital. What amazed me was how so many firms were not. The fixation on accounting-based earnings was a puzzle, as it remains today. My experience in analysing how so many firms made accounting profits but destroyed shareholder wealth led to writing a book called *Corporate governance and wealth creation* (2003). Chapter 3 of that book was used by Joel Stern when he taught finance to MBA candidates at Columbia University in New York. A highlight during that time was an invitation to a live TV debate with Nobel Laureate and Yale University professor Robert J. Shiller, who was in Auckland promoting his book *Irrational exuberance* (2000). The 30-minute debate was on whether the New Zealand equity market was susceptible to irrational exuberance. The first round of the debate was gentle, and I was still standing given my knowledge of corporate New Zealand. Round two was 'ugly' and I quickly stepped back and left much of the remainder of the show to Professor Shiller, who was a gentleman. In an intellectual sense, I turned up with a bow and arrow; Professor Shiller had high power artillery. I learnt a lot by listening.

In 2004, I became the Global Head of Client Relationship

Banking at ANZ, based in Sydney. ANZ was a bank led by bankers. It was the most internationally minded of the Australian banks and it had great momentum under its then CEO, John McFarlane. I left ANZ at the end of 2006 and joined NAB, where I became Group Executive Business Banking (covering the whole business landscape – SMEs, corporate and institutional – as well as private banking and the bank's customer activities in Asia, the UK and North America).

At NAB, I went back to my CFMP education and we developed the Customer-led Innovation Strategy (CIS). The purpose was to put the customer, not the bank's products, at the centre of how bankers would think, talk and act. In a business where financialisation (productisation) and product cross-sell were dominant in the way that bankers behaved, we felt that we needed to develop a strategy that thought about the business based on a deep understanding of the customer. At ANZ, in the Institutional Banking business, we developed the 'CEO Agenda', which was centred on thinking about our customers through the lens of the things that preoccupy the CEO and the Chief Financial Officer (CFO).

The critical distinction in all of this is customer first, products second. No rocket science here, but it was contrary to how many banking businesses were being run.

LEADERSHIP AND CULTURE

In the years preceding the GFC, there was an emerging trend in Australia and in the UK of CEO and C-suite appointments into major banks of people who had little operational experience of banking. This was a significant and defining development. The CEO at the Bank of Scotland, an institution that has a history dating back to 1695, was an Englishman, Andy Hornby, who had also started his career at the Boston Consulting Group (BCG), before moving into high street retailing. HBOS was the epitome of conservative Scottish banking, but under Hornby's leadership, the first Englishman in that role, the bank almost collapsed, saved by a forced merger into Lloyds Bank. The UK Banking Standards Commission accused Hornby and his chairman, Lord Stevenson, of a 'colossal failure' of management. Harsh words, yet in many ways an understatement. A gentler in tone criticism was to be levelled at the CEO and chairman of NAB in 2019 who were accused of a defiant and tone-deaf response to the criticisms made by the Royal Commission.[5]

A similar story to HBOS revealed itself at RBS. Fred Goodwin joined RBS under the sponsorship of Sir George Mathewson, an engineer, who had come to banking late in his career (aged 47). Mathewson became CEO and then chairman of the bank and flooded the RBS executive with former colleagues from the Scottish Development Agency (SDA) in much the same way that in some other banks, CEOs imported trusted alumni from consulting firms. Getting close to his retirement age, Mathewson appointed Goodwin, first as Deputy CEO/CFO and then CEO. Goodwin had been a CEO of the NAB-owned Clydesdale Bank, a small Scottish bank with approximately 5000 employees, for less than 15 months, and had no real operational experience, as Ian Fraser described in vivid detail in his excellent book *Shredded – inside RBS, the bank that broke Britain* (2014). According to Fraser, Goodwin's entry to banking was thanks to NAB's Don Argus, who was impressed how the young external accountant had performed on the acquisition due diligence of Clydesdale Bank. And so in 1995 he hired him to replace the highly regarded Frank Cicutto who was scheduled to return to Melbourne. In his short time as Clydesdale Bank CEO, Goodwin managed to 'hollow out' the bank through aggressive

---

5 Smyth, J., 'NAB chief executive and chairman resign after critical report', *Financial Times*, 7 February 2019, p. 12.

cost cutting; an experience the bank never recovered from as it became a perennial problem for NAB. Goodwin's reputation at Clydesdale and later at RBS was described as that of an egotistical tyrant.[6] Notwithstanding that, he went from joining Clydesdale as his entry to banking as CEO, to becoming the RBS CEO within five years, which is impressive. The RBS board was woefully missing in action in oversighting Goodwin. This is an endemic problem with so many bank boards, as the Royal Commission and the CBA inquiry revealed. A theme for Chapter 8.

As I discuss in Chapters 6 and 7, I have often reflected on how bank boards could have miscalculated or misjudged the core competencies essential to managing and leading such important institutions. I have always believed that the leadership of a bank has to have a strong risk-orientation as Jamie Dimon has at JP Morgan Chase, David Murray had at CBA, Bob Joss had at Westpac, Don Argus had at NAB and John McFarlane had at ANZ. The CEO must be the 'Chief Risk Officer'. They must have a deep instinctive feel for risk and an inquisitive mind, constantly questioning cause and effect, always seeing the forest as well as the trees, moving from the dance floor to the balcony and back again. In a bank, this is an absolute core competency and it cannot be delegated, even if (as there should be) a Chief Risk Officer (CRO) is in the senior ranks. The loss of risk management competencies within the senior ranks of many banks was and is a serious governance miscalculation by boards and regulators; the Three Lines of Defence model, sound in theory, has become deeply flawed in practice, largely because of a series of CEOs and far too many C-suite executives with little instinctive knowledge of risk management. I return to this theme in Chapter 6 and again in Chapter 9.

---

6   Fraser (2014, p. 71) describes how Goodwin was close to transferring to NAB in Melbourne. One Australian banker who was at NAB at the time said, 'Fred was not well liked, and his wife Joyce didn't like us colonials. We were very grateful to her when she encouraged him to return to Scotland.'

CULTURAL COMPATIBILITY

Under the then CEO, Frank Cicutto, NAB acquired MLC in 2000 for $4.56 billion. At around the same time, CBA, led by David Murray, acquired Colonial First State for $9 billion. Westpac and ANZ made smaller bets on wealth management, with Westpac, under David Morgan's leadership, astutely buying BT at a relatively bargain price and ANZ entering into a partnership arrangement with ING. Inside NAB, to make the MLC economics work, particularly when Ahmed Fahour ran much of NAB's Australian franchise, there was a strategy of integrating MLC people into senior roles within the bank.

The lessons from CSV on culture and competencies mix struck me as being as true in 2007 as they were in 1987. During the period 2007–14, NAB was also characterised, at that time and in my mind, by a strange tribalism, which fragmented and diluted its culture and created a sense that what had made NAB a great bank had been lost. There was a lack of the strong sense of shared values that had once defined NAB. There was an MLC tribe, a management consultants' tribe, mainly from firms such as BCG and PwC, and an ex-CBA tribe reflecting widescale hiring from that bank following the earlier appointments from CBA of George Frazis and a quintessential banker in Michael Ullmer. The proliferation of ubiquitous servants of the banking system – the accountants, lawyers and consultants – into the industry disguised the lack of banking professional credentials. Accountancy is a profession superficially like banking, but also very different in fundamental ways. In aggregate, these tribes made NAB an interesting place to define in a cultural heritage sense. It also struck me just how few people there with banking backgrounds who had ended up in senior roles. As management consultants and MLC people were put into senior roles in the bank, they in turn appointed people they knew, so there were many senior executives with no instinctive feel for the business and this also added to the cultural confusion. In aggregate this also weakened the management fabric of the bank. Culture is fundamental to how a bank (a business) functions and cultural changes that have been allowed to grow deep roots inside many banks represent not just one of the gravest miscalculations, but also one of the most significant challenges the industry faces. I discuss this in Chapter 7.

I believe today, as I did then, that mixing incompatible cultures and capabilities from what are fundamentally different industries is an unsolvable problem and it makes the entire enterprise more fragile. I remember John Reed writing about this in the *Financial Times*:

> Traditional banking attracts one kind of talent, which is entirely different from the kinds drawn towards investment banking and trading. Traditional bankers tend to be extroverts, sociable people who are focused on longer term relationships. They are, in many important respects, risk averse. Investment bankers and their traders are more short termist. They are comfortable with, and many even seek out, risk and more focused on immediate reward. In addition, investment banking organisations tend to organise on product rather than customers. This creates fundamental differences in values.[7]

What John Reed wrote on the difference between commercial and investment banking is equally valid when comparing wealth management with commercial banking – very different businesses requiring very different competencies.

The reality is that cultural compatibility can be difficult to achieve across divisions that attract very different employee profiles, and where the business model and goals are different. The people employed in the financial markets, who are heavily incentivised

---

7   Reed, J., 'Our universal banking mistake', *Financial Times*, 15 November 2015, p. 32.

by revenue and bonuses, have little in common with the people operating in the branch network.

To add to the cultural mix at NAB, there was a 'mini-me' investment banking tribe in a division called NabCapital. The existence of the NabCapital business made the bank more complex and confusing. Complexity is not an absolute and it is not a function of size; it exists when the range of activities undertaken by the bank exceeds the competency bandwidth of management and the board. Some of the activities undertaken by NabCapital, such as synthetic debt securities including collateral debt obligations (CDOs) were so distant from the core capabilities of the bank's management and board (and had little if anything to do with its customers), that there was little surprise that they inflicted financial and reputational damage. That damage included a $1.1 billion provision on a portfolio of CDOs. All this was hugely unfortunate (and unfair) to the then CEO, Cameron Clyne. He was only months into the role when it happened, but it played to a historical investor file on NAB's management as being accident-prone. Given the history of NAB since the turn of the twenty-first century, it was hard to argue against that file. A file that arguably has now been opened on CBA.

One thing that did strike me following the NAB CDO debacle, was an accountability culture that was soft at best and, more accurately, very weak. This is a trait of the banking industry in Australia. Senior executives with their fingerprints all over many problems kept their employment status, while shareholders were badly burnt and, as is so often the case, the 'butterfly effect' or collateral damage meant hundreds if not thousands of junior staff lost their jobs. The Royal Commission starkly highlighted just how weak some bank boards are on accountability, and only in extremis is there any accountability accepted, often then when there is no other choice – walk the plank or be pushed overboard. I return to this subject in Chapters 7 and 8, and to the welcome introduction of the BEAR (Banking Executive Accountability Regime) legislation, which is discussed in Chapter 4.

FINAL OPENING REFLECTIONS

This is a book about banking and the critical role it must play in the economy. The reason I decided to commit the time to writing this book is because I have had a long and deep respect for and pride in the fundamental role that banks play in society and the economy, both domestically and internationally. The GFC and the Royal Commission have highlighted how, largely through the process of financialisation, the industry had lost its moral compass and had made many miscalculations. How did this happen? What can be done to restore banks to a position of trust and respect – can the toothpaste be put back in the tube? This book addresses these questions. In Chapter 9, I outline a blueprint for a path to recovery; a path that will only work with courage from policy, political and regulatory leaders.

Some advice to readers; as is often the case with books of this nature, some readers will be attracted to certain chapters more than others. The themes in each of the chapters are interwoven and the reader will get the most from this book if it is viewed holistically rather than as a series of discreet chapters. The interwoven nature of the chapters will be evident in the frequency in which reference is made to other chapters in the book.

In the Epilogue to this book I provide some reflections on the role that I played as a senior executive.

INTRODUCTION

PUBLIC trust in the banking industry is at an all-time low and the role and conduct of banks in society is front and centre of the public discourse. Since the GFC in 2007/8, Australia's major banks have appeared before numerous government or parliamentary inquiries, including the high-profile Royal Commission into Misconduct in the Banking, Superannuation and Financial Services Industry (2019) (the Royal Commission). The banking industry has also been subject to the Productivity Commission inquiry report, *Competition in the Australian Financial System* (2018) (the Productivity Commission). It is hard to conceive that such a crucial sector of the economy appears to have become so detached from the society it is supposed to serve, or an industry with such a damaged reputation. The *purpose* of banks and their *social licence* to operate is under considerable scrutiny. As it should be.

The crisis that the banking industry faces is a deep concern, as our major banks play a systemically critical role in our economy. The overall finance sector accounts for close to 9 per cent of Australia's gross domestic product (GDP), a 50 per cent increase from the 1990s and broadly in line with the contribution that the mining sector makes to the economy. In the UK, the finance sector, reflecting the prominent role that the City of London plays, is marginally higher at 10 per cent of that economy. Finance sectors are strong contributors to economic growth in smaller economies such as Singapore and Hong Kong, but weaker in other countries, for example finance contributes only 7 per cent to GDP in Canada, 8 per cent in the US, 8 per cent in Japan and France, and 4 per cent in Germany. In 2017, Australia's four major banks (CBA, Westpac, NAB and ANZ) contributed approximately $11 billion in corporate tax, compared to the aggregate of approximately $10 billion from BHP Billiton, Rio Tinto, Wesfarmers, Woolworths, Telstra and AMP combined.[8] In 2018, the major banks employed close to 160,000 people.[9] By any measure, the finance sector and banks in particular play an important role in the economy, but that importance cannot simply be measured by the contribution made to the nation's fiscal position. Banks are much more important than that.

Before exploring the role that banks play in the economy, it is helpful to address the misunderstanding that there is a 'financial services industry' as the Royal Commission into Misconduct in the Banking, Superannuation and Financial Services Industry implies. In so many ways it is a set of *industries* rather than a single *industry*. Ever since the iconoclastic marketing theorist and Harvard Business School professor Theodore Levitt wrote his paper on 'Marketing myopia' in 1960, businesses have tried to define their industry in broad terms. Railroad companies came to see themselves as in the transportation business and oil companies as in the energy business (before its collapse, Enron called itself a 'Gas Bank' given its extensive use of financial derivatives and its infamous use of

---

8   Hutchens, G. & Evershed, N., 'Ten companies pay 45% of all corporate tax in Australia', *The Guardian*, 13 December 2018.

9   PwC, 'Waiting for superheroes: the banking workforce of the future', *Banking Matters: Hot Topics*, November 2018.

mark-to-market accounting). Today it is fashionable for many businesses, including banks, to describe themselves as a technology company, when they are clearly not. Knowing what you are is important for several reasons and pretending to be something you are not is a serious miscalculation with follow-on consequences, sometimes serious, as evident in the example of Enron.

Many people are advised early in their careers, in all walks of life, to 'play to your strengths' and to strengthen your strengths.[10] In the case of a bank, building enhanced technology capabilities is an example of strengthening your strengths. However, for almost all established banks, technology is an *enabler*, whereas for FinTechs it can be a *definer*, with a new breed of neobanks being a mix of both, but digitally led. Knowing who you are is important. That is where your potential for comparative advantage lies. Not knowing who you are and attempting to pass yourself off as something that you are not is risky and can alienate employees, customers and other stakeholders, and you will most certainly eventually get found out. And so it is with traditional banks that describe themselves as 'technology companies', or in the 'consumer retailing business', for example. It is also the case for some FinTechs and neobanks, which can have an unhealthy tendency to exaggerate their yet unproven product and management capabilities. There is both a refreshing and sometimes concerning feeling about the youthful irrational exuberance that flows from some in the FinTech and neobank community globally, which is discussed in Chapter 2.

One major miscalculation that banks have made was to conceive of themselves as 'retail businesses' with 'stores' and having 'sales and cross-sale targets'. Lending someone more money that they

---

10 I remember the then Macquarie Bank CEO, Allan Moss, telling a group of senior executives at ANZ in 2004 that a mistake he often sees in commercial banks is that of overinvesting in weaknesses and consequently underinvesting in strengths; so if there are two businesses, a fourth-rated retail division and a first-rated business bank division, commercial banks are more likely to invest in moving fourth to third, even if it risks the number one positioned business slipping to number two.

can prudently afford might hit 'sales targets', but it may not be responsible lending, which is a principle enshrined in Australian law.[11] It can violate a sense of fiduciary duty that customers trust banks to exercise with care, and is implicit in their social licence, as well as the law. Imprudent or irresponsible lending has the potential to ruin lives and destroy families and businesses. Young and vulnerable people can have their credit history tarnished for life. There is nothing easier to sell in life than money and potentially there is nothing more reckless. An addiction to debt and inability to free oneself from its shackles has parallels for many in society to the harm done to families from 'pokies' addiction. Banks know this, yet some have behaved as if 'selling' money is their raison d'etre and this is one of the major reasons they have got themselves in such a mess. More on this later.

FUNDAMENTALS OF BANKING

The word *bank* derives from the Italian *banca*, the word for the wooden bench that moneychangers used to display their coins. Though simple in origin, banking is a multifaceted industry, which over time miscalculated the scope of what banking meant. The problem is that management started to make extravagant assumptions about their intrinsic capabilities and those of the bank, and so it is with the 'finance industry'. Commercial banks acquired wealth and insurance businesses as well as stockbroking and investment banks and none of this worked out well, not just in Australia and New Zealand. There was an industry joke told in all major financial centres about bank ownership of investment banks and stockbroking businesses: 'Why do banks own small investment bank businesses? They buy big ones and wait a few years.' So true.

---

11 See the *Australian Securities and Investments Commission Act 2001* (Cth).

An industry can be defined by a set of competencies, expertise, know-how, conventions, culture and regulation. Technology can change an industry by lowering the barriers to entry and extending boundaries, but in many critical industries, the key competencies remain largely the same. In this context the competencies to run a commercial bank are different from a wealth management firm and different from insurance and investment banking. Having an MBA or having worked for one of the major consulting firms does not change this reality. It is a miscalculation to talk about the 'financial services industry' as it is a composition of several industries, defined by unique competencies, different professional requirements and, in many cases, quite specific social licences to operate. The social licence to operate, as discussed in Chapter 3, is the defining feature. The relevance of this discussion will become apparent in Chapter 4 when the theme of professionalism in banking is explored.

Banks are, to use a medical analogy, the heart that pumps blood around the body or the finance around much of the economy. How they perform that task is as critical to an economy as a healthy heart is to any one of us. Banks operate payment systems, they are the major providers of credit to much of the economy (households and businesses, small and large), they provide trade finance and risk management services (interest rates and currency) and they act as a haven for depositors' funds, albeit with government backing for those institutions that are Australian owned. Banks also create the 'miracle' of liquidity through maturity transformation. They largely own illiquid loan assets such as 25-year mortgages, yet depositors and providers of short-term debt, who fund much of these loan assets, may want their money back on short notice or on demand. How banks manage the mismatch of assets and liabilities has been a major focus of bank regulators since the GFC and remains one of the most powerful things that banks do in the economy. In Appendix I, there is a high-level summary of what banks do.

Operating in a largely oligopolistic industry structure, Australia's major banks are both powerful and privileged; they are also very resistant to change, with powerful lobbying muscle to influence political will. Why would they change given the privileges and protection bestowed upon them? They enjoy what looks to many as a cosy structure that generates among the highest levels of profitability in the world. Yet, while our banking system is both strong and stable, customers do not enjoy the benefits of this. Instead, customers are exposed to the entrenched market power of the banks and often feel betrayed by them. No industry structure can be sustained with such a relationship dynamic with its customers and with society. This was self-evident long before the Royal Commission or the Productivity Commission reports. It is equally a feature of the New Zealand market, which is dominated by subsidiaries of the major Australian banks.

A societally-attuned and well-functioning banking system works in the public interest through the allocation of capital across the economy. Banks take deposits and borrow in domestic and international capital markets, and then channel those funds into lending to support investment, whether that is in housing, in small businesses looking to expand, in large businesses managing their liquidity and working capital, or in infrastructure investment. The sustainable health of the economy depends on how well this is done. Going back to the medical analogy, if a heart has a blockage restricting the flow to certain parts of the body, over time this can be damaging and often fatal. Many industries and businesses have closed or shrunk in size because banks, often sensibly, have scaled back their willingness to provide finance. This is a legitimate role for banks to play as the natural forces of creative destruction (Schumpeter, 1942) work through an economy, even when their support is replaced by government (taxpayer) money in the form of aid packages, as happened, for example, with the motor car manufacturing industry in Australia. To extend the medical analogy, sometimes limbs and organs must be removed if they are unlikely to recover and may cause greater damage if not addressed. If the system tries too hard to pump more blood than needed into certain sectors of the economy such as housing, then the risks associated with high blood pressure can result. As discussed in Chapter 2, this 'high blood pressure' risk is evident in the scale of lending to Australian and New Zealand households.

Central to the role that banks play in the financial system is their skill in dealing with what economists call information asymmetric problems or the 'lemon' problem (Akerlof, 1970). This is where borrowers know more about the risk in their investment decisions than the banks do. An example of this information asymmetry problem is where a business or an individual provides false information on income or expenses to get a loan, or where the real risk involved in a business growth strategy is much higher than the business discloses to the bank. The bank may therefore lend on a project that turns out to be a lemon – a disaster. To address this problem, banks need to apply risk management skills to assess and then price risk. They also must deploy policies for monitoring that risk once it is assumed. To do this efficiently, banks must act in an independent manner, absent of political interference. This vital investment and monitoring role that banks play is critical to a vibrant economy, just as a healthy heart is critical to our body.

Outside the four major banks – ANZ, CBA, NAB and Westpac – there are several so-called second-tier or regional banks, such as the Bank of Queensland, Suncorp and the Bendigo and Adelaide Bank plus a range of community banks and foreign bank subsidiaries. While not part of the oligopoly and not reputationally tarnished to the same extent, the second-tier banks can enjoy some of the fruits of the oligopoly as they can and do free-ride on changes in key product pricing such as mortgages and credit cards. The smaller banks often adopt a 'fast follower' or a tailgating strategy when it comes to pricing, using the air cover provided by the larger banks.

Why not when your bonus largely depends on financial results and relative Total Shareholder Returns (TSRs)?[12]

THE IMPORTANCE OF REGULATION

To understand the strength and potential of any economy, the relationship between the financial system and how investment decisions are made is pivotal. The concept of a financial system is defined by the combination of financial markets (banks, debt and equity capital markets, etc.) and financial institutions (banks, investment banks, wealth and finance companies, brokers, institutional investors, etc.). In a financial system such as in Australia and New Zealand, the banks play a major role. The effectiveness of the banks in allocating capital is central to the sustainable productivity of these economies. Capital, or debt, which fund assets that add to the productive capacity of the economy, is normally value-adding in a growth sense, as it creates jobs that have a multiplier effect in the economy. Debt that adds nothing to the productive capacity of the economy can, if done to excessive levels, be very harmful. Not all debt is equal in its economic impact and risks. The GFC reminded us of this truth, as have so many other past financial crises. The modern case of Ireland should be a reference for any Australian bank board and regulators on the risk of excessive debt in the housing market. There are several similarities between the Australian banks today and the Irish banks pre-GFC when it comes to appetite for real estate lending and what the Irish call 'loose lending'. A theme for Chapter 2.

Those who believe 'this time is different' are destined to find out

---

12 TSR is a measure of the investor return on a share by adding both the share price appreciation and the dividend received on the share and reflecting the total as a percentage of the share price at the beginning of the measurement period.

in a very painful way that it rarely ever is. It may take some time for that harm to manifest, but manifest it will. For those unconvinced and given Australia has not had a major economic downturn for close to 30 years, then Reinhart and Rogoff's excellent book *This time is different – eight centuries of financial folly* (2009) is a must read.

Regulation is an important feature of the banking market. The primary banking regulator in Australia is the Australian Prudential Regulation Authority (APRA) and in New Zealand it is the Reserve Bank of New Zealand (RBNZ). In Australia, another important regulator is the Australian Securities and Investment Commission (ASIC), which is concerned with market conduct and the integrity of the financial system. A third regulator, the Australian Competition and Consumer Commission (ACCC), has the role of promoting competition and fair trade. Economic theory suggests there are three core purposes of regulation: limiting monopoly powers, safeguarding welfare and dealing with externalities. The importance of regulation is a core theme throughout the book and was a major criticism of the Royal Commission.

In Australia and in New Zealand, as in some other countries, a few banks dominate the banking market. Over time this has been driven by mergers and acquisitions (M&A). On controlling monopoly powers, and evident in the findings from both the Royal Commission and the Productivity Commission (both discussed later in this chapter), there is a growing call for regulators to be tougher, more directional and interventionist in their dealings with larger banks to offset the potential for abuse of power and to address societies' disquiet with how banks have behaved. The welfare considerations are a desire to protect depositors and consumers, as well as dealing with the moral-hazard risk of banks taking on excessive risk in the belief that the taxpayer will bail them out. Regulators deal with this in several ways, including by insisting on minimum capital requirements and levels of liquidity held by banks. In a regulatory sense, externalities are primarily the risk that an individual bank can impact the wider system via contagion risk or spillover effects. Regulators do not just focus on the risk attached to individual banks, they also focus on the overall system. They are concerned with the stability and integrity of the system, and the need to avoid the risk of a 'domino effect' through contagion and systemic risk.

Regulators are not a cost to the financial system, they are in many ways the guardians of the system. Society has a legitimate interest in how effective regulators are at discharging their duties. The lessons from the GFC were as much about the follies of weak regulation in the UK and the US as they were about so-called 'casino banking'.

The GFC is a classic illustration of systemic risk and why it is important that regulators see the forest as well as the trees. Regulators also help financial markets and customers deal with the problem of asymmetric information in assessing the riskiness of a bank. Information asymmetries arise when the bank knows more about the riskiness of its business than is known in the market. There is another relevant economic concept when thinking about regulators and banks, and that is the principal–agent problem. This problem arises in the relationship between the principal (the owner) and the agent (the manager); how can the principal ensure that the agent does what they were hired or licensed to do? The problem is mitigated where the principal closely monitors the agent's behaviour and ensures that the design of the incentives does not create a conflict of interest. The concept of the principal–agent problem can be applied to how the regulator monitors the bank; how can the regulator seek to ensure that individual banks behave in desirable ways? This is an important theme that readers should keep in mind throughout this book: 'Have the principals (the bank boards on behalf of shareholders) been effective in monitoring the agents (the management)?' And how effective have regulators been in acting as principals on behalf of society in monitoring the banks?

INTRODUCTION

DRAMATIC CHANGE

Largely since the last decade of the twentieth century, banking has radically changed. Banks went from being routine, mundane almost civil service style institutions, focused on their customers and communities, to becoming far racier, more exciting and for those employed in them, particularly at senior levels, far more financially rewarding. The days of '3-6-3' banking (take deposits at 3 per cent, lend funds at 6 per cent and hit the golf course by 3 pm) were bound to change, but few could have envisaged by just how much. The equivalent of Mao's Cultural Revolution swept the industry. Banks no longer saw themselves as the simple custodian of depositors' funds; they became more complex in their activities, through product development and through M&A into activities that they viewed as congruent with their core business of banking – they attempted to extend the definition of the industry. Thus, banks acquired wealth management and insurance businesses, some built capabilities in investment banking including stockbroking and asset management, off balance sheet activities surged, and a trend began that the British economist John Kay (2015) described as the *financialisation* of the banking market and the economy. The asset side of the bank balance sheets outstripped deposits creating what is known as the 'customer funding gap'. This gap was filled by an increasing use of wholesale funding and in a rundown of liquid assets. Some of the financialisation activity was famously described by the then chairman of the Financial Services Authority (FSA) in the UK, Lord Turner, as 'socially useless',[13] or of no economic value. The 'socially useless' phrase could also be applied to the not-fit-for-purpose insurance policies that banks sometimes foisted on their customers, which are discussed later.

---

13 Monaghan, A., 'City is too big and socially useless, says Lord Turner', *Daily Telegraph* (UK), 26 August 2009, <https://www.telegraph.co.uk/finance/newsbysector/banksandfinance/6096546/City-is-too-big-and-socially-useless-says-Lord-Turner.html>.

All this was integral to the financialisation of the economy. The global financial system grew from approximately 110 per cent of global GDP in 1996 to over 400 per cent by 2007.[14] In the UK alone, total bank assets grew from £2 trillion in 2001 to £6 trillion in 2007, four times the size of the economy they were meant to be serving. In Australia, bank assets grew to more than $4.1 trillion, including almost $2.6 trillion of outstanding loans compared to Australia's annual GDP, currently just over $1.9 trillion (including the New Zealand economy),[15] which puts total bank assets at more than two times the size of the economy and outstanding loans at around 140 per cent of the combined GDP.

The financial deepening of most Anglo-American economies, including Australia and New Zealand, was evident in the significant increase in leverage, particularly in residential mortgage lending. It is also evident in the growth in the financial markets activities of the banks. An important public policy question is whether this significant financial deepening has delivered value to the real economy. Or has it stored up problems for the future? Financial crises can have long gestation periods. A topic for Chapter 2.

FOUR FACTORS

Much of this growth and change in the banking system was fuelled by four factors that fed off each other. The first factor was an influx into the banking industry of well-educated and highly intelligent professionals from other sectors such as management consulting and those who found accounting and law lacking in excitement. At NAB, for example, there was also a significant influx of management consultants into senior roles. All were hugely bright

---

14 Davis, S., *Banking in turmoil*, Palgrave Macmillan, 2009, p. 6.
15 Australia's economy is sized at $1.6 trillion, whereas the New Zealand economy is estimated at $280 billion.

and talented people, who understood the theory of business and how to pull together an impressive PowerPoint, but many were without any instinctive or intuitive knowledge of risk management and banking.

This was at a time when the financialisation of the banking industry, as John Kay (2015) describes it, was a global phenomenon and management consultants were emerging across the industry, including Cameron Clyne at NAB, Ian Narev at CBA, Andy Hornby at HBOS and Peter Sands at Standard Chartered Bank to name only a few. Brian Hartzer at Westpac had a consulting background, but he had gained deep operating experience at ANZ and then at RBS in the UK. Before Cameron Clyne at NAB, there was Ahmed Fahour, who ran NAB's Australian franchise. He had a background at BCG, with limited operational experience in banking. On his appointment, based on experience at Citibank and its insurance arm Travellers, Ahmed made it clear that one of his key briefs was to rev up cross-selling between the bank and its MLC wealth management operation.[16]

This change in the leadership profile at many banks coincided with the surge in MBA graduates from business schools, where financial economics and corporate finance became important topics of study and the world was viewed as being populated by rational actors. To the extent to which there may have been an ethics elective, it was never seen as an essential area of study for aspiring bankers. None of these hires wanted to work in a boring bank.

The second factor, aided greatly by development in financial economics academia (a greater application of mathematics to finance), was a self-belief that with the advent of financial technologies, including tools of financial engineering and derivatives, the banks could grow and shed risk. This was largely

---

16 Boreham, T., 'Generation next: bank ushers in a new breed', *The Australian*, 14–15 August 2004, pp. 33–37.

using financial derivatives and securitisation, which made banks believe that they had found new frontiers in risk management (e.g. VAR or value-at-risk technologies pioneered by JP Morgan Chase) and ways of creating greater balance sheet velocity through securitisation.

The so-called bundling, distribution of assets and the separation of risk from the provision of capital, spawned a range of new financial innovations such as MBS (mortgage backed securities) and CDOs. It was not unusual for senior executive discussions inside banks to focus not on understanding customer needs, but on how 'we can originate assets' that can be packaged and sold to generate fees. None of these developments ended well for commercial banks.

The securitisation market, which can play an important role in the funding of banks, can also be fraught with conflicts if not properly managed. Banks can originate loans with the intent of packaging them and then securitising them, but there is always a residual concern about the care and due diligence that went in to making the loan; the investment bank that arranges the securitisation is conflicted by the fee it will earn, even though it is duty bound to investigate the quality of the loans made by the bank before enticing investors to buy the securitisation paper. The size of the fee can however dull the due diligence senses. A big part of the GFC story was low quality mortgage lending in the US, which found its way into the securitisation market.

These derivative instruments were famously described by Warren Buffet as 'financial weapons of mass destruction' and this was no more clearly illustrated than when Singapore-based Nick Leeson caused the collapse of the venerable Barings Bank in 1995. Barings was founded in 1762 and collapsed due to a massive trading loss (£827 million) when Leeson ran an unauthorised trading exposure on the Nikkei 255 futures market. The senior management within Barings Bank in London had little understanding of the risks that

Leeson was running and were blinded by the high levels of profits he had been able to generate until it all began to unravel. There are scores of other Leeson-like stories and many of them became visible with the GFC, including within Australian banks such as the $1.1 billion provision that NAB incurred on CDOs. When the economic tide goes out, all sorts of hitherto apparently profitable and low- risk activity can be washed up upon the beach and shown to be something other than what it was understood to be. When the tide goes out, you find out who has been swimming naked.

Several banks formally developed what was known as an originate-warehouse-distribute (OWD) strategy – grant loans, hold them in a 'warehouse' until they could be bundled with other loans to create scale, and then sell the economics of the loans to investors. Most commercial banks excelled at the 'O' and 'W' but never quite nailed the 'D'. They simply did not have the skills or competencies or investor networks to do this well. Many investment banks, as the GFC highlighted, ran a 'originate-flog-forget' model, as *The Economist* unkindly described it, where they did not care too much about the assets they were originating as they were to be sold to unwary investors, without recourse to the originator. This was a big part of the first chapter in the story of the GFC – low quality mortgage loans, mixed into a lethal cocktail with MBSs, CDOs and CDSs.

The period became known as 'casino capitalism' or, perhaps more aptly, 'financial capitalism' or *financialisation*. The term 'casino capitalism' was popularised by Susan Star, professor at the London School of Economics, in her 1986 book of the same name. The rise of financialisation, as the former chairman of HSBC, Stephen Green (2009, p. 192) wrote, had entered mainstream culture: 'Even those who have not seen Michael Douglas's Oscar-winning performance in Oliver Stone's 1987 film *Wall Street* will know the approximate meaning of "pump and dump" and "short and distort".' The culture that this language reveals only grew and spread across the banking industry. One has only to read the juvenile exchanges that took place between financial market employees at various Australian banks in connection with the market interest rate rigging scandals to see this. More on that later.

The growth in financial markets and the use of derivatives and securitisation drove a surge in trading and fee-based income. For banks there are two good reasons to securitise assets such as mortgages – liquidity and capital. In securitising assets, banks create velocity in their balance sheet – that is, they get their money back immediately – so they can lend it again; and, because the buyer of the securitisation paper takes the risk, there is no need to hold capital. This is all part of a strategy to increase non-interest income as a driver of revenue and return on equity (ROE) growth. Banks are obsessed with ROE growth and this focus is fraught with risks, more so in banks than in any other form of business, as the incentive is to keep the 'E' as low as possible in order to drive a higher 'R'.

Momentum behind this trend was reinforced by the third factor, the introduction of Basel II measures of risk-weighted assets (RWAs), which began in 2006 and determined the amount of capital that banks needed to hold against certain types of assets. Basel II drove significant behavioural change as capital requirements became less onerous and certain asset classes were granted preferential risk weightings. So, lending on a residential mortgage may attract a capital weighting of 35 per cent, whereas lending to an SME would attract up to a 100 per cent risk weighting. Given this, and the almost cult-like focus on ROE, the invisible hand of self-interest created the incentive to do more residential mortgage lending. The influence of Basel II and concept of RWAs, with the powerful link to ROE and incentive, is a topic for Chapter 2.

The fourth factor was globalisation, which accelerated from the 1980s onwards. Progressively, the financial markets became even more globally integrated with many banks operating in all the major international financial centres and staff moving frequently from one bank to another and from one location to another. Australian banks, particularly NAB and ANZ, were active participants, with significant operations outside their home markets of Australia and New Zealand. NAB acquired banks in the US and the UK, whereas ANZ owned Grindlays Bank, which operated in developing economies such as India. A significant feature of globalisation was just how quickly contagion risk could spread across markets. This was an important development, which represented a huge challenge for regulators and governments. Another feature of globalisation was the degree of mimicking that banks adopted based on a perception of best practice; for example, Wells Fargo was the benchmark in retail banking for cross-selling products and many Australian management teams made the pilgrimage to San Francisco to learn how to be like Wells Fargo. The then Westpac CEO, Gail Kelly, repeatedly championed replicating Wells Fargo's customer culture and the number of retail products sold to consumers.[17] The irony of Wells Fargo's perceived capabilities will be evident to readers in Chapters 7 and 8.

All four of these factors fundamentally altered the size, nature and culture of banking, which went from being narrowly based servants of the economy, to being broadly based institutions aspiring to become 'Masters of the Universe'. In Australia, this might be exaggerating the point, but not by much when it came to CEO and C-suite remuneration. This phenomenon was illustrated in the case of former ANZ CEO Mike Smith, who was paid $88 million over the eight years he was in the role. Reconciling these rewards with shareholder outcomes is not easily done, even with the most sophisticated of balance scorecard algorithms.[18]

---

17 Kehoe, J., 'Wells Fargo scam a warning for Westpac and local banks', *Australian Financial Review*, 11 September 2016, p. 36.

18 Patrick, A., 'Inside story: how ANZ paid Mike Smith $88m for failed Asian strategy', *Australian Financial Review*, 28 July 2016, p. 39.

At then scandal ridden CBA, the CEO, Ian Narev, was awarded total rewards of $44.8 million for the five years he was in that role.[19] Bank executives saw themselves as part of a globally visible and information efficient community, which viewed Melbourne, Sydney, Hong Kong, Singapore, London and New York as no more than 'separate floors in the same building'.

IDEOLOGY

These trends in the financial markets led to the GFC, which in the UK saw the first run on deposits in 150 years (the first since Victorian times) when customers sought to take their savings out of Northern Rock, at that point the UK's largest mortgage lender. Ultimately that institution had to be nationalised (rescued) by the British government (taxpayer) in September 2007. The main cause of Northern Rock's failure was a reckless business model with an overdependence on short-term wholesale funds (mainly asset securitisation). A contributing factor was a gross failure in regulatory oversight.[20] The UK, like the US, was influenced greatly by the beliefs and principles of Alan Greenspan, chairman of the Federal Reserve Board from 1987 to 2007, who argued that regulators should not attempt to restrain financial markets because they could not have a better understanding of asset prices than market participants. Greenspan's claim derives from ideology rather than evidence, in believing that markets would self-govern and the invisible hand of self-interest would ensure nothing reckless would be done. Regulation therefore should involve a gentle nudge from time to time, nothing more. What a major miscalculation,

---

19 Robin, M., 'What Commonwealth Bank paid Ian Narev', *Australian Financial Review*, 14 August 2017, p. 48.

20 Berger, A., Molyneux, P. & Wilson, J., *The Oxford handbook of banking*, Oxford University Press, 2010, p. 3.

which Greenspan, to his credit, later acknowledged. Greenspan's ideology (the so-called 'Greenspan Doctrine'), however, was to carry powerful influence over more cautious and less market trusting politicians such as Britain's then 'New Labour' chancellor, Gordon Brown. Ironically, Adam Smith, often seen as providing much of the ideological foundation for free market economics, believed that banks should be regulated given the harm they can cause (see Cassidy, 2009, p. 35). Greenspan was a disciple of Smith, but conveniently chose to skip over the important qualifier that Smith applied to banks.

Following Northern Rock, a sequence of events occurred, largely in the US and the UK but also in continental Europe (e.g. Hypo Real Estate in Germany, Dexia Bank in Belgium and Fortis in the Benelux), which saw an almost complete meltdown of the financial system as institutions such as Bear Stearns, Lehman Brothers, RBS and HBOS either went out of business, were nationalised or were forced into the arms of stronger institutions. Some of the great icons of the global banking industry such as Citigroup survived only because of emergency government funding.

THE AUSTRALIAN GOVERNMENT

In Australia, thankfully, events were not so dramatic, though the government, with the benefit of the country's AAA credit rating, had to guarantee the wholesale funding of the banks, following the decision by the Irish authorities to do the same for their banks.[21] The government also introduced a guarantee on retail deposits up to $250,000, aimed at stabilising the banking system and avoiding a Northern Rock style run on any bank and the contagion risk that would almost certainly follow. Several non-

---

21 Which was quickly copied by Denmark, Britain, Germany, Belgium and Spain.

bank lenders such as Allco Finance, Opes Prime and Babcock & Brown did collapse. Non-bank mortgage lender RAMS – which was struggling to roll over $6 billion in short-term funding – was acquired by Westpac. The wholesale funding model at St George Bank, which was not dissimilar to Northern Rock, with a high level of short-term wholesale funding, was ultimately a factor in a sale to Westpac. Absent a sale to a stronger bank, St George Bank would not have survived the GFC.[22] Bankwest, because of problems with its UK parent, HBOS, as well as its stretched balance sheet, was forced into a sale to CBA in order to avoid a collapse.[23] (Prior to being acquired by HBOS, Bankwest had earlier been rescued by the Western Australian Government.) From a competition perspective, the Bankwest and St George Bank deals were not in the interest of the economy but can be sensibly understood in the context of maintaining stability in the banking system. The prospect of a bank getting into difficulty and potentially failing makes the competition issue a moot and somewhat academic point; either a bank is acquired by a stronger bank or it goes out of business, which would have been the likely outcome with Bankwest and St George Bank. The impact on competition is broadly the same, though the economic and social risks attached to a bank failure can be material and not worth running an experiment on. These events led one commentator to observe, 'In a few short months, we saw the biggest reversal of banking competition since the Depression.'[24]

The Australian Government had to announce a guarantee of all wholesale bank funding to avoid the contagion risk of international investors fleeing their exposure to Australian banks. At that time, Australian banks were exposed to a significant vulnerability as they

---

22 Durie, J., 'St George was broke if we didn't buy it: Westpac chief', *The Australian*, 13–14 October 2018, p. 29.

23 White, A. & Creighton, A., 'Bankwest buy fast-tracked to avoid collapse', *The Australian*, 8 September 2018.

24 Irvine, J., 'Big 4 must be held to account', *Sydney Morning Herald*, 27 November 2017, p. 18.

relied on international wholesale markets for over 60 per cent of their funding and a sizeable amount of that was in short-duration instruments. In 2008 some $220 billion of offshore wholesale borrowings were due to mature within a year.[25] This was clearly reckless risk management, but banks liked to focus on short-dated funding as it kept the cost of funding lower and therefore profits and ROE higher. They did this even though it exposed the banks to liquidity risk, which in banking and in business generally is much more serious than capital adequacy; when a bank runs out of liquidity, the consequences can be fatal. All other measures of substance can become insignificant and not immediate. Longer-dated debt is more expensive; the difference in many respects is like paying an insurance premium to cover the risks of disruption to capital markets.

The prospect of liquidity risk was a big lesson for the banks, who now pay much greater attention to the duration profile of their liabilities with a bias to extending them as required by regulators under the newly introduced Basel III liquidity and capital rules – the Basel rules are explained in Chapter 2. As *The Economist* noted:

> If boardroom discussions in the past decade revolved around the asset side of the balance sheet, the next decade will see managers focusing on the liabilities side – the amount of capital they hold to protect against losses, and the duration and sources of their funding. [26]

In the midst of the crisis, the Reserve Bank pumped liquidity into the financial system, fulfilling its role as the 'lender of last resort'. This was a strategy central banks around the world followed and so began a decade of 'quantitative easing', which helped stem the risk of panic and collapse, but time may inform us that it has sown

---

25 Maley, K., 'Revealed how the banks were kept afloat', *Australian Financial Review*, 8–9 September 2018.

26 'Rebuilding the banks: a special report on international banking', *The Economist*, 16 May 2010, p. 9.

the seeds of the next crisis in the way that it may have artificially inflated asset prices.

The intellectual climate within the Australian banking community post-GFC, created a dangerous feedback loop in which senior bankers believed that the success of their bank was due to their genius and this supported the case for ever increasing remuneration and a continuation of relatively laissez faire regulation. Humility is an important quality in a banker, so those who proudly claim that the Australian banks missed the fallout from the GFC and that this was a reflection on the management of the banks, should consider the important role played by the then Labor government. The government of the day, led by the then Prime Minister Kevin Rudd, his Treasurer, Wayne Swan, and the steady hand of Secretary to the Treasury, Dr Ken Henry, the Reserve Bank, headed by Glenn Stevens, and John Laker, who headed APRA, were the real heroes. If not for the decisive and skilful handling of the crisis by the government and its agencies, the outcome could have been dramatically different. The exposure of Australian banks to short-dated international wholesale funding markets was clearly imprudent and complacent, though at the time it was what everyone was doing. Those reflecting and who argue that the government guarantee on deposits was unnecessary, are ungracious and ignore the significant contagion risk if the community thought that banks could collapse.[27] Luck, of course, also played its part. The GFC came right in the middle of a tripling in many natural resources commodity prices with China's insatiable demand for Australian resources, resulting in an investment boom, which saw mining investment grow from 8 per cent to 20 per cent of GDP. This, together with the fiscal prudence of the Howard-Costello era (1996–2007), created the fiscal flexibility that the Rudd government needed and allowed a stimulus package of roughly

---

27 Kehoe, J., 'The GFC remembered: ten years ago it was all about saving the banks', *Australian Financial Review*, 5 October 2018, pp. 18–22.

5 per cent of GDP, including a $900 cash payment to many Australians. Not all went as planned. The 'helicopter' cash drop helped boost the level of gaming expenditure, given the fascination many Australians have for the gambling industry and in particular pokie machines. The government also never quite excelled in its school building and home insulation schemes, only to remind society that governments are moving outside their competencies when embarking on such initiatives and wasting taxpayer money. These facts are not to detract from the decisive actions taken by the government, which showed bold leadership when it was most needed. History books should record that, with gratitude, notwithstanding the fiscal and debt legacy it created (Australia's net government debt at the end of 2018 was $350 billion, equal to 22 per cent of GDP: it was zero in 2007). The alternative is not worth thinking about. Ask the British or the Irish or, closer to home, the people of South Australia, who up to two decades later were still feeling the consequence of the $3.1 billion rescue by the state government of the State Bank of South Australia in 1991. A similar story is that of the State Bank of Victoria, which was on the verge of collapse post its acquisition of the troubled Tricontinental, saved only by its acquisition by CBA in 1990. The near collapse of the State Bank of Victoria was a key factor in the defeat of the state Labor government led by Joan Kirner and the election of the Liberal Party led by Jeff Kennett in 1992. Banking crises can have consequences that spill over in the political arena.

THE IMPORTANCE OF CAPITAL

There were many lessons taken from the GFC that are well documented in other books and writings[28] so they will not be

---

28 Anyone interested in an excellent summary of the GFC should read Mervyn King, *The end of alchemy*, 2016, pp. 26–38.

repeated here, except to mention two important facts about banks that the GFC reminded us of. First, banks are among the most highly leveraged (i.e. debt relative to equity) of any type of business. With equity cushions of say 10 per cent, banks, particularly under regulatory capital risk weightings, can borrow 15–20 times their equity. Some Australian banks, because of the low RWAs assigned to mortgages, which fell from a risk weighting of 50 per cent pre-Basel II to as low as 15 per cent in some banks, create leverage as much as 30 times their equity. Due to the concerted effort by APRA, the average leverage ratio of the major banks has reduced from 29 times their equity in 2013, to 19 times at the time of writing in 2019; a figure that is arguably still too high. Lord Turner, the former head of the FSA in the UK, argues that major banks should hold common Tier 1 equity of between 15 and 20 per cent, compared to the 10.5 per cent demanded by APRA.[29]

In the UK, Barclays at one point had leveraged its balance sheet over 40 times its equity base; there were examples of even higher leverage, such as Deutsche Bank and RBS, who got as high as 70 times. Also, banks everywhere ran down their liquid assets, which weakened a critical form of liquidity risk management. As King (2016, p. 97) notes, 'in less than fifty years, the share of highly liquid assets held by UK banks declined from around a third of their assets to less than 2 per cent.' In summary, the approach to capital adequacy and liquidity was of a magnitude that would cause the great bankers of yesteryear to either shake their heads in disbelief or turn (several times) in their graves. Banking had developed characteristics more akin to a highly leveraged gambling business obsessed with growing ROE. The lower the 'E', the higher the 'R'.

Equity in a bank's capital structure (in any business) is like an airbag in a car. It is rarely used and in the hands of a safe driver (good manager), it may never be used, but if there is a crash, then

---

[29] Boyd, T., 'UK regulatory expert backs call for higher bank capital', *Australian Financial Review*, 18 March 2019, p. 48.

the bigger the airbag the better. The bigger the car (the bank) and the faster it is driven, then the bigger the airbag must be to ensure survival. The GFC highlighted just how many banks were being driven like large cars at top speed with little in the way of airbags (the GFC started off as a liquidity crisis but quickly became a capital crisis). The influx of a new management philosophy from outside the traditions of the industry meant that banks had to become faster, more exciting cars, away from the days where they went largely unnoticed on the highway of the economy, there to serve rather than be seen. No bank epitomised this change more than RBS. In several places in this book, we will return to the dangers of ROE as a measure of profitability and determinant of incentives. Banks have become highly proficient at 'optimising RWAs' in order to further leverage their equity, to the extent that ROE is not adjusted for risk but flattered by it.

The second important fact history tells us is that, irrespective of internal and external controls, any sense of a lack of confidence in an individual bank or in a group of banks can signal a potential disaster as contagion quickly spreads. It is as much the prospect of the event as the actual event itself that matters. This reminds us that banking is a business where trust and confidence can be defining. Banks need markets and depositors to trust them. The irony of this will not be lost on some readers who will reflect on how much customer and community trust banks have lost. How can you lose customer and community trust, but maintain the trust of the financial markets? Can this dynamic be sustained over time?

It is primarily for these reasons that bank regulation is so important. Ultimately, when it comes to large domestic banks, regulators and governments cannot allow them to fail given the damage that can then flow into the economy. Banks are not true private sector firms capable of going bust and this creates what economists call *moral hazard* problems – that is, a lack of incentive to guard against risk when one is protected from its consequences.

For this fundamental reason, major domestic banks are quasi-nationalised or, as the British would say, semipublic institutions. Hence the importance of their social licence to operate, a topic explored in Chapter 3. The GFC illustrated how in many developed economies, government (taxpayer) bailouts were followed by austerity measures, which impacted millions of families who then became the innocent victims of the reckless management and flawed governance of the banks. A conservative estimate of the cost to the US economy from the GFC is close to US$14 trillion (Luttrell, Tyler & Rosenblum, 2013).

Thankfully, due to skilful handling of events by government agencies, the Australian banks largely avoided these issues and continued to grow beyond the GFC and became the most profitable banking sector in the developed world, as shown in Table 1.

TABLE 1: AUSTRALIA NUMBER ONE FOR BANK PROFITS

Rank	Nation	Bank profit share of GDP %
1	Australia	2.9
2	China	2.8
3	Sweden	2.6
4	Canada	2.3
5	Netherlands	1.9
6	Spain	1.8
7	France	1.7
8	Japan	1.4
9	US	1.2
10	UK	0.9

Source: The Banker, IMF, TAI calculations (2016)

It is an impressive achievement that a largely domestic banking business in an economy of 29 million people (including New Zealand) can produce, among the big four banks, profits after tax in the range of $30–35 billion. In an ROE sense, the major Australian and Canadian banks are standouts (both markets have a similar oligopoly structure), see Figure 1. The Australian banks benefit also from their New Zealand franchises where ROE has been even higher.

FIGURE 1: BANK ROE COMPARISONS

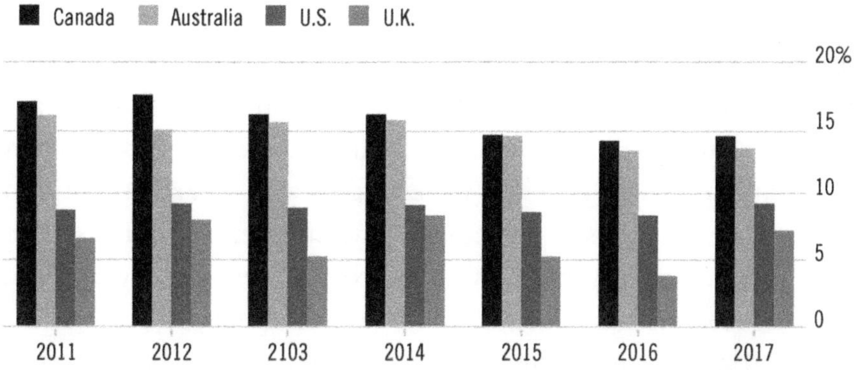

■ Canada   ■ Australia   ■ U.S.   ■ U.K.

Source: Bloomberg   ** Average return-on-equity for each country's biggest banks*

With profitability consistently sitting at the top of the global league table, such an achievement would normally be a badge of honour, a source of national pride, if it were not for a lack of competition and the poor conduct of the banks.

MARKET POWER: CORRUPTING AND ANTI-CAPITALISM

The pricing power of the major banks makes the maintenance of high ROEs an achievable priority and everything else becomes a secondary consideration. So, when their cost of funds rises or the burden of compliance costs increases, banks use these events as an excuse for shifting these costs to their customers – because they can.[30] The ability to pass on costs without consequences is quite wonderful if you are running such a business; just like one never-ending warm bath. It is, as one journalist described it, the industry's own version of Shangri-La.[31] There is little questioning of the high economic rents already earned and why they should be maintained. It is important to note however that it is entirely appropriate that banks should make a profit and earn a return in line with their risk-adjusted cost of capital. This is important for all businesses. What raises questions is when those profits are above the 'normal' level expected in a competitive market, and where 'super-normal profits' or 'economic rents' are being earned, that is profits above the risk-adjusted cost of capital. When that happens, there is prima-facie evidence of weak competition and privileged industry structures, with high entry barriers. The ability to constantly pass on rising costs when already earning excessive economic rents is, as a first-year economics student would testify, prima-facie evidence of market power, that is, a lack of competition. The Productivity Commission (2018, p. 11) clearly saw this issue:

> Simply accepting lower returns on equity is uncommon among Australia's financial institutions – banks in particular. Rather, it appears that achieving ROE targets is an important factor in major banks' interest rates decisions, and one that has tended to lead to higher rates charged to existing borrowers, rather than aggressive discounting intended to expand market share.

---

30 Crowe, D., 'Interest rates to rise as big four protect profits', *The Australian*, 1 December 2017, p. 1.

31 Boyd, T., 'Hayne exposes bankers' Shangri-La', *Australian Financial Review*, 29–30 September 2018, p. 48.

These words are both an indictment on the customer values of the banks, and an accurate statement of the motives behind repricing. The Productivity Commission insights are yet further evidence of the dominance of the so-called Friedman Doctrine (that the only legitimate goal of business is to maximise profits) in the way banks think about their purpose – although more accurately, a distortion of the Friedman Doctrine, as discussed in Chapter 3. The passing on of costs is shorthand for protecting monopoly rents. Exploiting customer loyalty is done in the knowledge of a high level of customer inertia, weak regulatory oversight on competition and a significant marketing budget to create a more caring front. There is also the comfort of knowing that all major banks act in pretty much the same way, with many second-tier banks as grateful 'fast followers' or tailgaters. The major banks with their stranglehold on the market are also largely undifferentiated in nature. John Dahlsen, a former ANZ director observed, 'There is a huge sameness about our banks ... you could switch the brand names of our banks and no one would know the difference. It is very incestuous.'[32] This sameness was amusingly told in a book on culture within British banks (Weeks, 2004), when a member of the internal audit team at NatWest arrived in Bristol from London to conduct a branch inspection. He decided to visit a nearby pub for some lunch prior to conducting the inspection. Having consumed several pints of beer, he made his way to the bank. Several hours later having completed his work, he went to see the branch manager and then discovered that he had mistakenly undertaken an inspection at Lloyds Bank and not NatWest! The strong similarities between the institutions meant that the inebriated internal audit officer could not distinguish between the banks, and the staff at Lloyds Bank saw nothing unusual.

More so today than with the UK banks, our banks operate as a

---

32 Dahlsen, J., 'Regulators running riot', 31 May 2018, p. 5.

pack and in the knowledge that they are insulated from individual criticism and, if things do go wrong, taking comfort from the ageless advice of John Maynard Keynes (1931): 'a sound banker, alas, is not one who foresees danger and avoids it, but one who, when is ruined, is ruined in a conventional way along with his fellows, so that no one can really blame him.' Keynes's observations hold as true today as they did in 1931; banks like to be 'in the pack' and not an outlier, in case something does go wrong. It is also a good cover for explaining excessive fees and margin on products such as foreign currency credit card transactions: 'it's market practice'.

The equally concerning reality is that the high level of profits were also made, as the Royal Commission highlighted, not just in an environment of weak competitive forces but one of customer abuse, with evidence of reckless lending practices, a culture of poor professionalism, of arrogance and all driving an all-time low in trust. How could this have happened?

It is true that Australia had avoided any major financial collapses since the HIH Insurance collapse in 2001 and the near collapse of Westpac in 1992 (noting the demise of the State Banks of Victoria and South Australia), and there has not been an economic recession since the early 1990s. Perhaps such a prolonged period of benign economic conditions and a false sense of superiority from navigating the GFC created a sense of complacency and arrogance. It is easy to convince oneself that superior management drove the strong profitability of the banks and discount the benign economic conditions that lasted for close to three decades. The bank-friendly macro-economic conditions coincide with a rising property market, an oligopoly industry structure and historic levels of low bad debts, all of which may have flattered management and driven an overinflated sense of capabilities. As Kay (2015, p. 156) observed, 'When economic conditions are benign, almost everyone who gambles in the property market with highly geared equity stakes makes money. And, like all gamblers, they interpret their success as evidence of their skill.' The truth is that in such conditions, it does not take a lot of skill to do well; the skill is in not messing it up. The puzzle is why did industry leaders mess it up?

SUCCESS IS TOXIC

The answer to this puzzle can be understood in the wisdom of the chairman of the Finnish telecommunications company Nokia, who described the collapse in the fortunes of that company, from a position of global leadership, as being due to 'success is toxic'.[33] In 2007, Nokia accounted for 40 per cent of global handsets and had a market capitalisation of US$290 billion. Because of its complacency towards industry change and emerging competition from Asia, together with a lax attitude towards software, Nokia's market capitalisation at the end of 2018 was US$35 billion. This 'success is toxic' hypothesis as to why our banks have seen their reputations so badly damaged, was summed up by former Treasurer Peter Costello:

> Our banks are absolutely immune from market discipline, living in a highly profitable cocoon; they think all these high returns are from their own brilliance, but what they haven't understood is they have a unique and privileged regulatory system which has delivered this to them.[34]

What the Nokia chairman was acknowledging is that the great success the company once enjoyed had sown the seeds of its downfall through a culture of arrogance and complacency. These characteristics were also evident at the cross-sell darling of the banking industry, the US-based Wells Fargo, whose success was finally revealed as that of faking accounts. In fact, what Wells

---
33 'Telephone tower v rubber boots', *The Economist*, 10 March 2018, p. 65.
34 Creighton, A., 'Peter Costello's blast at the banks: bring in some competition', *The Australian*, 19 August 2017.

Fargo was accused of – discussed in Chapter 8 – was mirrored by at least one Australian bank, CBA, who admitted to manipulating children's accounts to meet sales targets.[35] The manipulation of data within the industry for marketing purposes is endemic; for example, the number of customer bank accounts declared by the major four banks add up to 47 million for customers over 15 years old, according to the 2017 annual reports (CBA 17 million; Westpac 13 million; NAB 9 million and ANZ 8 million).[36] Given the population size (including New Zealand), adjusted for those under 15 years old and assuming that some customers may have more than one account, it is hard to understand the math no matter what assumptions are used. The data discrepancy can however be understood if there is a link to executive incentives.

Arguably NAB in the early 2000s stood on the 'success is toxic' banana skin as CBA did in 2018. History suggests that the 'success is toxic' hypothesis holds when you reflect that CBA was the standout bank performer in a financial sense over the decade to 2018, NAB was in the 1990s and Westpac was in the 1970s, with all three stumbling badly through arrogance, complacency and hubris. The irony is that in missing much of the fallout from the GFC and believing it was down to their skilful management, Australian banks became exposed to the 'success is toxic' syndrome and their very own Australian financial crisis (AFC). This is not a crisis in the sense experienced by the UK banks, where absent government support, some of the banks were in peril, instead this is a crisis of legitimacy, of reputation and of purpose. There is overwhelming evidence to support this hypothesis, in particular from the cultural traits, which were starkly highlighted by the Royal Commission and are discussed throughout this book. This 'success is toxic' trap can also impact

---

35 'Commonwealth Bank admits to manipulation of children's accounts', *ABC News*, 19 May 2018.

36 Smyth, J., 'Probe exposes Australian banks' abuse of customers', *Financial Times*, 1 May 2018, p. 7.

regulators, as was the case in the UK. Regulators too can become complacent and drop their guard. Modern history highlights how regulators can struggle to tame and hold accountable powerful actors and industry groups. Banks with a deeply ingrained sense of invincibility, even after the criticism of the Royal Commission, have a deep-seated dismissive attitude towards regulators.[37] This almost unconscious arrogance is exacerbated in a closely knit and shallow business community, where powerful people regularly bump into each other at cultural and sporting events, dining clubs and at the chairman's club at airports. Being a strong, independently minded regulator is not an easy task.

The business world, not just the banking world, is full of examples of how once iconic institutions, trapped inside their culture of superiority, complacency and arrogance, have fallen from grace. The example of the once iconic General Electric (GE) in the period up to 2019 is informative. During the tenure of the legendary Jack Welch from 1981 to 2001, GE's market value grew from US$15 billion to over US$400 billion. In 2017, after the 16-year tenure of Jeff Immelt as CEO, GE's market valuation had fallen close to US$150 billion. During Jeff Immelt's tenure, GE shares fell 36 per cent, while the S&P 500 rose 118 per cent.[38] At the time of writing, GE is in a state of crisis with a market valuation of US$70 billion and debt of US$150 billion. What the GE story tells us is that no company, regardless of its once formidable reputation, is exempt from culture-inflicted inertia or the risk of 'success is toxic'. The iconic GE had become a 'horror movie'.[39] The same can be said of the once mighty Deutsche Bank, as was the case with RBS and Citigroup to mention only a few banks. At the heart of the problem that affected these and other

---
37 Danckert, S., 'ASIC attacks bank attitudes to regulation', *Sydney Morning Herald*, 15 March 2019, p. 22.
38 Crooks, E. & Fortado, L., 'Activist Trian wins GE board seat', *Financial Times*, 10 October 2017, p. 27.
39 Lex, 'GE considers a break-up', *Financial Times*, 17 January 2018.

once great institutions was a culture that lacked effective board oversight, weak risk management and a culture of arrogance. These are themes for Chapters 6, 7 and 8.

CRISIS OF TRUST

More than any other type of business, banks are built on trust. Building an organisation's reputation for trustworthiness takes time and is founded on a robust ethical culture. Trust is also strongly related to fairness. Studies show that the experience of unfairness quickly erodes trust (Kramer, 2009). Because of the way the banks have conducted themselves, a crisis of confidence and trust hit the broader financial services market, see Figure 2.

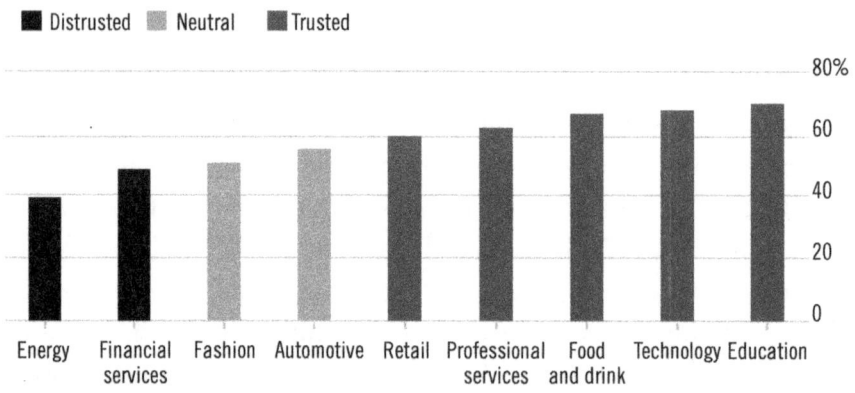

FIGURE 2: TRUST DEFICIT
Only energy companies are more distrusted than banks in Australia

Source: 2018 Edelman Trust Barometer

In part, the crisis of trust in banking must be understood in a context where societal trust in liberal values, capitalism and institutions has generally been in decline. Restoring trust should not be considered as yet another marketing campaign. There are no silver bullets: 'trust arrives on the back of a tortoise and leaves on the back of a galloping horse'.

When the shift in social attitudes and seeds of this mistrust took root is difficult to pinpoint. Political thinkers such as Stanford University's professor Francis Fukuyama point to the GFC.[40] Others, however, argue that the GFC was the time the seeds of discontent grew rather than were established. The GFC certainly inflicted damage to capitalism as an ideology, but arguably unfairly so. As discussed in Chapter 3, the original ideals of capitalism as espoused by Adam Smith have been corrupted by weak corporate governance, principal–agent problems and the dominance of monopolist or oligopolist industry structures. The problem is not with capitalism per se but how unchecked forces have been allowed to corrupt capitalism. This reality is more evident in banking than in other industries.

The debate on the social licence that should be granted to banks rages on in the UK and the US and has come to life in Australia as a result of the Royal Commission, even though there is resistance from the wider business community to the idea of a social licence to operate.[41] There is a growing feeling that society needs to reclaim banking for the good of society, not for the good of bankers and shareholders. Greater granularity and insights into the collapse in trust in Australian banks was provided in research conducted by Deloitte in 2018, which took a broad view on how society sees banks, as summarised in Figure 3.

Deloitte's research is insightful: on keeping promises to customers, only 26 per cent of respondents believe banks do; on having their customers' interests at heart, only 21 per cent of respondents agree; and on whether the banks are ethical, only 20 per cent thought they were. These are a disappointing reflection on a once proud profession.

---

40 Fukuyama, F., 'The coming collapse of America', *Australian Financial Review*, 28 December 2016, pp. 22–27.

41 Mather, J., 'ASX governance council dumps "social licence to operate" from guidance', *Australian Financial Review*, 27 February 2019, p. 18.

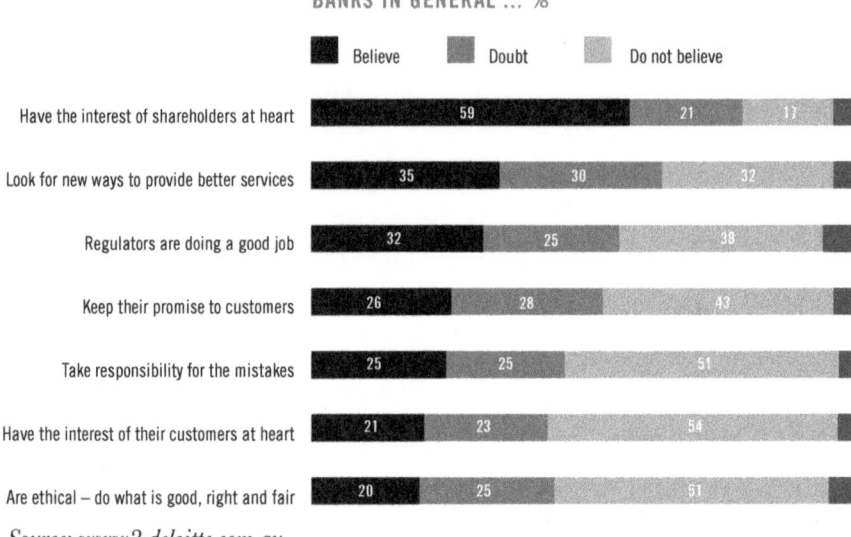

Source: *www2.deloitte.com.au*

The associated concern is that when society loses trust in an industry or in an institution, so eventually do employees, despite the avalanche of corporate spin and CEO tweets. Staff buy into the initial denial, as the corporate spin doctors craft messages that deflect and often deny that there is any truth in what is being said externally. Eventually when the evidence is overwhelming and there is the CEO mea culpa, everyone feels betrayed, let down and embarrassed that they have been peddling the corporate line until it was obvious they could no longer do so. Good people, as discussed in Chapter 7, become detached emotionally and in a values sense from the organisation; they leave who they are 'at the door' each day and go about doing their job as a hired hand. Discretionary effort is withdrawn and pride in the organisation evaporates. People feel that what they do lacks purpose.

Wells Fargo, in trying to distance itself from its past scandals, ran the campaign 'Established in 1852. Re-established in 2018'. It was a bold campaign but missed the point and highlighted just how deeply ingrained institutional arrogance can be. Both insiders and those outside the bank describe a damaged bank and a workforce held back by fear of repeating past mistakes, and the significant difficulty of drawing a line under the scandal-ridden period. Staff are said to still be shell-shocked by management reaction to the scandal, which included firing more than 5000 junior level employees, even though the core problem was with the bank's leadership and the culture it encouraged.[42] The Wells Fargo CEO got a pay rise to US$18.4 million despite the scandals that had engulfed the bank.[43] The subject of the societal disbelief with the nature of CEO remuneration is a subject that we return to in Chapter 8.

Banks, through their formidable marketing budgets, are exemplars at spin, which only reinforces community disbelief at how out of touch and insular they have become – establishing trust is not a call option granted to the bank; it is for customers and society to determine when trust is re-established. Such is the arrogance of many large institutions. As a British politician commented on the UK banks rebuilding trust with SMEs 10 years after the GFC: 'The idea that because the banks are not behaving as badly as they did a decade ago, it is all OK, is like inviting Hannibal Lecter to dinner because he hasn't killed anyone recently' (referring to the cannibalistic *Silence of the Lambs* character).[44]

This arrogance was also demonstrated by the banking industry trade body, the Australian Bankers Association (ABA), when in 2017 it ran a campaign titled 'The Banks Belong to You'; a campaign that was aimed at warding off the Royal Commission. The poorly advised campaign attempted to convey the message

---

42 Armstrong R. & Noonan, L., 'Wells Fargo repairing a damaged brand', *Financial Times*, 14 January 2019, p. 27.

43 Stampler, L., 'Wells Fargo CEO got a 5% pay raise to $18.4 million in spite of scandals', *Fortune*, 14 March 2019.

44 Megaw, N., 'Treasury rejects calls to reform UK laws on business loans', *Financial Times*, 11 January 2019.

that 80 per cent of bank profits are returned to shareholders, who comprise most Australians through their superannuation fund. The campaign failed to recognise that the excess profits earned by the banks came at a cost to Australians and it is the less powerful and disadvantaged bank customers that pay disproportionately towards the profits (e.g. anyone unable to clear their credit card balance and paying high rates of interest). The chairman of the Productivity Commission commented, 'The logic that it's ok to accrue a degree of oligopolistic rent as long as everyone's getting some is wrong.'[45] Every decent person in the country understands this, yet it appears that the banks do not get it. Another example of this disconnection and disrespect for customers is the way banks offer new customers better rates on products such as mortgages and credit cards. They are implicitly taking their existing customers for granted in a quite disrespectful way – the fact that other industries may do the same is not a justification. This was one of the telling signs behind the sales culture that eventually caused the collapse of HBOS, where the bank ended up paying £7 million in compensation to the 30,000 existing customers who complained, but nothing to the 400,000 customers who had not complained (Perman & Darling, 2012, p. 263).

A little more humility rather than arrogance from the ABA should have been the order of the day. A not dissimilar (equally lacking in credibility) quote was made in 2010 by the British Bankers Association (BBA), when it argued that new capital regulations would require the UK banks to 'hold an extra £600 billion of capital that might otherwise have been deployed as loans to businesses and households'.[46] This is a standard scaremongering ploy of the banks and it is false. As Admati and Hellwig (2013)

---

45 Creighton, A., 'Finance riddled with rent seekers: Productivity Commission's Michael Brennan', *The Australian*, 7 November 2018.

46 Treanor, J., 'Tighter banking rules will drain £1tn from financial system, study shows', *The Guardian*, 10 July 2010.

argue, this is nonsensical, sensationalised and false, particularly as to the use of the term 'capital'. The BBA would have the reader believe that the additional equity capital could not be leveraged and used as loans. More on this in Chapter 2. Banking industry associations, such as the BBA and the ABA, employ talented people, but they can sometime be devoid of any banking and commercial experience and senior management capabilities within the industry. They are more aligned to the spin from the political system, which is so distrusted by society. Unfortunately, their public utterances only serve to highlight their inadequacies rather than their talents. Which is a pity as they mean to do well.

ROYAL COMMISSION

Against a background of industry lobbying to prevent it, as well as government hesitancy, the Royal Commission was established in late 2017. The scope of its findings shocked the nation. It uncovered lying to regulators, falsifying documents, taking bribes, extracting fees from deceased customers and selling insurance products that were not fit for purpose.[47] Society was left feeling that this was only the 'tip of the iceberg' given the constraints placed on the inquiry. These and other ethical, moral and legal failings are illustrated in the following examples:

- *Fee for no service*: It is estimated that the major banks and AMP have taken more than $1 billion in fees that they were not entitled to, by charging customers for services that were never asked for or were never provided. CBA and NAB even managed to charge fees to the estates of customers who had been dead for a decade. CBA was made aware of the problem, but decided to do nothing for almost two years, even though

---

47 Cadman, E., 'A decade of banks behaving badly is being laid bare in Australia', *Bloomberg*, 30 April 2018.

the law requires that ASIC is informed within 10 days. A CBA executive agreed with the proposition that the bank would 'be the gold medallist if ASIC was handing out medals for fee for no service'.[48] As with CBA, this was a problem at NAB compounded by the failure to report this issue in a timely manner as required by law and internally discussing the concept of a 'strawman' to deceive the regulator.[49]

- *Risky financial advice*: CBA, ANZ and Westpac provided numerous cases of inappropriate advice from financial planners, which resulted in customers losing millions of dollars.
- *Introducer Program*: NAB ran an 'Introducer Program', which rewarded people for introducing mortgages, a program that was subject to fraudulent abuse. The arrangement was in place for over a decade and from 2014/15 had originated $24 billion in mortgages and paid $100 million in commissions to external parties, some of whom were connected to NAB staff. The program was originally designed to incentivise professionals who worked in adjacent industries, such as accountants and advisors, to refer mortgage loans to the bank. It soon took on a life of its own. One introducer was a tailor in western Sydney who referred $122 million in home loans and was paid $488,000 in fees as a result. A similar example was a Sydney gym owner who received hundreds of thousands of dollars in introducer commissions. A third example was in Melbourne where a photocopier technician received almost $800,000 in commission for introducing loans. There were allegations that the bank's staff received bribes in return for approving fraudulent home loans, which in turn helped the

---

48 Grattan, M., 'Australian Government should be ashamed of past performance on banking sector', *The Conversation*, 20 April 2018.

49 Roddan, M. & Butler, B., 'NAB scandal heading to court', *The Australian*, 18–19 August 2018, p. 25.

staff 'smash' their sales targets.[50] One Ferrari-driving retail banker pleaded guilty to one account of obtaining financial advantage by deception after tricking customers into signing an introducer form. An investigation of the program by KPMG in 2015 found serious control issues with bankers falsifying documents to issue bogus loans.[51] This conduct was largely motivated by sales-based commission bonuses paid by the bank to employees. Significant problems with the program were evident for over a decade, with evidence that the bank's senior management turned a blind eye to this activity given the rewards it bestowed.[52]

- *Branches selling superannuation*: ANZ encouraged unqualified branch staff to push the bank's own Smart Choice Super contrary to ASIC guidelines. The bank had sold $3.6 billion of superannuation this way and was fined $1.25 million as a result. The profits ANZ will make from the $3.6 billion remained intact.
- *Selling insurance policies that were not fit for purpose*: NAB and CBA were accused of selling loan related insurance cover that some customers felt was a condition of receiving a loan, only to find that the policies were not fit for the purpose that they were sold. NAB is alleged to have continued selling the insurance knowing that it was 'worthless' and was accused of 'unconscionable conduct'.[53] NAB, through the expensive lessons of mis-selling insurance in its once UK-based subsidiary, Clydesdale Bank, should have known better.

---

50 Danckert, S. & Yeates, C., 'NAB staff accepted cash-stuffed enveloped as part of alleged bribery ring', *The Age*, 13 March 2018, p. 24.

51 Frost, J., 'NAB kills scandal-plagued home-loan referral program', *Australian Financial Review*, 25 March 2019, p. 228.

52 Durkin, P., 'Everyone wanted a piece of the action: NAB's internal war over home loan referrals', *Australian Financial Review*, 17–18 March 2018, pp. 24–25.

53 Bailey, S. & Roddan, M., 'NAB and wealth arm MLC face class action over card insurance', *The Australian*, 28 September 2018, p. 34.

Senior executives at CBA ignored warnings from second and third lines of defence on the suitability of loan related insurance products and continued to sell the products when they were knowingly not fit for purpose.[54]

- *Disrespect for the regulator, the law and parliament*: Westpac was accused of resisting compliance with the law on responsible lending. NAB admitted that its Introducer Program had breached responsible lending laws, exposing the bank to both criminal and civil charges.[55] NAB was accused of keeping the regulator in the dark on the scale of compensation payable to the superannuation customers who had been ripped off. NAB wanted to 'remain in the pack' and not be viewed as an outlier, ahead of its annual results announcement. NAB also admitted to the Royal Commission that it failed to provide the inquiry with a crucial document showing that the board of the bank knew about the fraud and bribery related problems in its home loans operation in 2015.[56] The Royal Commission accused NAB, on a number of fronts, of having a 'total disregard' for the law and regulators.[57] There was also evidence of criminal law breaches among some of the banks.[58] The APRA initiated review of governance, culture and accountability at CBA suggested that the bank never took the regulator seriously in the five years to 2018: 'it repeatedly ignored or responded with legalistic defensiveness when called to account by APRA.'[59]

---

54 Durie, J., 'All talk, no action as Comyn ignores the problem', *The Australian*, 20 November 2018, p. 17.

55 Chau, D., 'NAB to scrap scandal-plagued Introducer Program', *ABC News*, 25 March 2019.

56 Butler, B., 'NAB's sad tale of fraud and dodgy loans', *The Australian*, 15 March 2018, p. 17.

57 Ferguson, A., 'Disregard, lack of respect: NAB leads poorly behaved pack', *Sydney Morning Herald*, 25 August 2018, p. 25.

58 Butler, B. & Roddan, M., 'CBA, NAB "committed crimes"', *The Australian*, 25–26 August 2018, p. 27.

59 Boyd, T., 'CBA facing $500m risk fix', *Australian Financial Review*, 2 May 2018, p. 48.

On scandalous conduct and weak ethical and moral values, Australian banks are no Robinson Crusoe operating on an isolated island. Many of these conduct issues had parallels in the UK, particularly the selling of Payment Protection Insurance (PPI), which was often sold to customers by creating a belief in the customer's mind that it was a condition of obtaining the loan. Augar (2018, p. 261) summed up the situation:

> PPI was an insurance policy to cover debts in the event of illness, accident or unemployment. It had been a lucrative business for banks for over a decade, earning the twelve largest distributors of PPI products premiums of £3.8 billion and profits after tax and cost of equity of £1.4 billion; return on equity was an extraordinarily high 490 per cent. If ever there was a case of something being too good to be true, this was it, and exactly the kind of signal the board should have picked up. Instead of asking why returns were so high, though, the banks loaded sales credits for PPI; by 2009, Barclays sales people could earn two and half times more commission for selling a loan with PPI attached than for selling a straight loan. Not surprisingly, they went at it with a will.

The British banks have made provisions of £49 billion ($89 billion) to compensate customers mis-sold PPI alone, with NAB shareholders through its then UK subsidiary, Clydesdale, paying a proportional share of that cost. These provisions however appear totally inadequate. Between 2002 and 2012, Barclays alone generated revenues from PPI, net of claims and provisions for alleged mis-selling, of £940 million. PPI comprised between 32 per cent and 42 per cent of Barclays' UK retail and commercial bank pre-tax profit between 2001 and 2005 (Salz, 2013, p. 57). Fines and penalties imposed on banks for this unethical and sometimes illegal conduct highlight how inadequate the deterrent system is and how it fails societal expectations. If the penalty for misconduct is 'chicken feed' for the banks in the UK, in Australia it is barely a crumb on the profits that banks make.

The Royal Commission investigation came about despite the banks using their significant political capital to lobby hard against it. They argued that there was no case to answer and that it was a waste of public funds. They claimed that the call for the Commission was yet more evidence of populist 'bank bashing' and that any negative findings would only damage the reputation of banks internationally, which would be unhelpful!

This posture only serves to highlight, again, how arrogant and disconnected both bank boards and senior management had become from society. In the modern era, it is hard to compare a miscalculated judgement of this magnitude, particularly from institutions that had spent heavily convincing society that they were there to serve, with customer interests at the front and centre of how they managed their affairs. The real damage to the reputation of the banks comes from their own complacency and unwillingness to change despite years of simmering community resentment, which dates back at least to scandals involving Opes Prime, Storm Financial, Timbercorp, Bridgecorp, Fincorp, Trio, Westpoint and Commonwealth Financial Planning. The truth is that it goes back long before these events and other examples reinforce a perception that the culture in the industry is 'rotten to the core' and that culturally banks are locked on a path dependent course.

The Royal Commission findings aside, there are numerous other examples of bank conduct being at odds with community expectations, and evidence of unethical or illegal practices undertaken solely in order to fuel even higher profits. One does not have to look far or dig deep to find examples, such as the financial planning scandals at CBA or when CBA admitted to systemically breaching anti-money laundering rules, allowing drug related monies to be transferred across borders.[60] Then there was the case,

---

60 Smyth, J. & Bland, B., 'How an Australian bank laundered money for Hong Kong drug gangs', *Financial Times*, 14 March 2018.

again at CBA, of fraudulently manipulating children's accounts in order to meet sales targets and qualify for bonuses. The CBA CEO apologised for a 'breach of trust',[61] but society was left feeling that this is an industry that will do anything to meet its profit goals and ride through any storm that media coverage might expose.

If all this was not enough, there was the case involving several major banks who reached settlements with the regulators on allegations of market manipulation by rigging the interbank interest rate setting mechanism, the bank bill swap rate (BBSW), which is Australia's version of LIBOR (London Interbank Offered Rate). How this rate is set impacts the pricing of billions of dollars' worth of bank loans. ANZ was alleged to have manipulated the rate to drive millions of dollars' worth of profits,[62] as was CBA, NAB[63] and Westpac.[64] Australians were left aghast at the evidence of bank employees exchanging much-caricatured, unethical juvenile emails and messages boasting how easy it was to manipulate a critical benchmark that set rates on billions of dollars of borrowing. Then there are the examples of the banks accused of breaching the law on responsible lending to grow its mortgage market share. An investigation found that eight out of ten of its core lending controls were found to be 'ineffective'.[65] The list goes on, but no more proof is needed that there are deep cultural and governance problems within the banking industry, problems that are not unique to Australia. Similar issues arose in the UK with the LIBOR rate rigging scandal, which led to the regulator insisting on the dismissal

---

61 'Commonwealth Bank admits to manipulation of children's accounts', *ABC News*, 19 May 2018.
62 Schmulow, A., 'Why rigging of the bank bill swap rate hurts everyone', *The Conversation*, 9 March 2016.
63 Smyth, J., 'Commonwealth Bank accused of "unconscionable conduct" as watchdog takes rate-rigging case to court', *Financial Times*, 30 January 2018, p. 13.
64 Gluyas, R., 'ASIC fails to sting Westpac for $58m', *The Australian*, 10 November 2018.
65 Long, S., 'Westpac exposed to civil action over irresponsible home loans', *ABC News*, 13 September 2018, <https://www.abc.net.au/news/2018-09-13/westpac-exposed-to-civil-action-over-irresponsible-home-loans/10238710>.

of Bob Diamond as Barclays CEO. As is often the case, banking practices in the UK seem to have parallels in Australia.

SNAPSHOT OF SCANDALS

TABLE 2: ENFORCEABLE UNDERTAKINGS (2013–18)

Reason for enforceable undertaking	Date	Bank
Rigging BBSW	July 2018	CBA
Unauthorised financial advice by staff	July 2018	ANZ
Unauthorised financial advice by staff	July 2018	CBA
Fees for no service	April 2018	CBA
Fees for no service	Mar 2018	ANZ
Rigging BBSW	Nov 2017	NAB
Rigging BBSW	Nov 2017	ANZ
Foreign exchange misconduct	Mar 2017	Westpac
Foreign exchange misconduct	Mar 2017	ANZ
Foreign exchange misconduct	Dec 2016	CBA
Foreign exchange misconduct	Dec 2016	NAB
CommSec compliance breaches	Dec 2014	CBA
Share price spike	Dec 2013	NAB

Source: ASIC as reported in Australian Financial Review, *23 November 2018, p. 15*

A snapshot of the scandals that engulfed the banks in the five years to 2018 can be seen in the number of enforceable undertakings that the banks have been subject to (see Table 2). An enforceable undertaking is an administrative sanction available to Australian regulators and is used in circumstances including an alleged breach of the law. The issuing of an enforceable undertaking is a method of settling the alleged violation and ensuring that changes are undertaken by the bank to avoid a repeat. It is a very weak form of 'punishment' that does not carry much weight, let alone form a deterrent

What is particularly disappointing and goes to the heart of values and ethics, is that these and other events occurred despite the marketing emphasis that banks placed on 'customer centricity', culture and trust. In 2015, the then CBA chairman, David Turner, promised that CBA 'will be the ethical bank, the bank that others look up to for honesty, transparency, decency, good management, openness'. As scandals unfolded within CBA, in part due to the campaign of a whistleblower, the then CEO, Ian Narev, defended the bank by saying 'the culture that we are building throughout the Commonwealth Bank ... is one with the customer at the centre of what we do'.[66] The then NAB chairman, Dr Ken Henry, provided similar reassurances in 2016 when he said:

> The way I think about it is that a bank that's focused on its customers is not going to treat them poorly or have significant conduct challenges. We have thought about this issue a lot at NAB, and it's actually [CEO] Andrew Thorburn's big messages to the board – we have to get closer to our customers.[67]

Fast forward two years, when the then NAB CEO made a public apology admitting that the bank tried to prevent the publication of correspondence showing more than 100 potentially criminal law breaches, including instances where the bank charged fees to the accounts of deceased customers. Having been forced by the

---

66 Rhodes, C., 'Command and control banks have got ethics and culture all wrong', *The Conversation*, 18 March 2016.
67 Gluyas, R., 'Are banks behaving badly?', *The Australian*, 18 April 2016, p. 11.

Royal Commission to disclose the documents, the CEO took to his Twitter account and sent the following message:

> This week we've been confronted at the Royal Commission with examples of where we have failed to serve our customer with honour. I'm sorry. And my commitment is that we will learn and get better, so we can once again be a bank you respect and trust.[68]

Despite the genuine apology and commitment to do better, the prevailing sentiment is that it only serves to highlight the magnitude of the cultural problems facing the banks. This was evident also in the UK, when the Barclays CEO, on learning of LIBOR rate rigging at Barclays, said that it was 'the worst day of my life'. We return to this theme later in the book, showing how these 'apologies' no longer carry any currency and are heard with a cynical ear by customers, given the deeply ingrained cultural problems including very weak accountability at senior levels. It is this equation of poor culture and weak accountability that is the Achilles heel of the industry and these attributes are consistent with an industry long locked on a path dependent course.

To highlight the uncanny similarities to the UK, several senior British bankers echoed a familiar tune of apology and commitment to do better (Salz, 2013, p. 77):

- In October 2010, Marcus Agius, then chairman of Barclays, stated, 'The leaders of our industry must collectively procure a visible and substantive change in the culture of our institutions … so as fundamentally to convince the world once again that they are businesses which can be relied on.'
- In October 2012, Stephen Hester, then CEO of RBS, said, 'Banks must undergo wholesale changes in their culture and refocus their behaviour on meeting the needs of customers to restore trust in the industry.'

---

68 Hutchens, G., 'NAB issues public apology after week of damning evidence at royal commission', *The Guardian*, 9 August 2018.

- In October 2012, Sir David Walker, then chairman of Barclays, said, 'Mistrust and the perception of inadequate standards have led to a crisis of confidence and it is severe ... We must not recoil from the shock waves, rather embrace the current reality and deliver the cultural change.'

Bank CEOs have learnt how to own up to 'mistakes', but society was left feeling that their profit maximising objectives were their overriding objective (adherence to their version of the Friedman Doctrine, as described in Chapter 3), and apologies were made simply because they had been caught. As the interim Royal Commission report states, 'Discovery of misconduct was "managed" by words of apology and promises to do better.'[69] The emperors were found to have no clothes, at least in an ethical and moral sense, even if legally the penalties for transgressions paled into insignificance as a 'cost of doing business'. As the chair of the Royal Commission said, the behaviour of the banks was not just immoral, but criminal. The punishment in Australia rarely fits the crime and it is the shareholders, rather than the offending executives, who pick up the bill. The culture of weak accountability is a topic expanded on in Chapter 7.

Another important lens on the banking industry was provided by the Productivity Commission report in 2018, which coincidentally overlapped with the Royal Commission.

PRODUCTIVITY COMMISSION

The Productivity Commission's report acknowledged that Australia has both a strong and stable financial system. While the oligopoly structure of the banking industry provides stability, that comes at a

---

69 Boyd, T., 'Hayne exposes bankers' Shangri-La', *Australian Financial Review*, 29–30 September 2018, p. 48.

cost to competition, a cost ultimately borne by the consumer. The report confirmed that:

- The banks were focused on shareholders over the consumer.
- The power of the banks enables them to game the regulations to maximise returns at the expense of the consumer.
- There is little product competition because of the general obfuscation with very minor product differences in price and features.
- Bank products lack transparency; they provide unclear and insufficient information for customers and ownership arrangements can create conflicts of interest at the expense of the customer.
- The regulatory environment distorts the market, with risk weighting differentials for the same asset class strengthening the power of larger banks and handicapping smaller banks. The design of the risk weighting framework also creates an imbalance between household and business lending.
- A void had opened on which government agency was responsible for the promotion of competition within the current regulatory framework.

The commission acknowledged that Australia needs a competition champion as this important economic function falls between the cracks of the current cohort of regulators overseeing aspects of the industry. The current regulatory arrangement is likely to be supported by the banks as it reinforces the oligopoly structure. In the UK, the principal bank regulator, the Financial Conduct Authority (FCA), has three objectives: (i) to protect consumers; (ii) to protect financial markets; and (iii) to promote competition.[70]

As in most industries, competition in banking is important and arguments that a consolidated market of a few powerful banks underpins stability is a self-serving myth — a nonsense.

---
70 <https://www.fca.org.uk>.

Competition and stability should be an *and* not an *or*. As the Productivity Commission reported (2018, p. 14), 'Competition and stability can, and should, co-exist'. Other countries, concerned about powerful banking structures and the damage they inflicted as evident in the GFC, have taken steps to strengthen regulation *and* promote competition. There should not be a trade-off if the institutional environment is properly set. In part the issue here, as the Productivity Commission highlighted, is the 'regulatory culture'. The call for change has never been louder or clearer. What passes for a stable banking system is also seen as one that is deeply flawed by many in society. While not all banks are sinners, the industry is tarnished by the deeds of many.

One of the more galling features of the banking system is the perception that banks take their customers for granted. The Productivity Commission report highlighted how banks reward new customers differently from existing customers in the implicit belief that existing customers will not leave. This exploitation of customer loyalty means that on average existing customers will pay 0.3 to 0.4 percentage points higher than the rates charged to new customers. This penalty on loyalty translates into $66 to $87 more per month on average mortgages for existing customers. In a separate study, the ACCC found that banks profited by $1.1 billion in revenue per annum by using a regulatory signal to slow down on investor-only loans, as a basis for increasing interest rates on such loans to existing customers.[71] The ACCC study also demonstrated how the banks 'rip off' loyal customers and in pricing mortgage loans act in a 'synchronised manner'.[72] The marketing and corporate rhetoric of putting their customers first is difficult to reconcile with this behaviour.

---

71 Crowe, D., 'Damning review finds big banks overcharge loyal customers $850 a year', *Sydney Morning Herald*, 10 December 2018.

72 Roddan, M., 'ACCC accuses banks of high mortgage costs rip-off', *The Australian*, 10 December 2018.

The four major banks – the so-called four pillars – routinely make annual profits totalling between $30 and $35 billion in an economy of just 29 million people including New Zealand, which equates to approximately $1200 in contributions by every single man, woman and child (remember this is *only* for the four major banks). The money made by these banks from fees alone is a staggering $13 billion a year, which means every Australian and New Zealand household is paying on average approximately $450 annually in bank fees. On a per capita basis, there is no domestic banking system anywhere in the developed world that earns such high economic rents while enjoying privileges such as an implicit 'put option' on failure to the taxpayer and the related cost of funds subsidy, estimated at some $4 billion a year.

The Treasury was critical of the banks, claiming profits had been propped up by a lack of effective competition, which led to a collective dulling of the sense of board members:

> Despite their conduct failures, many financial firms have continued to generate strong profits assisted by a lack of effective competition in the financial system. In these circumstances, boards have had their 'senses dulled' to the significance of the misconduct by their firm and its employees, and shareholders have had little incentive to intervene.[73]

The Productivity Commission report summed up the current environment in Australia, when it wrote:

> There is evidence that they [banks] have sustained prices above competitive levels, offered inferior quality products to some groups of customers (particularly those customers unlikely to change providers), subsumed much of the broker industry and taken action that would inhibit the expansion of smaller competitors in some markets. All are indicators of the use of market power to the detriment of consumers. (2018, pp. 4–5)

---

73 Frost, J., 'Treasury lashes boards "dulled senses"', *Australian Financial Review*, 27 July 2018, p. 4.

INTRODUCTION

CASE FOR CHANGE

The case for change is a strong one, but the banking industry is powerful. It spends millions of dollars each year on marketing and has the power to influence key voices in politics, as it did in watering down the Future of Financial Advice reforms in 2014. It employs hundreds of people in lobbying politicians and industry groups, and engages an army of lawyers and public relations specialists, all skilled at dry-cleaning reputations and in maintaining the status quo. To protect the status quo, the banks will argue that:[74]

- Australia is a small open economy and that it is desirable to have a few powerful banks.
- The banks need scale to invest in new products and technology.
- Strong, large banks are necessary to maintain capital market support for the Australian economy, particularly given the scale of our international borrowings.
- Competition may come at a cost to stability.
- To break up the banks would add costs, interest rates and threaten stability.
- Government should not interfere in the marketplace.

While there is merit in some of these arguments, they are largely self-serving and in the case of an argument that there is a trade-off between competition and stability, this can be viewed as a myth. There is certainly a trade-off between earning excessive profits and competition. Industry structure and competition matters and there is a need for structural reform, which will only happen where there are courageous political leaders. More on this in Chapter 9. The irony in the current market structure is that the economic rents earned by the banks and the poor level of trust in them is

---

74 I am indebted here to a paper written by John Dahlsen, titled 'Regulators running riot', 31 May 2018.

evidence that a consolidated market can result in anti-competitive behaviour and market failure, both of which can have far-reaching implications for the economy and for society.

Following the Royal Commission, all the major banks pledged to change and listen to their customers and to society. Most people hearing that commitment will be sceptical and for good reasons. Over the past 30 years, an endless line of bank CEOs have 'promised to do better'. The economics editor at the *Sydney Morning Herald*, Ross Gittins, recalled a column he wrote in 1990 saying that the banks' abuse of their customers' trust was getting them a bad name, so they should desist. He was referring to the fact that banks were abusing customer loyalty by offering better deals to new customers.[75] Culturally, nothing has materially changed in 30 years, except these culturally-based problems have dug even deeper roots and have weakened the foundation of the industry. A sceptical society should assume that nothing will change in the future unless there is government intervention. There is no competitive pressure to drive change and little political will to intervene, given the contribution the major banks make to the nation's fiscal position and the significant political lobbying power they hold.

In the same *Sydney Morning Herald* article, Gittins highlights an interesting paradox in the banking market. He argues that banking is both 'ruthlessly competitive and uncompetitive at the same time'. The banks are obsessed by a game of achieving higher market share and the highest increases in margin, profitability and share price. It is this competition, argues Gittins, that has kept bankers in a 'bubble of unreality, urging their minions on with KPIs and bonuses, and turning a blind eye to the rule-bending they lead to'. John Kay (2015, p. 136), in referring to the UK, wrote about 'bank CEOs competing like schoolboys to demonstrate that "my return on equity is larger than yours"'.

---

75 Gittins, R., 'Why the banks will ignore customer anger and match Westpac rate rise', *Sydney Morning Herald*, 4 September 2018, p. 29.

CONCLUDING REMARKS

Despite being among the most profitable banking system in the world, the issues plaguing the major Australian banks are there for all to see and are graphically illustrated by CBA, who have admitted that it provided dodgy financial advice; failed to update medical definitions on life insurance policies; settled allegations that it tried to rig a key interest rate; and fell foul of anti-money laundering and counterterrorism finance laws. CBA however was not alone. In so many ways, Australian banks may have missed the GFC only to find, 10 years later, they have their own post Royal Commission AFC, not in a financial vulnerability sense as was evident in the UK but nonetheless a crisis of culture, purpose and social licence, which may prove more challenging

This long opening chapter has focused on many of the problems with the current banking market structure and it paints a bleak picture. What the commentary in the opening chapter has not addressed and left hanging is the important question of what type of banking system do we need? To address that question, it is important first to understand what the current system looks like, how it operates, particularly in its pivotal function of allocating capital across the economy, and how it might distort the economy in significant and, in the long-term, unhelpful ways. This is the focus of the next chapter.

1
THE BANKING SYSTEM

THIS chapter is intended to give the reader a general overview of the nature of the banking market in Australia (which mirrors what is largely true of New Zealand). It is not a detailed commentary, but it is a broadly accurate picture on the shape of the market and its key drivers. In painting the picture, the reader is reminded that a core role of a well-functioning banking system is the efficient allocation of capital across the economy. It is a legitimate public policy matter as different categories of capital (e.g. lending to real estate versus SMEs) can perform different economic functions. It is not simply a question of how much lending banks do but what *type* of lending and what *sectors* that lending is allocated to.

Unlike the banking system in the UK or the US, the Australian banks are largely domestic in nature, if you include New Zealand in that definition. Equally, unlike the UK and the US, the Australian financial system is bank dominated, with a surprising shallow fixed income market given the size of the $2 trillion superannuation industry – Australia's pension fund allocation to fixed income is at 10 per cent, which is low compared to other Organisation for Economic Co-operation and Development (OECD) countries and the OECD average of 40 per cent.[76] So, in Australia and in New Zealand banks matter more in the financial system than they do in the UK and the US. Therefore, they should play a true leadership role in ensuring the financial system supports the real, or non-financial, economy. This is a reasonable societal expectation given the privileges bestowed on banks.

I am defining the Australian banking market in terms of customers, with a simple split into retail or personal banking (private banking, personal customers and very small businesses, such as the butcher, the baker and the candlestick maker) and business banking. Retail banking can then be most conveniently segmented by product and covers household mortgages, current and term deposit accounts and unsecured personal lending, most notably credit cards. Business banking on the other hand, is typically segmented by size into SME (businesses with a turnover of up to $50 million per annum),[77] Corporate (businesses with a turnover of up to $250 million per annum) and Institutional (the rest). Of course, businesses of all sizes can also then be segmented by industry such as property, retail, agriculture and financial institutions.

The emphasis in this chapter is on the lending role of banks and not on deposits and other important services. Before getting into the chapter a warning and an apology is warranted regarding the use of some jargon, which may at times feel overly technical and occasionally theoretical. Some readers may appreciate this, while others may not. For completeness, some of the technical commentary is necessary and will help those who wish to understand cause and effect. Those who prefer to skip the technical commentary will not be disadvantaged.

---

76 Organisation for Economic Co-operation and Development, *Pension markets in focus*, No. 14, 2017, <http://www.oecd.org/pensions/private-pensions/Pension-Markets-in-Focus-2017.pdf>.

77 Small businesses are defined as having a turnover up to $5 million, while medium businesses are defined as having a turnover from $5 to $50 million.

FOUR STRUCTURAL DEVELOPMENTS

In understanding the dynamics of the Australian banking industry, there have been four structural developments, which became apparent early in the twenty-first century and which both define the industry and have had material economic consequences. The first development, driven by Basel II and the favourable risk weightings on mortgage lending (which is explained below), resulted in a significant shift to household mortgage lending, away from business lending. The second development was the diminution in competition caused by a consolidation of the banks through M&A resulting in the four major banks – the so-called four pillars – controlling approximately 80 per cent of the market (with market share varying by product but broadly in this range, see Table 3).

TABLE 3: BANK MARKET SHARE

Bank	Business (%)	Housing (%)	Total (%)
ANZ	14.6	15.3	15.0
CBA	16.9	25.6	23.8
NAB	21.0	15.4	17.5
Westpac	18.0	24.7	22.0
Subtotal	**70.5**	**81.0**	**78.3**
Macquarie	1.1	2.1	2.0
Bendigo	1.6	2.2	2.3
BOQ	1.4	1.6	1.5
TOTAL	**74.6**	**86.9**	**84.1**

Source: APRA, March 2019. Business lending covers all lending to businesses excl. non-bank financial institutions. SME lending is a subset of business lending and the 80 per cent market share to the major banks is an estimate of the 70.5 per cent share shown above, noting that foreign banks are active lenders to large businesses hence the major bank market share is lower for overall business lending than it is for SME lending. Household lending covers mortgage lending only.

The third development was the emergence of brokers as major actors in the banking system, particularly in the mortgage market where brokers now originate over 50 per cent of all mortgage flow and close to 30 per cent of all new SME lending. The influence of brokers is discussed later in this chapter. The fourth development has been the progressive industrialisation of bank operating models, which has resulted in a dehumanisation of customer service, as banks sought to digitalise and standardise, and adopt a 'one-size-fits-all' philosophy and a rigid policies and procedures driven approach. ANZ CEO, Shayne Elliott, acknowledged this when he said that 'We engineered a production line to maximise efficiency and deliver those high returns ... as we learnt in the royal commission, while it was an efficient process, it did fail some people badly'. Elliott added that the systems that banks had set up to churn out strong profits were now being asked 'to deal with nuance, judgement and exceptions on an unprecedented scale'.[78] These developments were all largely aimed at achieving cost economies, a 'cookie-cutter approach' and reducing elements of operational risk. The bias towards mortgage lending also played to the desire of building simple products and simple processes, with six sigma specialists intent on attacking every cost line to further standardise and simplify. Soon, mortgage and credit card lending will most probably be totally handled by artificial intelligence (AI), as unlike business lending, consumer lending is conducted in a largely information efficient market and it does not require annual reviews – a classic example of 'set and forget' lending. Or is it?

These developments are also systematic of an industry focused on maximising shareholder returns in the safe knowledge that the oligopoly nature of the industry, and the herding behaviour of industry actors, should ensure that no one would upset the balance. It is the reverse of the 'prisoner's dilemma' with banks

---

78 Maley, K., 'Healing the scars', *Australian Financial Review*, 4–5 May 2019, p. 19.

acting in their own self-interest, knowing that other banks will do the same. The 'prisoners dilemma' is an important game theory that explains much of what happens in banking. The dilemma shows how two or more rational actors might not cooperate, even if it appears that it is in their best interest to do so, as they have been accused of the same crime. There is no such dilemma when it comes to repricing consumer lending products as the banks tend to move in lockstep, as if they were coordinated.

THE RISE OF MORTGAGE LENDING

Post-GFC, retail banking benefited from a benign interest rate environment to deliver strong mortgage growth, which fuelled rising property prices. By the end of 2018, bank lending to the household sector reached $1.8 trillion,[79] of which $1.68 trillion was in residential mortgages, with 33 per cent ($557 billion) of that lending to investors or buy-to-let borrowers.[80] In contrast, the business banking market is estimated at $760 billion of outstanding loans, of which approximately 40 per cent ($300 billion) is in SME lending. Total business bank lending within the banking system is at 49 per cent of GDP, down from a peak of 62 per cent in 2008 – a material drop – whereas household lending sits at over 100 per cent of GDP. Figure 4 illustrates the shift from business to household lending.

---

79 Australian household debt is approximately 200% of disposable income, with total household liabilities at $2.466 billion, representing one of the highest indebted household sectors in the world, 18 January 2018, <https://www.businessinsider.com.au>.
80 APRA statistics as at August 2018, <https://www.apra.gov.au>.

FIGURE 4: BANK LENDING – HOUSEHOLD AND BUSINESS
Banks' lending structure

Source: APRA, 2018

In New Zealand, total bank lending at the beginning of 2019 was NZ$445 billion, comprising NZ$268 billion to households (NZ$260 billion in mortgages) and NZ$176 billion to businesses (including NZ$63 billion in the agricultural sector). The SME sector, excluding agriculture, is estimated at approximately NZ$35 billion. Household lending is approximately 95 per cent of GDP and business lending is approximately 60 per cent of GDP. According to the Bank of England, as at the end of 2017 the UK bank market had household debt of £1.6 trillion (76 per cent of GDP) of which residential mortgages compromised £1.3 trillion. Total business lending to nonfinancial businesses in the UK was £460 billion, of which £164 billion was to SMEs. The stock of SME lending to GDP at less than 10 per cent is very low and evidence of a widely acknowledged market failure in the UK, and a warning to what might happen in Australia and New Zealand absent any policy intervention.

The clear shift towards household lending could be described as a bias within the system in how banks fulfil their purpose of allocating capital across the economy. A significant factor, but by no means the only factor, behind this shift has been more favourable capital weighting driven by the regulatory prescribed RWAs following the introduction of the Basel II changes in 2006. The higher the risk weighting the more capital a bank must allocate, and the lower the risk rating, the less capital that is needed. The lower the capital requirements, all other things being equal, the higher the ROE.[81] In turn, the higher the ROE, the higher the executive remuneration. So, the cause and effect formula can be understood – lend more into households, use less capital, generate higher ROE, drive higher bonuses. In 2018, mortgages represented 46 per cent of bank profits in Australia, delivering an ROE of 36 per cent.[82]

As readers go through this book, they should remember a simple formula in banking: the lower the 'E', the higher the 'R'. So a bias to mortgage lending is perfectly rational if the private self-interest of the bank is all that counts. The problem arises, however, if all the banks do the same, as they tend to do. Where all the banks are gripped by more than a dash of the 'animal spirits' that Keynes wrote about, the greater the risk of asset bubbles and of market failure. Keynes also wrote how banks operate in herds, so should things go wrong no individual bank takes all the blame – there is comfort and some protection from being in the crowd rather than standing alone. It is as close as a senior banker gets to a bulletproof vest.

---

81 ROE is a measure of profitability that divides net profits after tax (NPAT) by the average equity capital employed during the year, i.e. $7 billion NPAT on an equity capital base of $45 billion generates an ROE of 15 per cent. If the equity is reduced to $40 billion, the ROE created by $7 billion NPAT increases to 17 per cent. Equally, if the equity capital increased to $50 billion, the ROE on $7 billion NPAT is reduced to 14 per cent.

82 Deutsche Bank research, 'Australian banking sector', 17 January 2019.

RISK-WEIGHTED ASSETS

Some readers might find this brief commentary on RWAs rather dry, but it is worth understanding given how it influences and can distort the function of the banking system. Figure 5 shows the risk weightings against individual asset classes and Table 4 provides a high-level summary.

FIGURE 5: MAJOR BANK RISK WEIGHTS SUMMARY
Major Banks' Risk Weights

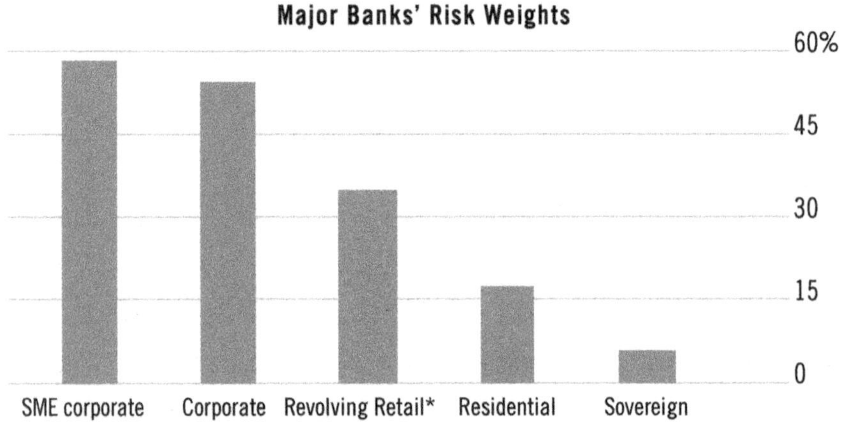

Excludes retail SME Source: APRA; RBA

If the equity capital base of the bank is 10 per cent of total assets, then the amount of capital allocated against each $100 of loan assets will be adjusted by the weighting, so that a 100 per cent risk weighting would mean that the allocated capital is $10 ($100 loan x 10% x 100% = $10). If the risk weighting is 25 per cent, then the allocated capital would be $2.50, that is, $7.50 less ($100 loan x 10% x 25%). Under the first scenario (100% RWA), $100 net profit after tax (NPAT) generates a 10% ROE (100/10=10); under the second scenario (25% RWA), $100 NPAT generates a 40% ROE (100/2.5=40). This is big difference. You would always do more of the latter if ROE and incentive maximisation is the primary goal. Absent any macro-prudential intervention, that is exactly what banks will do. It is exactly what the major Australian banks have done.

Table 4 shows how different loan classifications attract a specific risk weighting. SME loans, for example, are classified into two categories: (i) those that are treated as retail loans because they are under $1 million; and (ii) those that are treated like business loans (i.e. 'corporate lending'). Table 4 also looks at proposed changes in category risk weightings under Basel III compared to Basel II (this jargon is explained shortly). A noticeable difference is that SME corporate lending moves from a 100 per cent risk weighting under Basel II to 85 per cent under the new Basel III rules.

TABLE 4: STANDARDISED CREDIT RISK WEIGHTINGS

Type of lending	Basel II Standard risk weightings	APRA Prudential standard 112	Basel III Standard risk weightings	APRA Discussion paper (in response to Basel III)
	%	%	%	%
SME lending covered under retail lending	75	100	75	85
SME corporate lending	100	100	85	85
Lending for/secured by commercial real estate	100	**	80–130 (depending on LVR)	
Lending for land development			150	
Residential property	35	35–75 (depending on LVR and mortgage insurance)	25–55 (depending on LVR)	30–85 (depending on LVR)

Source: Productivity Commission, 2018   LVR = loan-to-value ratio

The most important point from Table 4 is that SME lending is normally 100 per cent risk-weighted, although it can be lower if appropriate residential security is held. This is one of the reasons why 90 per cent of all SME lending by the major banks is real estate secured, often on the entrepreneur's residence (SME lending essentially becomes a mortgage loan in disguise). Rather than taking a more granular approach, absent property as security, a single risk weighting of 100 per cent is applied, with no delineation allowed for size of borrowing, the form of borrowing or the risk profile of the SME borrower. Australian regulators apply higher risk weightings to SME borrowers than is the case in many other countries, causing many bank executives to view SME lending as 'capital hogs'. Canadian and European regulators, for example, take a more positive approach to SME risk weightings where there is no property as collateral, making SME lending more attractive to their banks.[83]

For more technically minded readers, the determination of an RWA is primarily driven by three internally assessed inputs into the model:
- Probability of default (PD): an estimate of the level of risk of a borrower defaulting.
- Exposure at default (EAD): an estimate of total facility exposure at the time of default.
- Loss given default (LGD): an estimate of the potential economic loss on the facility exposure as a result of the default. So if the loan is unsecured, the LGD could be estimated at 100 per cent.

---

83 Productivity Commission, p. 435.

PROBLEMS WITH RWA DETERMINATION

RWA determination (and therefore the amount of capital required) in the case of the large banks is based on their own in-house, 'advanced accredited' model, which delivers lower RWAs than the 'standardised' models used by non-major banks and used in the examples in Table 4. Regardless of whether it is advanced or standardised, RWA determination remains far from a perfect science. Instead it is highly subjective, which encourages creative thinking to economise on capital, with material behavioural and competition implications. As executive remuneration is in large part determined by ROE outcomes, there is every incentive to engineer the 'desired' outcome. RWA and 'capital optimisation' programs, a euphemism for tweaking models so that loans are less risky and thus require less capital, is standard fare in many banks.

This subjectivity was highlighted by a test carried out by the FSA in the UK[84] on a sample of 13 banks, which showed a 'huge disparity' in the 'probability of default' data. On one typical corporate loan, with an 'A minus' credit rating, the cautious estimate of risk was 100 times greater than the most bullish. This translated into risk weightings ranging from 30 per cent to 189 per cent of the value of the loan. *The Financial Times* noted:

> Multiply that kind of differential across the loan book and suddenly all the fine efforts of global regulators to set a unified capital standard of seven per cent, look rather hollow. As the Bank of England has said, some reported capital ratios could be as much as a third higher than they should be.[85]

Studies between 2012 and 2016 conducted by the Basel Committee

---

84 Due to the regulatory failure of the banks in the GFC, the FSA was abolished in 2013 and its responsibilities were then split between two new agencies of the Bank of England: the Financial Conduct Authority (FCA) and the Prudential Regulation Authority (PRA).

85 Jenkins, P., 'Time to work out the real odds in the weighting game', *Financial Times*, 3 May 2011, p. 20.

on Banking Supervision highlighted alarming discrepancies between similar banks' so-called RWA densities in similar lending categories.[86] Given the latitude of the subjectivity that can be applied, there is always the temptation to take an aggressive approach in order to minimise the amount of capital. Evidence of this was highlighted in the case of Metro Bank in the UK. The bank's share price dropped close to 50 per cent when it was discovered that they were misclassifying certain commercial loans secured on property and certain buy-to-let loans. The ramifications of this error were profound, requiring the bank to raise more than £350 million of new equity when the bank's market capitalisation at the time was £1.4 billion. Investor anger resulted in demands that the chair and the CEO resign.[87] The *Financial Times* wrote:

> Metro Bank, once the darling of Britain's challenger lenders, has lost half its stock market value ... There has been no nasty loan loss, no vast money laundering scandal and no funding squeeze to rival the nightmares visited on other trouble banks. Metro's problem is far geekier. But as the share price slump shows, being found out by regulators to have miscalculated your risk weighted asset tally – and overreported your capital ratios as a result – is a serious gaffe ... the Financial Conduct Authority is to examine whether the miscalculation resulted in a false market in Metro's shares.[88]

The example of Metro Bank is a useful case study in the problems with RWA calculations. With total assets of £22 billion, Metro's RWAs were stated at £8 billion, before the miscalculation was found. The error required a restatement of RWAs and the need for £350 million more equity.

---

86 Bank for International Settlements, *Regulatory consistency assessment programme (RCAP) – Analysis of risk-weighted assets for credit risk in the banking book*, April 2016, <https://www.bis.org>.

87 Jenkins, P., 'Over the Hill: why Metro Bank and its founder are past it', *Financial Times*, 28 January 2019, p. 18.

88 Jenkins, P., 'Metro gaffe highlighted banks' flimsy risk arithmetic', *Financial Times*, 4 March 2019, p. 20.

On a smaller scale but equally embarrassing for the bank, the Reserve Bank of New Zealand (RBNZ) revoked ANZ New Zealand from using its own models for assessing the operational risk capital requirements, due to a 'persistent failure' in its controls. This problem with the model existed despite the ANZ New Zealand directors attesting that all controls were in place and working. As a result of having to move from the more favourable internal advanced model, ANZ had to inject an additional NZ$277 million of capital into its New Zealand subsidiary.[89]

Lord Turner, then chairman of the FSA, commented on the RWA subjectivity:

> This is a hugely important issue. We have spent a lot of time over the past two years devising a standardised definition of capital as the numerator in capital ratios. It would be sensible now to look in more detail at the denominator and examine whether risk-weighted calculations are comparable and consistent across banks and across countries.[90]

Similar variations exist in Australia. APRA's chairman, Wayne Byres, noted when he said that efforts to strengthen confidence in the banks' ability to withstand future shocks:

> are being undermined somewhat by an increasing lack of faith in the use of internal models by the largest banks to calculate risk-weighted assets … doubts about the reliability of risk measurement in the denominator mean that the resulting ratios lack credibility as a reliable measure of financial strength.[91]

The current approach materially favours large banks. This distortion was highlighted by the Murray Inquiry (2014), which

---

89 Chalmers, S., 'ANZ shares tumble as New Zealand's central bank calls out "persistent failure"', *ABC News*, 17 May 2019.
90 Lord Turner, 'Drive for global standard on banks', *Financial Times*, 3 May 2011, p. 1.
91 Letts, S., 'Bank debt ratios expose Basel's faulty risk weightings', *ABC News*, 18 June 2015.

recommended that the mortgage risk weightings gap between major and small banks be narrowed by increasing the risk weighting required by major banks in assessing mortgage risk.[92] The current arrangement can result in perverse outcomes, which are difficult to explain to anyone, particularly the reasonably educated 'man on the Clapham omnibus'. For example, a customer borrowing from a major bank may have a risk-weighted mortgage of 25 per cent because that bank uses the 'advanced' model; when the customer refinances through a regional bank, that risk weighting may increase to 50 per cent, even though the underlying risk (PD) is exactly the same. The system benefits the major banks, creates an uneven playing field for smaller banks and is anti-competitive.

This is a hugely unhelpful distortion and an opportunity for regulators to apply common sense judgement, which in turn would do much for competition. The Bank of Queensland highlighted this problem in its submission to the Federal Government's Financial System Inquiry; they noted that 29 per cent of CBA's then $341 billion housing mortgage portfolio was risk-weighted at just 2.9 per cent: 'This risk-weight translates into a requirement that the bank holds only 26 cents in equity against every $100 in loans. In contrast, a regional bank with the same loan portfolio would have to hold around $3.15 per $100 of loans.'[93] In other words, the CBA can achieve leverage on its loans of around 380 per cent compared to a regional bank's maximum leverage of 31 per cent.

The RWA advantage granted to the major banks (and Macquarie Bank and ING) represents a regulatory granted source of competitive advantage. Jamie McPhee, CEO of ME Bank, a second-tier largely household lender, summed this up:

---

92 Shapiro, J., 'Murray Inquiry's key recommendations', *Sydney Morning Herald*, 7 December 2014, p. 22.
93 Ibid.

The average capital risk weights of the standard banks is around 39 per cent, the major banks average around 25 per cent, and the actual cost of that difference equates to around 15 basis points in margin, so it's not insignificant at all.[94]

This RWA bias to household lending is true in all developed market banking systems. The Australian banks however have a greater appetite for property-backed lending, and specifically residential real estate and commercial real estate, than most other countries. The bias to household lending has caused several commentators, and former NAB CEO Don Argus, to describe Australian banking as a 'building society system'.

This bias to property lending is much more pronounced in Australia in comparison to other markets (Figure 6), underlining the quip from Don Argus.

FIGURE 6: AUSTRALIAN BANKS ADDICTED TO PROPERTY
Proportion of book exposed to Residential and Commercial Property

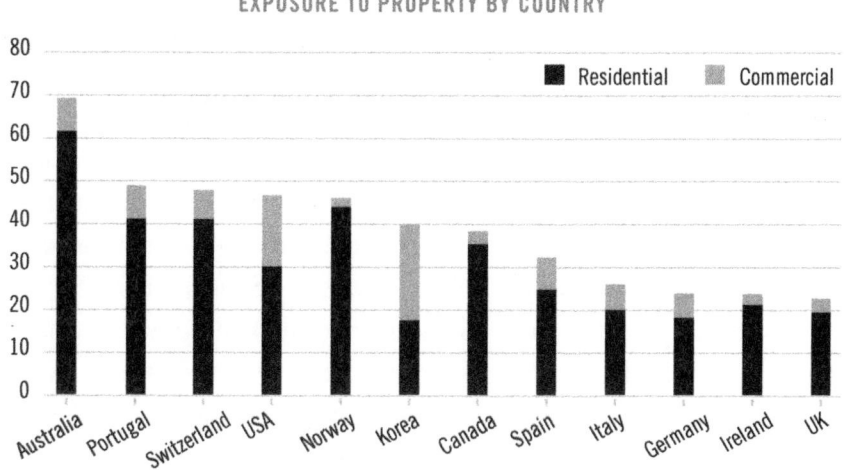

Source: IMF Macquarie data Q1 2018

---

94 Janda, J., 'Do big banks deserve the mortgage cost advantage gifted by regulators?', *ABC News*, 1 August 2018, <https://www.abc.net.au/news/2018-08-31/do-big-banks-deserve-mortgage-cost-advantage/10057756>.

BASEL

The reader will note the reference to Basel and the influence it has on the banking market. Established in 1974, the Basel Committee of Bank Supervisors (BCBS) is a global forum of bank supervisors – APRA and its equivalents – aimed at establishing uniform global standards to govern banks. Its charter mandate is:

> To be the primary global standard base setter for the prudential regulation of banks and provide a forum for cooperation on banking supervision matters. Its mandate is to strengthen the regulation, supervision and practice of banks worldwide with the purpose of enhancing financial stability.

An important point is that the BCBS does not have any legal or formal authority within each country. It relies on the commitment of members such as APRA to achieve its mandate and a convergence of rules and regulations across member countries, subject always to national laws. One of the reasons that the banking industry focuses on Basel is because of the capital requirements that it imposes, particularly the need to maintain a minimum equity capital ratio. In 1997, the Basel Committee issued its *Core principles for effective banking supervision*, which Australia through APRA and the other 48 member countries adhere to, thus creating a powerful policy network (Schooner & Taylor, 2010). Bank regulation is primarily concerned with ensuring that all banks are financially sound and well managed. While emphasis is placed on the capital base as a measure of bank strength, following the GFC, regulators moved to strengthen the liquidity of banks and the durability of their liabilities. So, under what came to be known as Basel III, emphasis was placed on the customer funding ratio (deposits) and the stable funding ratio (long-term debt plus deposits). This is in essence about extending the maturity and stability of the liabilities on bank balance sheets. This is an important development as many banks, and particularly Australian banks, were relying on the international short-dated wholesale funding markets, for example, the securitisation market. This reliance on wholesale funding as distinct from deposits created new risks as it was demonstrated to be a less stable source of funding, as was evident in the demise of Northern Rock and the problems that caused St George Bank to merge with Westpac. As highlighted earlier, a liquidity crisis for a bank can be deadly. Another reason the banking industry focuses on Basel is to ensure that there is competitive equality across international markets and that no single market operates under less rigorous rules, creating a competitive advantage for that market. In 2004, the Basel II so-called three pillars were declared:

- Banks are subject to minimum capital requirements, which individual national regulators can increase.
- Banks can determine their own capital levels through an internal assessment of RWAs, which are then subject to regulatory review and supervision.
- Strengthen the disclosure of risk management frameworks and portfolio composition as a market discipline to complement regulatory oversight.

The Murray Inquiry (2014) into the financial system called for Australian banks to increase their capital ratios and become 'unquestionably strong' to prevent a financial crisis that could cost the economy as much as $2.4 trillion. The Murray Inquiry recommended that Australian banks should be in the top quartile of international banks in terms of capital strength.[95] It is not unusual to hear bank lobbyists complain that additional equity capital restricts lending or that equity is expensive. Finance students

---

95 Shapiro, J., 'Murray Inquiry's key recommendations', *Sydney Morning Herald*, 7 December 2014, p. 22.

know that these arguments are weak. When there is more equity in a balance sheet, the riskiness of the debt and equity comes down and wholesale lenders are willing to accept lower returns. The airbag is bigger and the car passengers safer. Investors buying equity can look to the Capital Asset Pricing Model (CAPM) or a deviation of that to price the required return to compensate for risk. The lower the risk, the lower the required return – investors care about making sure that the reward they receive compensates them for the risk they are assuming. So a well-capitalised bank, all other things being equal, represents a lower risk than a less well-capitalised bank. Finance students also know the Miller and Modigliani (1958) theorems on the mix and cost of equity and debt, in a world free from tax distortions and transactions costs. A simple model, but one that reminds us that the more debt there is in a balance sheet, the higher the risk to equity, therefore loading up a balance sheet with lower cost debt only transfers the risk premium in the cost to equity as investors seek higher returns. These simple but powerful theories of finance highlight the limitations of the argument that equity is 'too expensive'. (In the real world, taxes do impact some assumptions and banks do benefit from low cost deposits.) As Admati and Hellwig (2013, p. 112) argue 'the notion that the required ROE is fixed and independent of the funding mix is as fallacious for banks as it is for nonfinancial corporations.' In a similar vein, Hyun Song Shin, chief economist at the Bank for International Settlements (BIS), said, 'Higher bank capital is associated with greater lending [because of] the lower funding costs associated with better capitalised banks.'[96]

---

96 Creighton, A., 'Kiwis show the way on regulation', *The Australian*, 28 December 2018, p. 19.

COST OF CAPITAL

Back to CAPM. This is a widely known framework for measuring a business's cost of equity and therefore understanding how its ROE should compare. In competitive markets, investors should expect an ROE to broadly equal the CAPM determined cost of equity. If this happens, investors are growing their wealth as the return on investment is equal to the riskiness of that investment. Anything over and above is called 'excess' or abnormal returns, and sometimes known as 'economic rents'. A bank's CAPM cost of equity is determined by three inputs:

- The *risk-free rate* – the rate the investor would earn on a ten-year government bond.
- An *equity risk premium* – the margin over the risk-free rate to compensate for the equity risk of the market.
- The *beta* – a variation to the equity risk premium to reflect the unique risks associated with a company; this may be greater or less than the risk premium for investing in the market.

To use the formula to determine the cost of equity for a domestic bank, the risk-free rate for the 10-year government bond is known and at the time of writing is 2.50 per cent. A reasonable conservative assumption on the equity risk premium is 6 per cent. Then the equity risk premium is adjusted up or down depending on the risk of an individual bank. Large domestic banks normally have a risk profile equivalent to the overall market, so their beta of 1.0 is applied to the 6 per cent. Adding the risk-free rate and the beta adjusted equity risk premium together, you get a bank's cost of equity at 8.50 per cent (2.50 + (6.0 x 1.0) = 8.50). If the beta was greater than 1.0, say 1.5, then the cost of equity would be 11.50 per cent (2.50 + (6.0 x 1.5) = 11.50). This simple illustration ignores taxes, which have to be factored in and would lower the numbers in these examples. Assuming therefore that the bank's cost of equity is 8.50 per cent, this compares to an ROE earned by the major banks, which varies in the range 12–15 per cent (post-tax). This means that the excess profits or economic rents earned by the banks is between 3.50 per cent and 6.50 per cent before considering tax, which would further increase these rents as it lowers the cost of equity. These are big numbers, which banks in most other markets could only dream about as they find competitive forces compete these abnormal profits away to the benefit of consumers.

Occasionally, commentators point out that bank ROEs are broadly in line with the average earned by ASX100 firms. This of course is not a valid or meaningful comparison given the unique characteristics of banks relative to other industries. No business outside the banking sector would be allowed to operate on the financial leverage that banks are allowed to adopt.

HIGH LEVEL OF HOUSEHOLD DEBT

A natural consequence of the bias of the banks towards household lending has been a strong growth in household debt, resulting in one of the most highly indebted household sectors in the world in a period of low interest rates.

As illustrated in Figure 4, going back to 1990, lending to businesses accounted for two-thirds of the aggregate bank portfolios, whereas in 2018, it has shrunk to approximately one-third. Since the GFC, every dollar the banks have lent to businesses has been matched by $5 to homebuyers and housing investors. When compared to the SME sector, which is approximately 40 per cent of total business lending, the $5 to housing contrasts with $0.40 to SMEs (the remaining $0.60 flowing to larger businesses). The banks will argue, RWA and ROE incentives aside, that they are simply responding to a demand from households and housing investors. This demand is driven by a tax system that favours property both because of the capital gains tax exemption on owner-occupied housing and the capital gains tax discount, and when combined with negative gearing and depreciation allowances, this makes the buy-to-let property asset the investment of choice for many Australians. Another factor true of other Western economies is that with real interest rates at close to zero, housing offered an attractive investment. Consequently, bank debt in Australia sits at 190 per cent of household income. In the US between 1986 and 2006, household debt rose from under 70 per cent of total household income to almost 120 per cent, and from 90 per cent to around 140 per cent in the UK (King, 2016, p. 23). Later in this chapter, the concept of property as a speculative financial asset rather than a home is discussed.

FIGURE 7: GLOBAL HOUSEHOLD DEBT

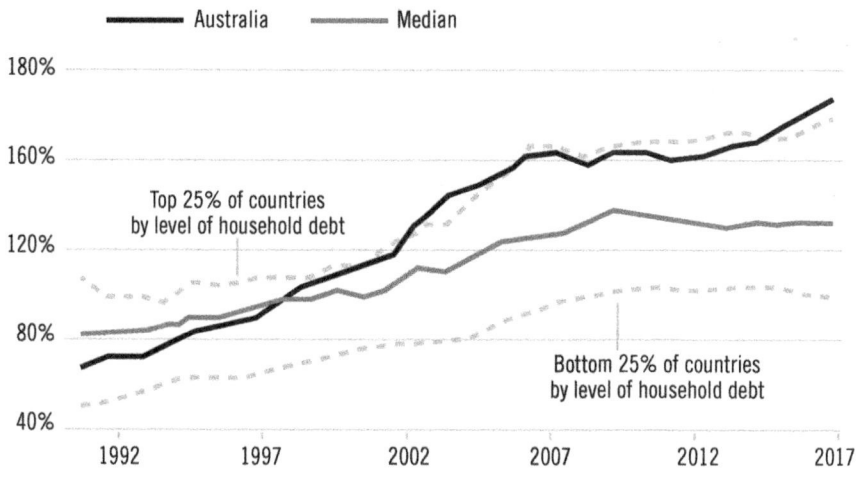

Source: OECD, RBA

Morgan Stanley looked at household debt levels across 11 countries, focusing on three key measures, the debt-to-income ratio, the debt-to-assets ratio and the debt servicing ratio, to create a global risk indicator. Australia is at or near the top of all three measures, as shown in Table 5.

TABLE 5: HOUSEHOLD DEBT LEVELS – INTERNATIONAL BENCHMARKS

Country	Debt levels (percentage of income)	Debt gearing (percentage of assets)	Debt servicing ratio (percentage of income)
Australia	189	20	16
US	101	19	8
Euro Area	95	20	5
UK	125	14	9
Japan	72	17	7
New Zealand	156	18	14
Canada	165	16	13
Switzerland	195	19	10
Norway	224	38	15
Sweden	176	30	11

Source: BIS, Haver, Morgan Stanley, October 2018

The Morgan Stanley report noted, 'Our Household Deleveraging Risk Indicator suggests that Australia is the economy most at risk of household deleveraging, coming near the top across all three aspects.'[97]

The high household debt levels need also to be understood in the context of speculative residential real estate investment, with interest-only loans at around 33 per cent of all mortgage lending

---

97 Letts, S., 'Australians face $700b wealth wipe-out as debt levels rated riskiest in the world: Morgan Stanley', *ABC News*, 30 October 2018, <https://www.abc.net.au/news/2018-10-30/australia-most-country-to-risks-of-rising-household-debt/10445814>.

in 2018 – it was closer to 40 per cent before APRA intervened, with more than 60 per cent of interest-only loans held by investors rather than home owner-occupiers. This is an alarming level and if left unchecked by regulatory intervention, there is no knowing where that figure might have reached as bank risk management systems and culture failed to address this. Admati and Hellwig (2013, p. 56) remind us of a universal truth:

> Careless lending also occurs if bankers do not have the right incentives to engage in due diligence when making loans. In real estate lending, a boom may actually feed of itself, because rising house prices make bankers feel safer in lending and induce them to lend more, allowing homebuyers to bid up prices even more until the 'bubble' bursts.

The easy availability of mortgage debt can play a major role in driving asset price cycles, which in turn drive credit supply in a self-reinforcing and potentially destabilising manner. When asset prices are rising, bankers become overly optimistic, as do investors. Lord Turner summed up the risks:

> Increased asset prices in turn drive expectations of further price increases which drive demand for credit: but they also improve bank profits, bank capital bases, and lending officer confidence, generating favourable assessment of credit risk and an increased supply of credit to meet the extra demand.[98]

As discussed earlier, in a banking system that has become culturally 'sales driven', as was also the case in the UK, there is evidence of lax credit standards, particularly in assessing a household's expenditure and thus loan affordability. In order to save costs, in assessing household expenditure, a benchmark known as the

---

98 Lord Turner, 'What do banks do, what should they do and what public policies are needed to ensure best results for the real economy?', CASS Business School speech, 17 March 2010.

household expenditure measure (HEM) was widely used by the banks. Under this approach, banks assessed borrowers using broad-based demographic information, such as a typical income in the suburb in which the borrower resides or plans to purchase the new property in. This is done instead of assessing the borrower's specific financial circumstances. Hardly a prudent or responsible approach. Some evidence of lax standards comes from an estimate by investment bank UBS of $500 billion of 'liar loans'[99] (loans where documentation or information provided was incorrect or fraudulent) and accusations levelled at Westpac, for example, for irresponsible lending. To criticism of lax lending standards, banks argue in response that on average, their portfolio is performing well, as the bad debt graph below would support, with the overall level of bad and doubtful debts (BDDs) at unsustainably low levels (the historically low level of bank debt is a major, and unsustainable, factor in the current levels of bank profits).

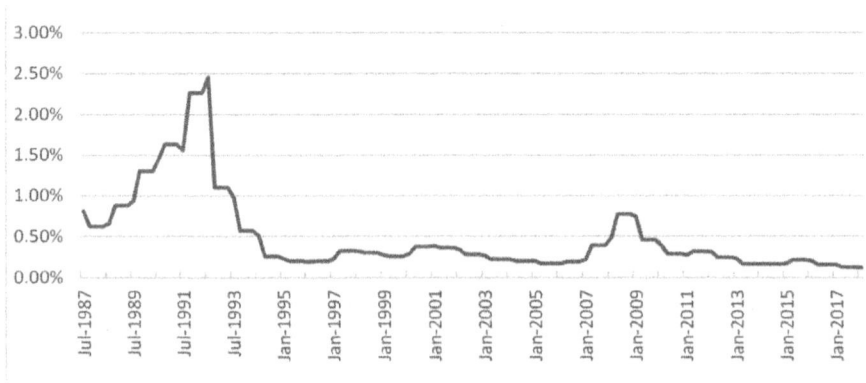

FIGURE 8: AUSTRALIAN BANKS LOAN LOSSES
Loan losses as a % of total lending are at historically low levels
The '92 commercial property collapse saw Westpac lose $1.6bn & recapitalise to survive

Source: *CLSA, Company*

---

99 Shapiro, J., "'Liar loans' hit $500 bn, mortgagors are "more stretched" than banks believe: UBS', *Australian Financial Review*, 11 September 2017, p. 18.

THE DANGER OF AVERAGES

Averages in banking are very dangerous measures. It is like saying to the non-swimmer that it is safe to walk across the river because it is a metre deep on average, only to find that it is three metres deep in the middle. A lot of important information is lost in averages. History reminds us that a core cause of the GFC was subprime home lending in the US and a factor that triggered the crisis was when the five-year adjustable rate mortgage could not be refinanced and borrowers faced steep increases in their interest costs. The parallel to Australia is when the interest-only and fixed rate interest loans are reset, borrowers may see material increases in interest costs at a time when banks may tighten their credit standards and become more disciplined in their responsible lending.

At HBOS, the board took comfort in managements reporting that close to half of the mortgage book had a loan-to-value ratio (LVR) of 28 per cent and only 3.5 per cent of the portfolio was over 90 per cent. The asset cover was there, but what about borrower capacity to service the debt? The banks also had lender mortgage insurance (LMI) in place to cover higher LVR loans, but this proved a false sense of security. The HBOS mortgage portfolio had close to 25 per cent of its lending in buy-to-let or self-certified mortgages, a figure that totalled £60 billion. Eventually when the market corrected, HBOS took losses on its mortgage book of £7 billion. So much for averages.

RISK CULTURE

An illustration of the cultural difficulty banks face in moving from a 'sales' to a prudent banker mindset is provided in Figure 9. The data shows that in the year to September 2018, there was a $19 billion or 85 per cent increase in residential property loans approved by lenders that fell outside their own tightened credit criteria, according to analysis conducted by APRA.[100] The focus of the analysis was on debt serviceability standards, that is the borrower's capacity to comfortably service the loan. The analysis suggests that while publicly committing to responsible lending, banks continued to demonstrate weak risk management discipline. While this is emphatically a leadership and cultural problem, the underlying dynamics of which are explored in Chapter 7, there should be no surprise in this as banks struggle to self-regulate and their attitude towards light touch regulation is dismissive in practice while compliant in their public utterances.[101]

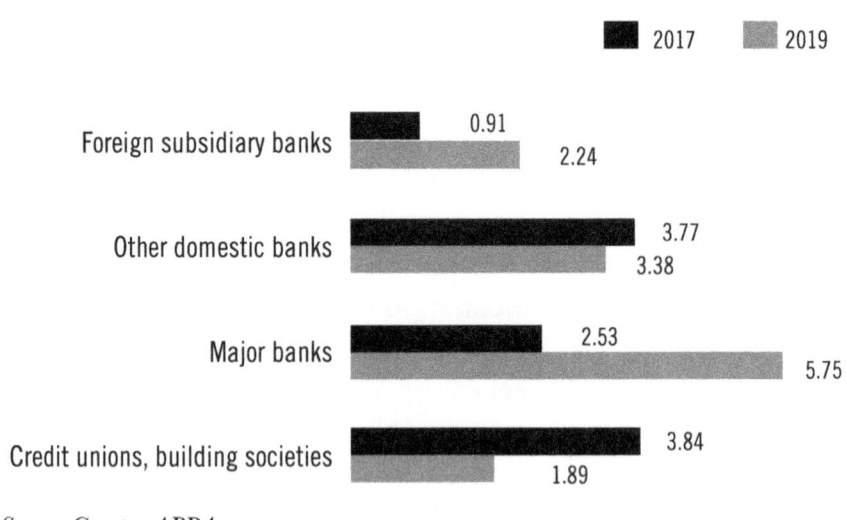

FIGURE 9: CREDIT RISK APPETITE DISCIPLINE
Missing the mark
LOAN VALUE APPROVED OUTSIDE OF SERVICEABILITY BY LENDER TYPE (%)

Source: Canstar, APRA

---

100 Hughes, D., '$19b in property loans breach new rules', *Australian Financial Review*, 25 October 2018, p. 21.

101 Danckert, S., 'ASIC attacks bank attitudes to regulation', *Sydney Morning Herald*, 15 March 2019, p. 22.

If banks are true to their commitment to be responsible lenders – and society needs them to be – a consequence will be that so-called interest-only 'liar loans' may find it particularly difficult to refinance when they convert to principal and interest, as was the case in the US. With so many households skating on thin ice in a financial sense, banks must accept that imprudent lending practices, combined with claims of misconduct, are likely to come home to roost. This is one of the burning issues with the bias to household lending, amplified by the evidence of 'loose lending'. A high concentration in investor interest-only loans is manageable in a property market when house prices are rising. When capital gains become uncertain, borrowing rates rise to 5 per cent or more and the net rental yields are less than the 10-year bond rate of 2.7 per cent, then the economics of such an investment strategy becomes challenging. This is not a new movie, as experienced bankers and regulators would (should) know. The concern is that the refinancing of interest-only loans is highly likely to reveal how unsuitable this product is in a weak property market. In many ways it is hard not to see that lending at high LVRs on an interest-only basis for investment properties (buy-to-let) is gambling on asset price inflation. Casino banking. It is not prudent or responsible banking. It contrasts, as discussed in Chapter 5, with the challenges and frustrations that SMEs find in getting access to credit.

When it comes to debt, economic history has taught us that this time is rarely different. Research by Jorda, Schularick and Taylor (2015) shows that a rising level of mortgage debt is a better predictor of financial crises than surges in other forms of lending and that the impact of a correction caused by high levels of household debt results in deeper recessions and slower recoveries. The dilemma for banks in managing the demands of equity investors, and the challenge of prudent risk management (discussed in Chapter 6), is that the growth in banking profits in Australia has largely been driven by the growth in household debt (see Figure 10).

FIGURE 10: RATIO OF HOUSEHOLD DEBT TO BANK PROFITS IN AUSTRALIA

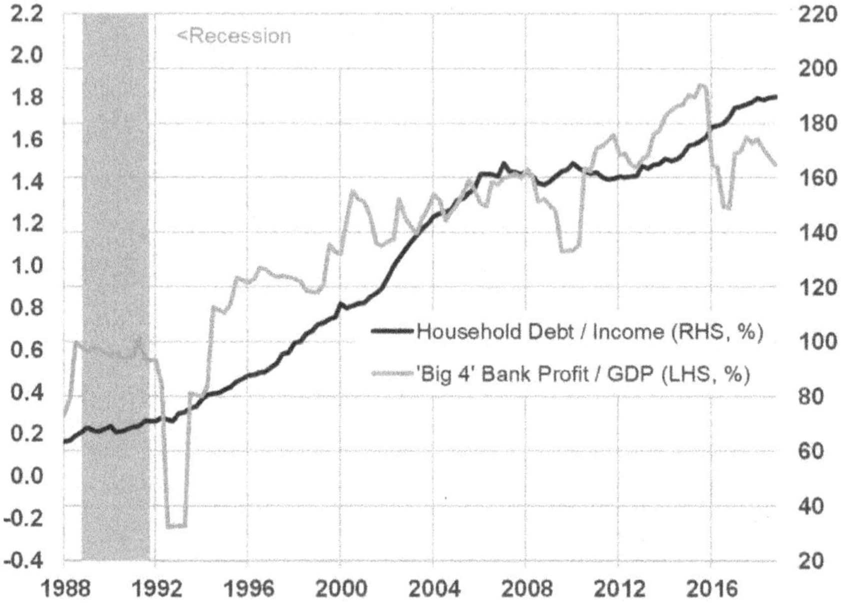

Source: Minack Advisors

With household debt levels among the highest in the world, an obvious reaction is to be cautious. A directionally similar trend was evident in the UK prior to the GFC, which caused Lord Turner, former FSA chairman, to comment:

> The easy availability of mortgage credit can generate a credit/asset price cycle and can encourage households to select levels of income leverage which ... Increases vulnerability to employment or income shocks ... And it can tempt some individuals, in pursuit of prospective capital gain, into debt contracts which harm their individual welfare rather than maximise it.[102]

---

[102] Lord Turner, 'What do banks do, what should they do and what public policies are needed to ensure best results for the real economy', CASS Business School speech, 17 March 2010, p. 19.

Widespread excesses if allowed to be prolonged are dangerous. In his *General theory* (1936), Keynes highlighted the dangers of excessive savings – the opposite of borrowing. He argued the 'paradox of thrift', where it might be rational for an individual to save, but if everyone saved then spending would drop and so would economic prosperity. This is the problem Japan faced post its crisis in the 1990s. Excesses both in debt and in savings can have lasting implications for an economy.

PROPERTY AS A FINANCIAL ASSET

With the proliferation in investor (buy-to-let) mortgages, there is a school of thought that the traditional supply and demand explanation of house prices does not always explain why prices are high. This theory argues that rising house prices has more to do with the financialisation of housing, or the easy access to low cost mortgages.[103] The supporting logic is that investors look at housing assets as a financial asset, which produces income and incurs costs, including the interest on debt, that can be matched against each other sometimes resulting in a tax credit. This results in investors looking at housing and comparing to other investment classes to determine the opportunity cost of buying a property for investment purposes. The behavioural bias towards property can lead investors to view it as a one-way bet. John Kay labelled this kind of behaviour as 'tailgating strategies' – riding an unsustainable trend in the hope that you will be clever enough to get out ahead of the crash.[104] The surge in debt financed property-based investment by the self-managed superannuation fund (SMSF) community is evidence of speculative behaviour. And this by a clientele that should have a risk profile more weighted to wealth preservation.

---

103 'Home economics', *The Economist*, 24 November 2018, p. 69.
104 Kay, J., 'Tailgating blights markets and motorways', *Financial Times*, 19 January 2010.

Loans to SMSFs to acquire property, which have limited recourse to the borrowers' other assets (unless there is a personal guarantee in place), reached $39 billion in 2018 compared to $418 million in 2008.[105] Thus, argued *The Economist*, it is not supply and demand imbalances that are driving house prices but low interest rates and financialisation. This theory on a large part of the housing market is consistent with speculative gambling (or casino banking) on an asset price appreciation and again raises questions on social licence when a significant part of the economy, the SME economy, struggles to access bank lending.

BANKS AND REAL ESTATE

A similar market dynamic to what we see in Australia existed in the US, the UK and the Irish housing market pre-GFC. While bank risk management systems will argue that the risk in housing is low because of history and it represents a geographically diversified portfolio, as with the dangers with averages, the US housing crash illustrated just how correlated the risks on mortgages are in a falling housing market.[106] It could be argued that the Australian banking market, because of RWA/ROE and remuneration linked incentives, is functioning as the invisible hand of self-interest would have it function. It is perfectly rational for the individual banks to allocate capital and funding to the assets with the highest return. Ironically, what may be rational for an individual bank can create outcomes that are not rational for the wider economy; in other words, rational irrationality! This outcome occurs for two reasons: first, if all banks focus on certain assets classes such as housing, they can create inflated asset prices, or housing bubbles;

---

105 Roddan, M., 'Super loans trigger alarms', *The Australian*, 14 January 2019, p. 1.
106 Holden, R., 'We should know how this property movie ends', *Australian Financial Review*, 8 January 2018, p. 31.

and second, there is the opportunity cost of under investment in other sectors of the economy that do not offer as attractive RWA/ROE outcomes (noting that RWA reflects a subjective and questionable measure of risk). Both reasons, of course, are driven by the remuneration linked ROE maximisation motive.

To the economy, the absurdity of this is that it results in a banking system that makes it more attractive for banks to lend the marginal dollar on a weekend holiday home than to a small business – arguably a perverse outcome and one difficult to reconcile with the traditional role and societal expectation of banks in recycling savings by lending to encourage productive investment and economic growth. Such a banking system does a substandard job in supporting the real economy. This is why public policy, or macro-prudential policy, needs to distinguish between different categories of lending and the different economic functions each category represents. The interest rate elasticity of demand can be different for each category, particularly in a rising property market.

As Keynes observed in 1931, banks are prone to 'herding' type behaviour. This herding of the banks in fuelling even higher leverage in an already over leveraged household sector is not to be dismissed as a remote risk. In many ways the excessive lending into the household sector is reminiscent of the philosophy of then Citigroup CEO, Chuck Prince, in 2007, when he said, 'As long as the music is playing, you've got to get up and dance. We are still dancing.'[107] This rather unfortunate quote is reflective of how banks think: so long as the household market wants to borrow, we are there to lend to protect market share. It sometimes appears that banks, like kangaroos, have no reverse gear. Absent regulatory intervention (history says that boards do not do this well), Chuck Prince was expressing the reality of the dilemma he and other bank CEOs face. His choices were to (i) stop dancing and run the

---

107 Nakamoto, M. & Wighton, D., 'Citigroup chief stays bullish on buy-outs', *Financial Times*, 9 July 2007.

risk of being fired for losing market share; (ii) dance half-heartedly in which case investors, employees and customers may desert the bank; or (iii) dance with as much zeal and energy as he could until the music stops and then get fired. He chose the third option and lost his job four months after making that statement. Citigroup subsequently went into intensive care for many years, saved only by US government support. What Chuck Prince was articulating is the classic game theory problem of the prisoner's dilemma that bank CEOs can face – should we slow down mortgage lending and therefore lose market share? It can be safer for a CEO to stay on the dance floor (keep dancing), and if the music stops, then no one will blame them in isolation; they will have their fellow CEOs to take their share of the blame as Keynes prophesised, and they will collectively blame externalities and 'black swans'. (A 'black swan' event as described by Nicolas Taleb (2007) has three characteristics: first, it is a highly improbable event; second, should it occur, its consequences can be severe; and third, after the event, it is clear that it should have been foreseen, for example a housing market crash.) The type of prisoner's dilemma faced by Chuck Prince is commonplace in banking and explains how what appears as the rational behaviour of an individual bank can result in a bad collective outcome. So when the CBA CEO was asked why the bank continued with broker commissions when he, in a previous role, had recommended that they move to a flat fee and avoid an inherent conflict of interest that worked against the customer, he said that the then CEO was concerned about losing market share if other banks stayed with the commission arrangements.[108] Courageous leadership, despite high remuneration, is not something senior bankers are renowned for.

The GFC highlighted how distorted incentives can create asset bubbles that eventually burst. As King (2016, p. 47) notes, 'bad

---

108 Chalmers, S., 'Banking royal commission: CBA backtracked on mortgage broker plan for fear of losing market share', *ABC News*, 19 November 2018.

investments' are encouraged by low real interest rates. The GFC revealed that much misplaced investment went into housing in markets such as the US, Ireland and Spain. In the UK, because of the aggressive posture of HBOS and RBS in particular, there was a lot of 'bad investment' in commercial real estate.

Readers may get the impression that in highlighting the risk with current levels of household mortgage lending there is a residual question on the economic value of such lending. The efficiency of capital allocation is vital to the long-term productive potential of the economy; so too is investment in new housing stock and the life cycle consumption smoothing of ready access to mortgage credit. Mortgage credit for the existing stock of housing does this and, indirectly, helps finance new investment in housing. The rate of growth in mortgage lending however and the opportunity cost it represents (as evident in the challenges SMEs have in accessing credit, as discussed in Chapter 5), does come at a cost and at a risk to the economy. It is prudent to assume that the rate of growth in mortgage lending, particularly in the speculative 'buy-to-let' market, carries more economic risk than upside. Time will tell.

In the UK and the US, it was the ROE and bonus maximisation motivation of bankers, as well as the absence of meaningful regulation, that were the fundamental underlying drivers of the GFC. This was evidenced by a huge bias towards household lending, some of it poor quality (subprime), high bank balance sheet leverage and an excessive use of short-dated funding markets. The GFC was a cocktail of three miscalculations, which today has *some* parallels to banking in Australia.

TWO BIG QUESTIONS

That ROE incentives drove a prioritising of household lending regardless of systemic risk raises two residual questions that this chapter has emphasised: first, is this bias to housing consistent with an efficient allocation of capital?; and second, what are the long-term economic implications of this bias? These questions were considered by Cecchetti and Kharroubi (2018) who concluded that finance sector growth benefits disproportionately high collateral/low productivity projects. This outcome reflects the fact that periods of high financial sector growth often coincide with the strong development in sectors such as property construction, where returns on projects are relatively easy to pledge as collateral but productivity (growth) is relatively low. They argue that periods of high credit growth coincide with lower growth in total factor productivity.[109]

Anyone looking at the skylines of the central business district (CBD) in Melbourne, Sydney, Auckland or Queenstown would readily understand the argument that is made in this research. The crowding out effect of excessive lending to housing over business is a legitimate public policy matter and the evidence that this has occurred is overwhelming. The banks have operated in their private self-interest, devoid of any social licence obligations or any recognition that their collective ROE-maximisation-driven strategies can create significant systemic risk, which may be ultimately met by society.

BROKERS

Another factor that concerned the Royal Commission has been the conflicted role that some mortgage brokers play in the market. Brokers act as an intermediary between borrowers and lenders, and account for the origination of over 50 per cent of all mortgage lending. They are currently incentivised by a commission linked to

---

[109] Cecchetti, S. & Kharroubi, E., *Why does financial sector growth crowd out real economic growth?*, BIS Working Papers, No. 490, 2018, <https://www.bis.org/publ/work490.pdf>.

the size of the loan, with trailing commissions over the life of the loan. That commission is paid by the bank. The incentive therefore can be to encourage the borrower to take out a larger loan, which is potentially in conflict with the role of the bank as a responsible lender. It may also be in conflict with the customer's interests. Despite a regulatory obligation, critics argue that brokers have no real incentive to validate the income and expenses of customers they are promoting to banks, yet there was evidence that the banks rely on what the brokers submit. The Royal Commission heard of four cases in which brokers at Aussie Home Loans, which is owned by CBA, falsified home loan applications so they could earn more commission. Another problem is the industry practice of paying trailing commissions, which can act as a disincentive to look for better deals for customers that brokers have previously introduced to a bank. Absent trailing commissions, brokers would have an incentive to find the best possible deal for the customer. The requirement of acting in the interests of the customer is further clouded by the fact that many of the large brokers are owned by the major banks. Problems with broker introduced mortgages were a feature of the UK market, where brokers originated close to two-thirds of all mortgages. A BBC investigation found evidence of brokers encouraging borrowers to lie about their income in order to get loans based on five to six times their income. The BBC estimated that up to 30 per cent of self-certified mortgages were obtained on fraudulent income figures (Perman & Darling, 2012, p. 327). Though arguably a casual coincidence readers will note the similarities to the $500 billion estimate of 'liar loans' by UBS ('liar loans' are loans obtained using false information largely in support of income and expenses), which equates to approximately 30 per cent of the Australian housing loan market. The similarities between the UK and Australian banking markets are uncanny in many important respects.

Chapter 6 returns to this theme and how it supports the

hypothesis that the first line of defence in a bank's risk management framework has been allowed to fall into a state of disrepair and is arguably broken. In Chapter 9, the important role brokers play in the market and why they can be a force for good in getting better consumer outcomes is discussed, as is the problem of having brokers owned by banks.

SME BANKING

In understanding the nature of the banking lending market, it is helpful to summarise in this chapter some of the issues facing SMEs, a theme that is explored in more detail in Chapter 5. While households have various options when accessing mortgage or credit card products and larger corporates can access deeper funding markets such the capital markets and foreign banks (as well as being self-financed), SMEs are almost totally reliant on the banks. The major banks control 80–85 per cent of all SME lending. According to the Australian Bureau of Statistics (ABS), small businesses are around twice as likely as large businesses to identify a lack of access to finance as a barrier for growing their business. Moreover, less than a fifth of small businesses actually sought external finance in 2015/16, according to the Reserve Bank of Australia (RBA).[110] This demand however should not be read as indicating the level of latent demand, more as a reflection of the difficulty businesses perceive there to be in obtaining finance, thus many self-select not to pursue finance to fund expansion. Estimates showing that 90 per cent of SMEs seeking finance are successful in obtaining it should be read with care, as data in Chapter 5 will show.[111]

---

110 Connolly, E. & Jackman, B., 'The availability of business finance', *Reserve Bank of Australia, Bulletin*, December quarter, 2017.
111 Productivity Commission, p. 435.

Why should we be concerned about SMEs? There is a very important reason why. SMEs are the engines of the Australian, New Zealand and most modern economies. In Australia, they employ seven out of ten people in the private sector and account for 56 per cent of GDP. Bank lending provides the fuel that drives the growth in SMEs and thus an important contribution to economic growth. Banks, more than any other part of the financial system, are critical to SMEs. SME lending is very different from consumer or large corporate lending, primarily because SMEs are informationally more opaque. That is, to use economic jargon, the SME market is information inefficient, while both the consumer and large corporate markets are largely information efficient. In other words it is easier to lend to a consumer or a large corporate than it is to an SME. Lending to SMEs takes a little bit more effort and commitment.

Few topics unite the SME community more than that of the frustration in dealing with banks, who they see as unresponsive, bureaucratic and risk averse. That the Australian banking system has a bias to the household sector is hard to refute. A central theme in this book is that the SME sector has been disadvantaged as a result of this bias, and that there has been a market failure. SMEs are being left behind by a banking system that does not adequately meet their needs. Most SME lending in Australia (as is also the case in the UK) is a disguised form of mortgage lending. The problem of SMEs getting the support they need from banks will only be exacerbated as the digital and intangible asset economy grows, with serious long-term implications to the innovation potential of the economy.

Haskel and Westlake in their excellent book *Capitalism without capital – the rise of the intangible economy* (2018) capture this. They point to the evidence that the financial system does a poor job in meeting the needs of the real economy and this is a public policy concern across much of the developed world, a problem that will only grow as more and more new business are light on tangible assets; the new economy is one where intangible assets become more prominent and banks struggle to ascribe value to these assets and therefore assess risk.

Many SMEs decide not to apply or are unable to access a banker to help shepherd their interest in obtaining finance. This problem highlighted one example of where the broker market is important to the economy, as brokers will do what banks used to do. When SMEs do access finance, the availability of housing collateral has a significant effect on the cost and availability of finance, with lenders having a limited appetite for cash flow based or partially secured lending (Connolly, La Cava & Read, 2015). The fact that an estimated 90 per cent of SME lending is property secured may reduce the risk to the banks but it also means that viable businesses may not get access to finance when the owners are unwilling to provide the security of their residence, given how that concentrates their risk should the business fail. The economic cost of the investment that would otherwise occur is not easy to estimate, but it is reasonable to assume that it is not immaterial. Many net present value positive projects go unfunded.

A related issue is that the process in obtaining finance from banks is lengthy and onerous. SMEs report that banks have extensive information and documentation requirements and take a long time to decide whether to provide the finance (Connolly & Bank, 2018). In a business setting where time is of the essence, such a process is another reason that SMEs decide not to pursue positive net present value opportunities. Investments that would otherwise be made, are not. As discussed in Chapter 5, the opportunity cost of not having a well-functioning banking system is estimated at $83 billion in credit extension and a multiple of that in economic consequences.

Research demonstrates that larger banks tend to become more impersonal (dehumanise) in their engagement with SMEs, increasingly pointing them to highly impersonal but, for the banks, hugely functional call centres (see the letter to 'Joe' in Chapter 5). Where there is relationship management coverage, cost-cutting motivations result in a 'light touch' proposition where the banker is responsible for hundreds of SMEs and is often disempowered to make any decisions regardless of their experience and credentials to do so. Banks have also tended to develop standardised products, which do not suit all circumstances. This means that the banks either refuse to grant the loan, or the SME gets a loan product ill-suited to their needs. Bankers have very little or no authority to vary standard products and any exceptions sought are rarely granted, and when they are, they can be extracted only after considerable time and effort; weeks and months, not days. The increasingly bureaucratic and rigid policy framework that banks operate in, means that 'one-size-fits-all' is the philosophy and the fear of losing a job or being 'gated' (a yellow card in a sporting sense, with firing being a red card), means that the natural tendency is to be inflexible, even when common sense might dictate a better course: 'Sorry I wish I could help; I fully understand your position, but our policies say …'.

In an oligopoly industry where standardisation and a sales culture have replaced a service culture, the customer experience is collateral damage. This experience is exacerbated by the drive to 'dehumanise' service through the increased use of technology. While retail banking tends to attract political and media interest, the greatest victims of this trend are SMEs, who in so many ways have been left behind by the banking system. SMEs feel that when it comes to the banking system, they have the triple 'U' virus – unloved, unwanted and undervalued. While SMEs are victims of the trends to industrialise and dehumanise, so too are the dedicated bank employees who are often frustrated and embarrassed by their inability to do the right thing by the customer. Poor staff morale is a sure predictor of poor customer service. More on this in Chapter 5.

FINTECHS, NEOBANKS AND CHALLENGER BANKS

The term 'FinTech' covers a very broad ecosystem, and according to KPMG, there are more than 650 firms in the FinTech sector in Australia.[112] Much has been written about the emergence of FinTechs and neobanks, and how they will change the competitive landscape in banking. There is little doubt that the banking system, at least in its intermediation role, will face greater competition from new entrants, including technology companies. Financial intermediation is an attractive business, which McKinsey & Company (2018) estimate to generate margins of 190 basis points (bps) on average, within a range of 350 bps for deposits and lending to 60 bps for funds management. This competitive risk has caused one large bank to reportedly describe itself as a FinTech, having announced it will replace 6000 staff with 2000 tech experts, with some staff retained as technologists.[113] This thinking outside the box is commendable but as Andrew Hill wrote in the *Financial Times*,[114] wanting to be a technology-based company does not make you one. This is different from saying that all banks must have a clear technology agenda that reflects state-of-the-art developments, including the undoubted scope for AI. There are good reasons for banks to want to promote their technology strengths, including the halo effect flow into their share price. Hence the growing trend of banks to invest in and in some cases buy FinTechs. As discussed in Chapter 1, miscalculations are made and confusion reigns however when the core competencies of the bank are defined by technology, when they are clearly not. This is something that we at Judo Bank discussed at length in an

---

112 KPMG, *Australian fintech landscape*, September 2018, <www.home.kpmg/au/en/home/insights/2017/08/australian-fintech-landscape.html>

113 Eyers, J., 'Andrew Thorburn explains the fintech forces reshaping NAB', *Australian Financial Review*, 7 May 2018, p. 36.

114 Hill, A., 'Not every company is a technology company', *Financial Times*, 15 October 2018, p. 31.

early stage – was technology a *definer* as it is with FinTechs, or is it an *enabler* of a great customer and employee experience? We saw it clearly as an enabler – a powerful enabler. The other reality is that major banks are handicapped by legacy technology, which has increasingly become a burden. Fixing that problem should be a priority, so customers can confidently rely on basic services.

The digital transformation of banking is a hugely positive development, but banks have always been in the information business, all that is happening today is that they are in a much better position to utilise the data and to make it easier for their customers to do business and exchange transactions through the bank. Digital transformation however must not distract from the core culture issues plaguing the banks, which centre on customer trust. The potential for technology will be defined equally by the customer; it would be a miscalculation by a bank in the era of digital transformation and big data to fall into the trap of thinking of their customers as mere 'data'. The dehumanisation of banking is drifting in that direction, whereas, even with the positive advent of AI, the core banking skills of understanding the customer, credit risk, risk management more broadly, regulations, compliance, banking operations and professional ethics remain just as important. This is particularly so in the case of SMEs. The core challenge for all businesses, be they longstanding traditional banks or new entrants, is to be clear and focus on the things it does uniquely well. From that foundation new capabilities can be developed where its unique capabilities can further strengthen its comparative advantage over others.

Adapting to digitisation has significant potential for banks, but for most banks it is a daunting task given the incredible complexity and archaic nature of the system, with some banks having to find programmers still fluent in computer code written in the 1980s. The significant challenges to this kind of transformation are not to be underestimated; notwithstanding the costs, which are eye-watering, as is the level of operational risk. Many major transformational programs are launched with much fanfare and economic promise only to then peter out, quietly disappear and then eventually get expunged from corporate-speak and memory, as if they never happened. It takes a very brave CEO to embark on such an adventure.

It is too soon to say how successful the FinTech sector will become. It is also too early to understand the comparative advantage that each actor brings to the market. However, the potential for digital transformation in the payments space is obvious and exciting. We only need to look at the progress of Ant Financial, the US$150 billion valued affiliate of China's ecommerce giant Alibaba, to get a sense for the potential.[115] The volume of mobile payments in China reached US$8.6 trillion in 2016, compared to US$112 billion in the US.[116] Cash payments are becoming increasingly the exception in cities such as Shanghai and Beijing, and Chinese travellers to the West feel that they are stepping back in time when they look at the current state of mobile payment capabilities, and this is before considering the array of other mobile digital services on offer in China from Ant Financial, Ping An, Baidu and WeChat (Healy, 2018). There is also scope in the short-dated receivables finance business, where specialist providers are both emerging and flourishing.

The FinTechs and neobanks offer real potential, but there is a risk of it becoming exaggerated. Some early forecasts have proven to be wildly optimistic, such as the 2015 report from Morgan Stanley, which forecast that peer-to-peer lending would reach $22 billion in Australia by 2020 ($10.4 billion in the unsecured personal loan market and $11.4 billion in small business lending).[117] What we can

---

115 Special report: banking, *The Economist*, 4 May 2019, pp. 21–28.
116 'Innovation in China', *The Economist*, 23 September 2017, p. 17.
117 Eyers, J., 'Morgan Stanley says peer-to-peer loans will soar to $22bn in Australia by 2020', *Sydney Morning Herald*, 22 May 2015, p. 26.

say is that their success will be determined not only by the quality of their technology and the part of the industry value chain that they seek to compete in, but also critically by their management competence. Looking around the world, so many FinTechs appear long on 'Tech' and short on 'Fin' (TechFins), raising questions on whether they have the management capabilities to build scalable businesses and to manage that business in an economic downturn when credit risk is heightened. Building scalable new financial services businesses requires experienced and stable management teams; experience in particular is vital. As former Citibank CEO Vikram Pandit said, 'If you're in the credit card business I want to see people who understand how the business works. It's not only about technology ... There is comfort from seeing the right kind of people in management.'[118] He has invested $350 million in FinTechs through his venture Orogen. Too often the public portrayal of FinTech executives is that of 'cool' millennial-style entrepreneurs, who boast 30–40,000 customers on their platforms. The residual questions are: Do they have the management capabilities to build scalable businesses? Will their 'signed-up' customers make them any money? The internet mania in the late 1990s and early 2000s had a similar look and feel.

Neobanks are different from FinTechs and challenger banks. Neobanks originally emerged in the UK in the form of Monzo, Atom Bank, Revolut and Starling. A neobank is a digital bank that exists without any branch network. They take aspects of traditional banking and use mobile phone enabled apps and other forms of digital banking to provide mobile customer services and are predominantly focused on retail customers, but they can also play a meaningful role in supporting SMEs in meeting their payment needs. There is tremendous potential for neobanks in the SME payments and cash management space. Neobanks will

---

118 Noonan, L., 'Out with the old, in with the new', *Financial Times*, 16 January 2019, p. 35.

also carry much appeal to millennials, as they have in the UK.

The McKinsey & Company report (2018) highlights the big threat to banks from technology-led firms such as Amazon and Apple; Amazon is already disrupting the traditional credit card market in partnership with JP Morgan Chase and is in discussion with a number of banks on the creation of transaction banking products. Amazon has also signalled its intention to enter the mortgage market. There are many other examples, including tech firms such as Alibaba.

Challenger banks come in many forms, but their core characteristic is that they are seeking to challenge the traditional banks in certain markets and address pockets of the market that are underserved, such as the market failure in SME banking. Building a credible challenger bank is a significant task and successful players tend to be characterised by leadership with proven skills and experience. In the UK, Metro Bank, Shawbrook, OakNorth, Aldermore, TSB and Clydesdale characterise themselves as challenger banks. New challenger banks, such as Judo Bank, blend a mix of old and new. Old in the sense of traditional relationship values focusing on the SME market and new in the sense of modern technology platforms. The challenge for challenger banks is to avoid becoming a 'mini-me' of the larger incumbents by seeing strategy as a David versus Goliath battle. To avoid this, challenger banks must be free from the five legacies that imprison the larger banks: dated technology; large infrastructure assets; complex business processes and systems; traditional management and board thinking; and a culture set in concrete.

Combined with pro-competition measures such as Open Banking,[119] there is no question that technology is and will

---

[119] Open Banking is the application of the Consumer Data Right in the banking sector. It gives consumers the right to access their bank-held data and transfer it, free of charge, to trusted third parties. It is designed to encourage competition by giving consumers control over their credit and payments history. In theory therefore it removes a material barrier to entry for FinTechs, neobanks and challenger banks.

transform the way in which banking is delivered, including the potential offered by Cloud Banking. Technology will greatly assist in lowering the barriers to entry and it should greatly empower consumers. One way to think about the role of technology and the nature of large banks is to reflect on the insights of the great economist Ronald Coase (1937). Coase famously argued that large-scale firms make sense when the 'transaction costs' associated with buying things in the market exceed the hierarchical costs of maintaining a bureaucracy. In other words, much of large modern businesses were justified because of the scale and scope economies of size. The problem is that as a firm grows and becomes more complex, the more severe the problems are in properly managing and governing its activities – principal–agent problems become more apparent and diseconomies of scale set in, with the management and governance costs of size surpassing scale benefits. The Royal Commission provided ample evidence of this phenomenon as did the APRA review into CBA. This issue of diseconomy of scale is a reality that Australia's major banks and industrial firms such as GE, and arguably domestic firms such as Telstra are already facing.

While they are unlikely to compete head on with the incumbent banks, FinTechs and neobanks are well placed to attack certain aspects of banking as specialists rather than broad-based generalists. Some will focus on payments, others on specialist lending and others will go to parts of the banking industry value chain where technology can create an advantage, such as foreign exchange. In the lending business, FinTechs as SME lenders are likely to predominately position themselves further to the right on the risk curve, as illustrated in Figure 11.

FIGURE 11: NEW LENDING LANDSCAPE
Challenger Bank 'Sweet Spot'

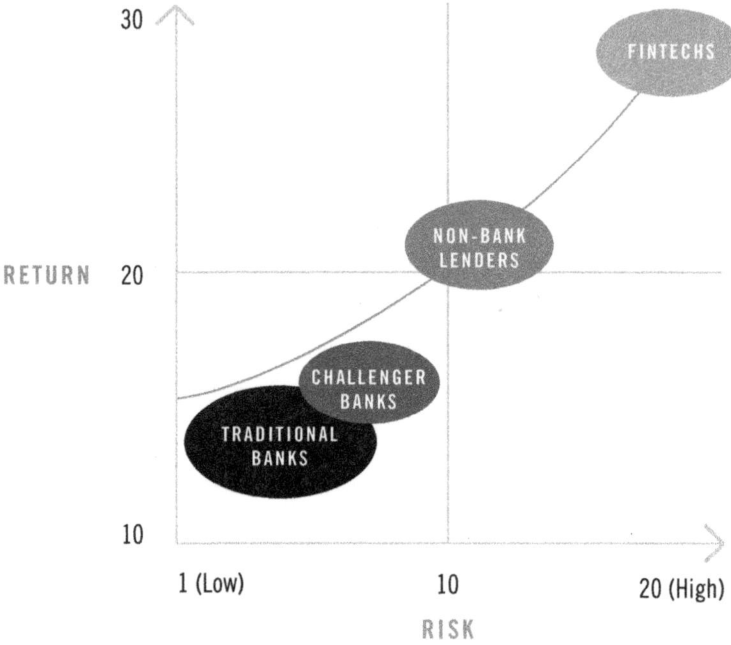

Source: Judo Bank

The new challenger bank model, which was successfully developed in the UK, is likely to emerge in Australia, based on the seven principles of a judo strategy (Yoffie & Kwak, 2002). A judo strategy is a natural choice for smaller banks because it values skill over size. If skilfully executed, a judo strategy is how challenger banks can compete and win against large incumbent banks. As discussed in Chapter 9, creating a meaningful challenger bank market will depend on a number of things, in particular the regulatory environment.

Finally, a growing feature of the financial system in many economies is the so-called non-bank lending sector, which includes a growing number of unregulated lenders. Somewhat provocatively, this is sometimes known as the 'shadow banking' system. The term 'shadow banking' is unfortunate as it creates a mind picture of being mildly sinister and dangerous. As regulated banks are increasingly subject to greater scrutiny, including reduced leverage, the concern is that the shadow system will grow and with it systemic risk, given contagion risk. Critics point to the regulatory arbitrage of this growing segment of the financial system. In the US, the shadow sector accounts for up to 30–40 per cent of total financial intermediation[120] and it is growing, as it is elsewhere including in Australia. A material part of that growth is in real estate lending, both residential and commercial. Will it result in a problem and create the potential for systemic risk? There is a reasonable prospect that it may, hence the need for some form of regulatory oversight. This happened in the UK in the late 1970s with the collapse of the secondary banking market, forcing the Bank of England to launch a 'lifeboat' to rescue a number of secondary lenders in order to avoid contagion in the main banking system. A regulatory regime that ignores the 'shadow system' is potentially making a grave miscalculation.

CONCLUDING REMARKS

Australia has a financially strong and stable banking industry that dominates the financial system. Australian banks are also among the most profitable in the world, having navigated through the GFC largely unscathed (at the time of writing, there is evidence that the high levels of profitability are coming under pressure, particularly given that the historically low bad debt charges (Figure 8) cannot be sustained). Despite this profitability, from society's perspective, the banking industry is problematic and lacking in trust. An obvious problem is that there is a significant and arguably unhealthy bias towards household lending resulting in one of the most highly

---

120 Porters, R., 'Shining a light on shadow banking', *London Business School Review*, vol. 29, no. 3, 2018.

indebted household sectors in the world. The corollary of this bias to the household sector is that the SME market has been neglected or exposed to the triple 'U' virus – unloved, unwanted and undervalued. Given this, the banks have failed in their role as impartial allocators of capital across the economy.

Another problem is that banks compete aggressively with each other to maximise ROE and market share. RBS and HBOS did the same, then imploded. The danger of this competitiveness was also epitomised by the then Deutsche Bank CEO, Josef Ackermann, who set a goal of 25 per cent ROE, which the bank achieved in 2008. In 2019, Deutsche Bank was a 'zombie bank'. Its market capitalisation at the time of writing is €13 billion and this after several rights issues raising €29 billion of new equity since 2010. The bank had managed to not just lose all the market value of the equity it had prior to the rights issues, but also €16 billion of the new equity raised. Time and time again, history has shown that ROE can be a dangerous measure of profitability in banks as it is largely driven by high leverage, which is aided by a generous RWA treatment. The core premise of RWA calculations – and thus the determination of capital that banks should hold – is clearly deeply flawed. The Metro Bank case highlights all that is wrong and why this issue must be addressed by regulators. Reform is long overdue and the need for a level playing field is critical if competition is a desired policy goal.

In the context of the housing market, a related theme was explored by Akerlof and Romer (2004) when they described the incentive for some banks to go for broke (gamble on success) and at society's expense. This risk is evident where there is passive regulation as society cannot rely on the corporate governance checks within banks. Firms, such as banks, that are protected by a government guarantee, or implicitly so through the 'too big to fail' commitment, can go for broke in say household lending in the safe knowledge that their reckless conduct is subject to taxpayer bailout, avoiding the risk of bankruptcy. They take comfort from Keynes' argument that banks fall in packs, so avoiding individual accountability. In the immortal words of Chuck Prince, they can keep on dancing until the music stops. That kind of private interest incentive driven behaviour is clearly contrary to the public interest and any sense of social licence.

With the bias of the banking system to household lending, which by any metric – debt-to-income, house prices-to-income or house prices-to-rent – has created the risk of an asset bubble and is no way congruent with prudent risk management. There are also broader macro-prudential policy issues of Australia's (and New Zealand's) financial concentration in the housing market. This extreme concentration is through superannuation funds, which will have a significant weighting in bank stocks, and through both owner-occupied and investor owned property. This is an important topic, which goes to the heart of the nature of a nation's financial system, not just its banking system. It is an important topic outside the scope of this book. It does feel however that the banks are behaving just like the grasshopper in Aesop's fable who ate to his heart's content during the summer instead of storing up food for the coming winter.

While this is not a book on the digitalisation of banking, which is a huge and important topic, there is no doubt that technology and AI will play a big role in reshaping the industry and the economy, as will changing consumer preferences, particularly driven by millennials. AI has the potential to automate personal lending including mortgages. In SME banking, unlike Retail/ Personal Banking, AI will never completely replace the human expert, given the importance of human judgement at critical stages of an SME's evolution. Machine learning and algorithms can be used to understand data and through sentiment analysis can help improve the effectiveness of human judgement. In SME banking, the quality of personalised service is the key differentiator.

The mantra at Judo Bank is a digitally supported but human-led approach to banking.

Much of this chapter has focused on the role banks play in allocating capital across the economy. In the next, much shorter chapter, the important connected themes of social licence and purpose are explored.

2
SOCIAL LICENCE AND PURPOSE

NOT so long ago the concept of social licence would have been politely dismissed within most boardrooms as another bit of fluffy corporate responsibility rhetoric, in the same way that the triple bottom line and corporate social responsibility (CSR) have, disappointingly, largely become. CSR in particular is increasingly viewed as empty rhetoric, as former BP chairman, Lord Browne (2015) describes it. Society feels that boards pay polite lip service to the virtues of broader social obligations. However, things are changing. Most large companies, and particularly major domestic banks, need a social licence to operate and that licence is subject to review when there have been scandals and major failures in governance. It is also open to review even when there have been no scandals but where there is a sense that the banks and other firms are abusing their power and neglecting their obligations to society. A bank's social licence to operate is intangible but it is very real, more so today than ever before.

BANKS ARE SPECIAL

The concept of social licence is more relevant to banks than to most other businesses because banks are 'special' and banks are 'different' from any other type of business. They are different, but not so when it comes to the laws of financial economics, which, like the laws of medicine, transcend markets and geographies. The special nature of banks has been the subject of many investigations, in recent times by the FSA, which noted that:

> Banks are different and society has a strong interest in bankers taking a different attitude to the balance between risk and reward to that which applies to the rest of the economy ... their failure is of public concern, not just a concern for shareholders.[121]

Sentiment echoed in the Royal Commission report. Thus in the case of banks, their social licence must be explicit whereas in the case of most other businesses, or industries, that licence may be implicit and subject to lower thresholds.

The reason banks are 'special' is not down to their divine qualities but because of the significant externalities that flow to the economy from their activities, which were discussed in Chapter 1. To recap, the special nature of banks is down to the role they play in:

- Providing finance to consumers, businesses and governments.
- Managing large parts of the payments system that provides the 'daily oil' to ensure that the economy functions smoothly.
- A safe haven for consumer and businesses to deposit their surplus funds given the existence of a government guarantee on domestic deposits held in licensed banks up to $250,000.
- The role they play as the primary transmitter of monetary

---

121 The Financial Services Authority, *The failure of the Royal Bank of Scotland: Financial Services Authority Board Report*, December 2011, pp. 4–5.

policy in the economy.
- The power imbalance and grossly unequal bargaining power banks have in 'negotiating' credit, particularly with consumers and SMEs.

Banks are also 'special' because, particularly for larger banks, they are deemed 'too big to fail', as we saw in the UK and in the US during the GFC. Because of this, if banks are poorly managed, then the implicit guarantee from government (taxpayers) would result in the bank being rescued; hence the view that major banks are essentially quasi-nationalised firms. To describe banks as pure creatures of the capitalist economy is misleading; if a business is not allowed to fail by the state, then it cannot be a pure actor in the capitalist market, where the risk of bankruptcy is a feature of a poorly managed business. Moreover, because of the so-called 'four pillar' policy, the risk of being acquired, another feature of a market economy that exposes weak management, is also removed. The prospect of being bailed out by taxpayers is not a remote risk, as the GFC highlighted, and it is based on the fact that bank balance sheets are more highly leveraged (debt-to-equity) than any other type of business. In terms of risk, as discussed in Chapter 1, banks are unique in the following ways:
- They have a high proportion of callable debt (short-term or on-call deposits) and other short-term debt relative to total debt and relative to assets.
- The duration of their assets is significantly greater than that of their liabilities.
- They have a small proportion of liquid or cash assets relative to total assets.
- They have a small equity capital base relative to assets.
- The collapse of one large bank could have material contagion risks throughout the banking system and therefore throughout the economy.

It is these fragile characteristics that caused the economist Hyman Minsky (1977) to argue that banks are inherently unstable and that the existence of a government guarantee on deposits is critical to the confidence in the banking system. The implicit government guarantee on Australian banks because of the 'too big to fail' view is worth an estimated $4 billion per annum to the banks in lower funding costs given the country's sovereign rating. The International Monetary Fund (IMF) estimated that the implicit subsidy to banks in major economies is in the order of US$200–300 billion (King, 2016, p. 97). No other private sector industry enjoys such a privilege.

The existence of the deposit and bankruptcy protection guarantees brings with it the risk of moral hazard behaviour on the part of the banks. What this means is that with the existence of the government guarantee on deposits and the implied 'too big to fail' taxpayer bailout guarantee, there is a risk that banks would build riskier portfolios than they would in the absence of these guarantees (an example would be excessive lending into the household sector or to commercial real estate). This was evident in the UK with the government rescue of RBS and Northern Rock, and its capital injections in Lloyds Bank following the hastily arranged merger with HBOS, together with similar examples in Ireland and in the US. The economic and social cost of bank rescues is huge. For these fundamental reasons, regulation and close supervision of how banks conduct themselves is in the public interest, and the concept of social licence becomes even more relevant. Even Alan Greenspan, a strong free market ideologist, acknowledged, 'I made a mistake in presuming that the self-interests of organizations, specifically banks and others, were such that they were best capable of protecting their own shareholders and their equity in the firms' (Cassidy, 2009, p. 5).

In his report on Barclays, Salz (2013, p. 78) summed up why banks are special:

Appropriate business practices are always important, but disproportionately so in higher-risk industries where key business concerns transcend growth, profitability and competitive advantage. In such industries, management focus on developing business practices which emphasise the importance of never compromising safety or of managing risk in a way that avoids a catastrophic loss. Banking certainly falls into the latter.

Due to a collapse in moral and ethical values within the industry, and a sense that the unwritten dominant values are 'let's see what we can get away with', investors increasingly worry about the threat to the social licence that banks have and how societal mistrust towards banks may encourage greater government and regulatory scrutiny, potentially leading to intervention. The Royal Commission highlighted deep cultural problems that violated any measure of ethical behaviour, and in some cases extended to allegations of breaking the law.

SOCIAL LICENCE

What do we mean by a social licence to operate?

The standard definition of a social licence to operate is the level of acceptance by communities and stakeholders of an organisation's activities. Many professions need a licence (lawyers, doctors and accountants) and certain industries such as banking, though the licence in the case of banks is issued to the institution by APRA, whereas in the case of other professions, the licence is issued to the individual, that is the doctor, the lawyer and the accountant have a professionally accredited licence to operate. We return to this theme in Chapter 4, as the decline in professionalism in banking has been a major contributing factor to the current problems facing the industry and highlights the case for bankers to be professionally accredited, just as lawyers, doctors and accountants are.

For a financial service company to describe itself as a 'bank' it needs to be licensed by APRA. In addition to this being a form of regulation, the granting of a banking licence is to certify to the public that a bank is subject to certain standards and oversight ensuring, at least in theory, that the public good is protected and principal–agent costs are being closely monitored. A social licence to operate goes beyond the approval of a licence by a regulator. Typically, according to The Ethics Centre,[122] a social licence to operate has three components: legitimacy, credibility and trust.

When it comes to business, how should we understand whether companies have sufficient social legitimacy to take on the responsibility for delivering essential services such as banking, health services, water, energy and telecommunications? A social licence can never be self-awarded, it requires that the activities of the business have sufficient credibility and trust in addition to legitimacy (Morrison, 2014). There are many examples of where social licences have been lost, such as BP in the Gulf of Mexico and Shell in the Niger Delta. Several banks, such as RBS and Wells Fargo, had their social licence curtailed in response to scandals. Facebook also faces the risk of its social licence being changed unless it addresses growing concerns on data security and the fact that it allows material to be published on its platform that can be harmful and even dangerous. Facebook does not intentionally cause harm to others, but its business model allows harm to occur.[123] Society is demanding that this be addressed.

One of the best summaries of the context in which social licence can be damaged was provided by highly respected Australian director, Graham Bradley, who warned on these issues in a speech to the Australian Institute of Company Directors in 2017:

---

122 The Ethics Centre, *Social licence to operate*, 22 January 2018, <https://www.ethics.org.au>.
123 'Facebook must recognise it is more than a platform', *Financial Times*, 3 December 2018, p. 14.

> In Australia, a series of sensational corporate events have challenged the reputation of boards and management of some of our largest firms and organisations: think CBA, Australia Post, CPA Australia, QBE, Seven Network. This has given rise to debate about whether corporations deserve their 'social licence to operate', which is essential to maintaining ongoing community support.[124]

Modern sentiment on this is very similar to that espoused back in 1935 by former US President Teddy Roosevelt, who proclaimed, 'I believe in corporations; they are indispensable instruments of modern civilisations; but I believe that they should be supervised and so regulated that they shall act in the interests of the community as a whole' (Micklethwait & Wooldridge, 2003, p. 182). What Roosevelt was referring to was the obligation of firms to operate under a social licence, which society, in extremis through government and its agencies, could amend or withdraw. The establishment of a Royal Commission to consider the conduct of, among others, commercial banks was in many ways a de facto review of the social licence of banks in the same way that in the UK the Vickers report investigated and then made recommendations on ring-fencing commercial banking from investment banking and in the US the Dodd-Frank Wall Street Reform and Consumer Protection Act recommended restrictions on certain banking activities. The banking sector is not alone in having its social licence amended by government when there is evidence of scandal or market power abuse. The energy sectors in some economies are subject to similar scrutiny.

It is important however to be clear on the scope of a social licence to operate. It is largely contextual to individual businesses, and sometimes to an industry. It is not a mandate to drift into social discourse that is more the legitimate domain of politicians.

---

124 Boyd T., 'Directors' guide to rebuilding trust', *Australian Financial Review*, 17 October 2018, p. 48.

There are many special interest groups that would have businesses participate in politically charged debates that are unrelated to the core activities of their business. Activists who would like to drag the business community into areas that are unrelated to the legitimate interests of the business point to CSR and ESG (environmental, social and governance) obligations. There is sometimes a legitimate business case for companies to be vocal on specific CSR and ESG related matters, but too often businesses can find themselves sleepwalking into topics that only serve to politicise businesses in a way that could ultimately be damaging to the company and its brand. This is a growing risk. Larry Fink, the head of BlackRock, for example, called for business leaders to take more responsibility for addressing social and economic issues such as environmental challenges, gender and racial inequalities, and the growing crisis in the provision of pension and health care. He argues that given mounting societal frustration, disillusionment and absence of trust with governments, business must fill the void.[125] Fink's comments in his 2019 letter to the CEOs of the S&P 500 captured this: 'Stakeholders are pushing companies to wade into sensitive social and political issues – especially as they see that government is failing to do this effectively.'[126]

Business leaders make very poor politicians and politicians rarely make good business leaders. This truism should be respected if miscalculations are to be avoided. The line between what is a legitimate CSR and ESG topic for a company to be an advocate on, and where it should leave the debate to the political classes and the media, must be clearly articulated by the board of each company. CEOs and chairs should never be allowed to use their position within a company to prosecute personal interest

---

125 Flood, C., 'BlackRock's Fink urges CEOs to tackle social issues', *Financial Times*, 17 January 2019.

126 Sorkin, A. R., 'Business must lead a divided world: Fink', *New York Times*, 18 January 2019.

agendas. There are many examples, as good corporate citizens, where it is important businesses are clear on social matters. An example would be a company's carbon footprint and commitment to diversity, family values, work-life balance, gender and racial equality. In doing these things well, businesses are making a positive contribution to society. Knowing where to draw the line is important. Warren Buffet was clear on this: 'I don't believe in imposing my political opinions on the activities of our businesses.'[127]

PUBLIC INTEREST VERSUS PRIVATE INTEREST

Chapter 1 briefly touched on the importance of regulation in the banking sector. Regulation, in its broadest sense, is a form of behavioural control, which was described by Selznick (1985) as a 'sustained and focused control exercise by a public agency over activities that are valued in a community'. The scope and nature of regulation is intertwined with a bank's social licence to operate. It should be clear, as President Roosevelt alluded too, whether banks should be operating in the public interest or in their own private interest. This fundamental question is at the heart of the regulator's role and it goes to the biases and risks in the banking system that are described in Chapter 2.

A public interest view would ensure that the banks allocated capital in a socially efficient and responsible manner, without compromising sound risk management principles and the need to achieve a satisfactory ROE. This implies a more active and directional involvement of regulators and other government agencies, either in directing existing banks or encouraging new entrants, which the Australian Government is endeavouring to do through its new licensing regime and initiatives such as 'Open

---

127 Ibid.

Banking'. This is what happened in the UK, where the banks were pressured to disclose their targets for lending to SMEs[128] with pressure brought to bear if there was evidence of that commitment waning.[129] Where there is a desire for greater public interest but strong resistance from the banks, who are protective of their private interest view, then the government can enter the market, particularly where there is evidence of market failure, and set up its own bank. In the UK, the government established the state-owned British Business Bank,[130] which was set up in 2014 with an initial £1 billion of government funding. The British Business Bank targets SMEs with a turnover of up to £25 million. As discussed in Chapter 5, the decision by the Australian Government to launch a $2 billion securitisation fund and an equity-based fund was motivated by the very same concern, that of market failure.

A private interest view places greater reliance on market disciplines, information disclosure and a light-handed regulatory approach. In this context, banks use their political connections and significant lobbying power to keep regulatory and political intrusion to a minimum. In a strict private interest view, banks are also allowed to engage in M&A, free from competition-based regulatory intervention and grow the scale and scope of their businesses, as has been a feature of the Australian market for several years (although NAB's attempt to buy AXA in 2010 was blocked by the Graeme Samuel led ACCC).[131] The private interest view was the dominant ideology in the US and in the UK leading up to the GFC, in line with the philosophy at that time of Alan Greenspan (the Greenspan Doctrine). In the UK, there was sustained political

---

128 Megaw, N., 'RBS unveils £1bn small business lending push', *Financial Times*, 25 May 2018, p. 33.

129 Binham, C., 'Banks "reluctant to lend" to small businesses, MPs told', *Financial Times*, 31 March 2018, p. 15.

130 <https://www.british-business-bank.co.uk>.

131 'ACCC to oppose NAB bid for AXA and to clear AMP bid', ACCC, 19 April 2010, <https://www.accc.gov.au>.

emphasis on the need for the regulator to take a light touch in 'order to retain the international competitiveness of the UK's financial system'. The regulatory report investigating the collapse of HBOS quotes the then British Chancellor, Gordon Brown, in 2005 as saying, 'There is no inspection without justification, no form filling without notification. Not just light touch but a limited touch.'[132] Brown had bought into the Greenspan Doctrine on regulation. The story of what happened to the UK banking sector during the GFC is well documented elsewhere as are the austerity costs that still plague that economy a decade and more later. The fact that Gordon Brown, a Labour politician with a strong social conscience and 'left' leaning sentiment on the political economy, should espouse such a view, is testimony to the strength of the laissez faire ideology at that time.

An area of legitimate public and regulatory concern is that of executive remuneration. Bank executives are well paid and, as discussed throughout this book, the link between ROE and incentives has been highlighted as corrupting of behaviour and conduct. As discussed elsewhere in this book, weak accountability for conduct outcomes has meant that even in the event of reputation damaging scandals, the financial consequences for senior executives can often be minimal. In the 2017/18 financial year, which by any measure was an *annus horribilis* (horrible year) for banks and their shareholders, allegations of law breaking, appalling conduct devoid of any ethical or moral values and serious failures in risk management resulted in bonuses being cut by 20–30 per cent. The reaction of many in society was that of disbelief that bonuses should be paid at all. What does it take to not get paid a bonus? More on this in Chapter 8.

---

132 Bank of England, *The failure of HBOS plc (HBOS): A report by the Financial Conduct Authority (FCA) and the Prudential Regulation Authority (PRA)*, November 2015, <https://www.bankofengland.co.uk/-/media/boe/files/prudential-regulation/publication/hbos-complete-report>.

On the topic of banker remuneration, which most in society consider excessive given the largely annuity nature of revenues and the oligopoly structure of the industry, it is important to address a misconception. Most bank employees receive respectable salaries and very modest (if any) bonus incentives. They are also held to a level of accountability not applied to their leaders, yet they are largely tarnished by the same brush. This is deeply unfair.

The executive bonuses, and other examples, raise legitimate questions on how attuned banks are to their social and community obligations. They highlight the risks that this lack of sensitivity – despite decades of promoting CSR in annual reports – represents to the social licence of the bank and to the capitalist ideology. It is hard to build a case that banks have not violated at least two of the three components of a social licence – legitimacy, credibility and trust.

PURPOSE

Today, there is emphasis placed on the *purpose* of a firm – the enduring statement on *why* a business exists, which is closely aligned to its social licence. As with social licence, purpose is highly relevant in banking given the central role that banks play in an economy. It is important not to confuse purpose with a company's vision or value statement. A purpose statement should define why the business exists. A clear statement of purpose should also anchor all strategic decisions. In the 1990s, Harvard's Christopher Bartlett and LBS's Sumantra Ghoshal argued that firms need to move away from an over emphasis on strategy-structure-systems and empower their people through an engaging corporate purpose. That purpose gives a firm a single shared goal that sums up why the firm exists; it gives direction and meaning to everything the firm does. At Judo Bank, for example, our purpose is 'to be Australia's most trusted

SME business bank'. Every strategic move that we consider must be based on a clear alignment with our sense of purpose. Society, including many investors, want to see clarity on purpose beyond profits and dividends. Banks (and all large businesses) must stand for something more than making money.

It is also important that purpose is properly defined and put in context, given its unique nature to each firm. A focus on shareholder value has the benefit of specificity, but it is an incomplete statement of legitimacy, let alone success. Most executives and directors with a business school or professional training will look to economic logic as the key driver of a firm's performance. Given this paradigm, they come to look at purpose in the same way that many looked at CSR. Yet an authentic higher-level purpose can ignite latent enthusiasm and engagement within a firm, as Bartlett and Ghoshal describe.

The growing importance of purpose was succinctly captured by BlackRock CEO, Larry Fink, in his 2018 letter to the CEOs of the S&P 500:

> Without a sense of purpose, no firm, either public or private, can achieve its full potential. It will ultimately lose the licence to operate from key stakeholders. It will succumb to short-term pressures to distribute earnings, and, in the process, sacrifice investment in employee development, innovation, and capital expenditure that are necessary for long-term growth.[133]

In his 2019 letter, Fink argued that 'Purpose guides culture, provides a framework for long-term decisions and ultimately helps sustain long-term financial returns for shareholders.'[134] What Fink

---

133 Ignatius, A., 'Why BlackRock CEO Larry Fink is not a Socialist', *Harvard Business Review*, 12 March 2018.
134 Flood, C., 'BlackRock's Fink urges CEOs to tackle social issues', *Financial Times*, 17 January 2019.

is arguing for is purpose-driven capitalism in a shared value sense. Implicitly there is an acknowledgement that all businesses live in a political and socio-economic system that can define the success of a business; therefore, rather than narrowly focusing on profit, businesses have to do a lot more if they are to be sustainable.

Integral to purpose and social licence is trust, particularly in banking. Many bank CEOs over the last decade have gone to great lengths to emphasise how they are committed to building trust with their customers and society. In 2010, the then NAB CEO, Cameron Clyne, in a speech in Melbourne to the Australia-Israel Chamber of Commerce (AICC), talked about the bank's commitment to rebuilding trust with a focus on transparency. He acknowledged that rebuilding trust would be a 'marathon not a sprint' but the bank was committed to taking a lead and in doing so balancing the needs of all stakeholders. He acknowledged that the closure of branches and the nature and level of fees charged was undermining public trust. The bank received many plaudits for abolishing a lot of fees at the time of its 'Break-up' campaign, which conveyed a sense of purpose, captured in the bank's marketing position of 'more give, less take'. As a CEO, Cameron Clyne was ahead of his time in thinking through the social acceptance of banking practices and was genuinely committed to having NAB take a lead in shaping a fairer and more customer friendly bank. The outcome at the Royal Commission for NAB may well have been profoundly different had Cameron Clyne been the CEO.

In addition to a reassuring humility, he was deeply in tune with societal sentiment towards the banks. Having taken a leadership position in addressing much of society's misgivings with the fees and service provided by banks, as is so often the case, NAB then drifted back into the comfort of the pack and the sense of purpose in 'Break-up' was lost. The 'Break-up' campaign was a bold move that was highly popular within the bank and with the media. The financial markets however did not like it and pressure was put on NAB to get back in the pack. The truth is that building or rebuilding trust is easier said than done. The challenge in rebuilding trust, some eight years after the commitment made by Cameron Clyne, is starkly highlighted in the well-publicised scandals that have plagued NAB and the industry since then. Consistent with a path dependent thesis and as with Ross Gittins's sceptical view mentioned in Chapter 1, history informs us that banks simply will not change if left to their own devices. It would be a naive miscalculation to assume otherwise, despite the genuine intent of many leaders such as Cameron Clyne. The reality also is that CEOs and C-suite executives change every four to five years and a new CEO inevitably does two things: first, they will rewrite history and present a revisionist view of how well their predecessors performed, often presenting them in a poor light, if not explicitly then almost certainly implicitly; and second, they will often redefine the purpose, values and strategy in order to stamp 'their' personal brand on what the bank stands for. This revisionist tendency was evident when Cameron Clyne's successor as CEO, Andrew Thorburn, told the Royal Commission that the bank had no purpose for some time and that he and the chair had landed on 'Back the bold'.[135] The new CEO at CBA, Matt Comyn, wasted no time in criticising the management team under his predecessor, Ian Narev.[136] This is normal, though not always so publicly aired.

BANKS AND SHAREHOLDER VALUE

In the late twentieth century, there has been a battle between two apparently conflicting ideas of the firm: the stakeholder

---

[135] Whaley, J., 'NAB chief admits fee-for-no-service scandal "absolutely wrong" amid claims the bank no purpose in recent years', *Herald Sun*, 26 November 2018.

[136] Janda, M., 'CBA CEO Matt Comyn heaps blame on predecessor Ian Narev for dodgy credit insurance', ABC News, 28 November 2018, <https://www.abc.net.au>.

idea, which argues that firms are responsible for a wide range of stakeholders, and the shareholder idea, which argues that the firm has a primary responsibility to their shareholders. The concept of 'shareholder value' has been discredited in the minds of many. This is because it is unfairly associated with CEO greed, short-termism, underinvestment and corporate scandals. It remains however one of the most influential ideas in business and represents a philosophy that is understood and practised by the best-managed firms in the world. The idea of shareholder value is important in a market economy. The fundamental problem is not with the idea, but with the weak corporate governance that has allowed abuses and sometimes eye-watering scandals. *The Economist* summarised the reality of how shareholder value should be understood:

> Outbreaks of madness in markets tend to happen because people are breaking the rules of shareholder value, not enhancing them ... That such fiascos occur is a failure of governance and human nature, not an idea.[137]

There is a growing sense that the capitalist ideas, which have spurred economic growth and created so much prosperity, are under siege. The chairman of the ACCC summed up the reputation problem facing businesses when he said, 'Too many firms mislead their customers or treat them unconscionably and the incentives that encourage bad behaviour often outweigh incentives to put the customer first.'[138] As *The Economist* noted in an uncharacteristically understated way: 'Anglo-Saxon capitalism has had a bad decade'.[139] This was not how the founder of capitalism, Adam Smith, had intended it to be.

In the minds of many, a discussion about purpose brings into

---

137 'Analyse this', *The Economist*, 2 April 2016, pp. 58–59.
138 O'Dowd, C., 'ACCC boss hits out at bonuses', *The Australian*, 14–15 July 2018, p. 25.
139 'Capitalism for the people', *The Economist*, 2 December 2017, p. 59.

focus more fundamental questions about the ongoing relevance of the capitalist model. This however confuses two ideas that can be reconciled by Adam Smith. First on the principal–agent problem in how people managing other people's money can never be trusted. Smith's insight was echoed by Berle and Means in their classic work *The modern corporation and private property* (1932). The authors argued that the divorce of ownership from the management of a company created agency problems that were insurmountable and aggravated when ownership was widely dispersed. They were restating a concern prophetically seen by Adam Smith (1776, p. 741):

> The directors ... being the managers rather of other people's money than of their own, it cannot well be expected that they should watch over it with the same anxious vigilance with which the partners in a private firm frequently watch over their own. Negligence and profusion, therefore, must always prevail, more or less, in the management of the affairs of such a company.

Smith's insights into corporate governance, stated some 250 years ago, will tell the thoughtful reader that little has changed in corporate governance terms in a world that has changed beyond recognition since 1776. This is a puzzle and a reason why Milton Friedman sought clarity of purpose when he wrote about the social responsibility of business in what became known as the Friedman Doctrine. When you set aside much of the corporate spin of Australia's major banks, their focus on ROE and incentives together with their disappointing abuse of customer and community trust, they have been exemplars of the Friedman Doctrine that 'the social responsibility of business is to increase its profits'. Yet as explained below, they have done Milton Friedman a great disservice, as he would never have approved of how his doctrine has been so abused. Moreover, the leadership within the banks have not served their shareholders well in recent years based on TSR, with the share price of some banks below where they were five years ago, in some cases a decade ago. It is a more accurate statement to say that banks have been run to optimise senior executive remuneration than in the interests of their customers or shareholders, yet 'shareholder value' has been tarnished as a legitimate business goal.

The University of Chicago economist and Nobel Laureate Milton Friedman famously wrote:

> There is one and only one social responsibility of business – to use its resources and engage in activities designed to increase its profits so long as it stays within the rules of the game, which is to say, engages in open and free competition without deception or fraud. (Freidman, 1962)

Friedman's words remind us that the debate on social responsibility is not new. He argued that the notion of social responsibility is analytically loose and vague and can result in businesses drifting into the domain that is legitimately the area of government, politicians and special interest groups and of shareholders acting in a private capacity. Equally, the vagueness of social responsibility creates conflicts that can damage one stakeholder over another. For example, the board of a business heading into difficult times may decide that the right thing to do is to cut the workforce. In doing so there may be community implications, but not doing so may result in greater societal cost in the long term. How is this dilemma to be solved?

Friedman argued that the clarity of purpose around maximising profits in a legal and ethical manner avoided confusion regarding purpose and the principal–agent costs of boards allowing companies to stray into territory that is mapped out by others in society. Friedman's views are criticised today partly because they have been taken both literally and absent the context in which the comments were made – competitive markets, legal and ethical purpose.

SHARED VALUE

The counterargument to the Friedman Doctrine is presented by Nobel Laureate and Harvard professor Oliver Hart and the University of Chicago's Luigi Zingales. In their view plenty of shareholders have ethical and political concerns on a range of matters such as climate change, the environment more broadly and gender equality, which they correctly want to see the business endorse. Related to this perspective is the concept of shared value, popularised by Harvard's Michael Porter and Mark Kramer (2011). They argued that the capitalist system is under siege, largely because companies are trapped in a narrow sense of shareholder value as the primary goal. Their response was the concept of shared value, where companies bring business and society back together to generate economic value and, in doing so, also produce value for society by addressing its challenges. A shared value approach reconnects business success with social progress.[140] This is a powerful idea and one that bank boards would be strongly advised to spend much more time on. A clear insight into how this important discussion can manifest itself is captured in an interview with the then co-CEOs of Citigroup, the urbane banker John Reed, and Sandy Weill, the cavalier financial conglomerate deal-doer (Langley, 2003, pp. 324–5):

> 'The model I have is of a global consumer company that really helps the middle class with something they haven't been served well by historically. That's my vision. That's my dream,' said Reed. 'My goal is increasing shareholder value,' Sandy [Weill] interjected, glancing frequently at a nearby computer monitor displaying Citigroup's changing stock price.

---

140 Porter, M. & Kramer, M., 'Creating shared value', *Harvard Business Review*, Jan/Feb 2011.

Weill eventually convinced the Citigroup board to oust Reed and appoint him as the sole CEO. Within eight years, Citigroup's share price was wiped out and the bank rescued by the US government. The position of Citigroup's shareholders and other stakeholders would likely have been so different had the board backed Reed over Weill. A serious miscalculation.

In a similar vein, ICI, once headed by Sir John Harvey-Jones, was once seen as one of the most respected firms in the UK. Up until the 1990s its purpose statement read, 'we aim to be the finest chemical company in the world'. In the 1990s, at the height of the Friedman Doctrine, ICI changed it purpose statement to 'we aim to maximise shareholder value'. This change was a serious miscalculation and proved disastrous. The firm lost its purpose, suffered declining performance and in 2008 was acquired by AkzoNobel. A once iconic firm is no more. Replacing ICI as most respected firm in the UK, according to Paul Collier in his excellent book *The future of capitalism* (2018), is John Lewis Partnership, which is a firm that is unusual in its ownership structure in that it is owned by a trust run in the interest of the firm's employees. Reflecting this, employees receive a substantial part of the firm's profits as a profit share (a bonus and a profit share can be two quite different things), with the CEO getting the same percentage of base pay as a profit share as the most junior employee in the firm. John Lewis is a mutual company owned collectively by people with a direct interest in its culture and in how customers are served. This strong alignment of interests reduces the costs of agency problems that plague most other widely owned businesses.

ADAM SMITH ON PURPOSE, CSR AND ETHICAL CAPITALISM

Adam Smith is seen as the intellectual father of capitalism and modern economics, so what would he have to say about the state of capitalism if he were alive today, given that so much of the principles and conduct that passes as capitalism find their economic foundation in his work? The answer is easy. Smith knew that unbridled capitalism was not in the interest of society. In *The wealth of nations* he noted caustically that:

> The proposal of any new law or regulation which comes from [businessmen] ought always to be listened to with great precaution, and ought never to be adopted till after having been long and carefully examined, not only with the most scrupulous but with the most suspicious attention. It comes from an order of men whose interest is never exactly the same with that of the public, who have generally an interest to deceive and even to oppress the public, and accordingly have upon many occasions both deceived and oppressed it.

Despite his scepticism, Smith was an undoubted advocate for markets, trade and of small government, as was Milton Friedman. Smith saw the power of self-interest (the invisible hand) as being essential to wealth creation in competitive markets. Smith also saw wealth as equating to the wellbeing of people and his thinking was based on morality, justice and doing good. Smith regarded benevolence as admirable and a great virtue (Smith, 1759). Smith would have objected to corporate irresponsibility, to economic concentrations in monopolists or oligopolists. He would have viewed rent-seeking behaviour as distasteful. He saw competitive markets as creating efficiency through the profit motive that met societal needs.

The wealth of nations was in many ways a book on CSR, on the importance of the public interest.[141] Smith's invisible hand argued that the private search for profit advances the public interest and thus CSR. Greed and self-interest are not the same thing. Greed, in the ordinary meaning, is ugly and can be corrupting. It can lead to corporate obesity, to excesses that damage reputations and to unethical and sometimes illegal conduct; it also increases the prospect of bankruptcy or government intervention. In competitive markets, as Smith would have envisaged, profits come from 'doing the right thing' by producing goods that are valued by society. Smith's view on capitalism could be described as 'ethical capitalism'. What passes for capitalism today, which has prompted such societal backlash, is not what Smith had in mind, nor is it what Milton Friedman had in mind.

Perhaps then, rather than critics of capitalism looking to the Friedman Doctrine to justify their case, they should look to the father or patron saint of capitalism, Adam Smith, and learn again the true spirit of capitalism – ethical capitalism. Russ Roberts' excellent book *How Adam Smith can change your life: an unexpected guide to human nature and happiness* (2014), based on Smith's *The theory of moral sentiment* (1759), provides the insights that better explain the real meaning of capitalism. A true understanding of what Adam Smith stood for and how he viewed capitalism reveals that he was much more than a free market economist; he was passionate about the wellbeing of the less well off. He saw how ethical capitalism could create prosperity for all. He placed great virtue on the notion of the impartial spectator, asking that people have an internal conversation on moral values, asking 'what would you do'? In *The theory of moral sentiment*, he wrote, 'The wise and virtuous man is at all times willing that his own private interests should be sacrificed to the public interest.' There is little doubt that Smith would be appalled at the immorality of much of what is conducted today in the name of capitalism, particularly in the banking sector.

---

141 'Profits and the public good', *The Economist*, 20 January 2005, p. 68.

THE SCOURGE OF MONOPOLIES (AND OLIGOPOLIES)

In their important and well-researched book *The myth of capitalism – monopolies and the death of competition* (2018), Jonathan Tepper and Denise Hearn argue that slowing growth and rising inequality have become a toxic combination. While many blame an excess of free market capitalism for this politically dangerous mix, they convincingly argue that the opposite is true. What has emerged during the past 40 years is a predatory form of monopoly capitalism. The market, they argue, needs a resurgence of antitrust law, not just to protect consumers but to protect competition itself. The book could have been written solely on the Australian banking market and its central thesis would remain unchanged.

In today's banking world, the irony of the Friedman Doctrine will not be lost on the observant reader. The primacy of shareholder value, even though largely discredited as a primary guiding principle in running a business, is exactly what the Royal Commission and Productivity Commission reports highlight as the motivating principle for managing and governing our banks – profits before customers, employees and societal expectations. The banking system, on the surface, looks like an industry, at the heart of the economy but trapped in a self-serving interpretation of the Friedman Doctrine when the rest of society has moved onto a higher and broader plane, embracing shared value. But as argued above, Adam Smith saw the importance of shared value as a basis for capitalism. Both he and Milton Friedman, if alive today, would surely disassociate themselves from the conduct that has allowed our banks to generate the economic rents that they have. Both Smith and Friedman would also disassociate themselves from the rent-seeking behaviour present in so many industries, where competitive forces are weak and consumer interests are a second or third order consideration.

At the core of this problem has been a combination of poor public policy on competition and deep flaws in corporate governance. There is no debate on the supporting facts that capitalism has its flaws; to believe that all capitalists will behave honourably just because they are engaged in capitalism is akin to believing that all drivers of cars will drive safely just because they have a driving licence – some drivers are reckless, some cause injury and even fatalities, but the vast majority are safe and operate within the spirit as well as the letter of the law. The challenge is to mitigate many of the wasteful, damaging and corrupting features of capitalism, therefore making truly competitive markets and effective corporate governance together with effective regulatory and legal deterrents so important. As discussed in Chapter 8, boards today must think of governance as embracing a wider range of issues than it has traditionally done, while also not losing sight that the preservation of shareholder wealth is an important board objective, but not at all costs let alone exclusively. Shareholder wealth creation, societal purpose and being true to a social licence should not be in conflict: they can be an *and* instead of an *or*. They should live side by side.

The dangers of having an overly weighted bias towards and a poor understanding of sustained shareholder value outcomes were starkly illustrated by the events in the global banking industry during the GFC. These dangers were also visible by the corrupting behaviour in much of Australian banking, as highlighted by the Royal Commission. The corrupting nature of a sales culture in banking and the associated problems in the design of short-term incentives heavily linked to financial outcomes were the main reasons for the cultures that damaged so many great institutions such as **RBS**, **HBOS**, Deutsche Bank, Citigroup and, in recent times, Wells Fargo and CBA. All had at their source a culture that valued and rewarded profits over ethics and moral standards. As Professor John Kay reminded us:

People's behavior typically meets the expectations generated by the environment in which they operate. Incentives aren't an alternative to culture; incentives, appropriate or inappropriate, and trust and confidence, or its absence, are the product of the culture of financial organizations.[142]

Kay highlights how the single-minded focus on shareholder value can lead to decisions that emphasise financial considerations (and often by association, short-termism) over long-term value creation. There is no denying that banks are under pressure to deliver short-term results by the market and this is hardwired into executive remuneration, but this is not an excuse for the conduct and culture highlighted by the Royal Commission that has resulted in a record low level of trust in the banks.[143]

CONCLUDING REMARKS

Banks are different from any other business and they are rightly subject to public scrutiny. A concentrated banking system protected by a public policy framework and implicitly subject to a government guarantee is quasi-nationalised in nature or as the British would say, they are semipublic institutions. Banks have been granted special privileges and with those privileges come obligations and responsibilities to society to operate in the public interest, which need not conflict with a private interest view. In a corporate governance sense, this goes to the heart of *purpose* – why the banking firm exists – and to the social licence that it enjoys. This is an important theory of the banking market and arguments that large domestic banks should be regulated as a public utility are not without merit if they cannot be trusted to self-regulate, which history informs us that they cannot, even in the face of

---

142 Kay, J., *Kay review of UK equity markets and long-term decision making, final report*, 22 July 2012.
143 <http://cms.edelman.com/sites/default/files/2018-03/Edelman_Trust_Barometer_Financial_Services_2018.pdf>.

criticism such as that which came from the Royal Commission. There is a deeply ingrained arrogance within banks of 'let's ride out the storm and then get back to making money.'[144] Those that might argue that being a public utility would drive highly talented management out of the industry should reflect on the findings of the Royal Commission. Many of the issues evident in the Royal Commission and in the Productivity Commission report have their root cause in a decaying culture, which saw profit before customers and weak accountability; a culture that promotes what Milton Friedman called out in 1962 as the social responsibility of business – to increase profits (except Friedman placed the caveat 'to be done legally and ethically'). Australia's major banks embraced the Friedman Doctrine but took a casual approach to his caveats. Friedman, moreover, would have emphasised the importance of competition, as Tepper and Hearn (2018) so skilfully do. A Friedman Doctrine absent moral and ethical values, weak corporate governance and a market that lacks meaningful competition, leads to outcomes such as those highlighted by the Royal Commission. It encourages a culture of arrogance and customer abuse. It also damages what 'creating shareholder value' truly means. Creating shareholder value is a legitimate objective of any business, but it can never be the be-all and end-all. Rather it should be the result of a business doing well in fulfilling its purpose and meeting its social licence obligations. As John Kay (2010) described in his book *Obliquity*, the creation of shareholder value should flow from doing what is important, such as looking after customers.

A healthy culture is one that is based on a clearly articulated higher purpose for the bank; a higher purpose that is intertwined with the bank's social purpose. The shared value philosophy reconciles the dilemma that some boards grapple with on the

---

144 Danckert, S., 'ASIC attacks bank attitudes to regulation', *Sydney Morning Herald*, 15 March 2019, p. 22.

question of purpose. Oxford University professor Colin Mayer (2018) argues that to focus solely or predominantly on maximising shareholder value represents a betrayal of one of humanity's most accomplished inventions. The corporation, he argues:

> is not a vehicle for controlling our lives for the benefit of a small class of privileged owners. It is a body that can promote co-operation and collaboration in the realisation of purposes that individually we can neither conceive nor achieve with the same degree of integrity and credibility.

This is what President Roosevelt had in mind in his utterances in 1935.

One of the challenges facing the banking industry is how it aligns with its social licence to operate. There is a risk that, in the same way that unfortunately CSR has become nothing more than empty rhetoric for the banks, so too will a commitment to a social licence, even though, in so many ways, the Royal Commission was a de facto review of the social licence of the major banks.

The next chapter looks at evidence not just of a failure of banks to act in accordance with their social licence, but a concerning underlying cause, the decline of professionalism.

3
THE DECLINE OF PROFESSIONALISM IN BANKING

THE banking industry was once defined by trust. The Latin term for credit is *creditum*, meaning to believe, to trust. Trust and integrity were at the core of how the industry developed professional standards, but unfortunately these values declined progressively over the years. Today the industry's reputation has been shredded and the decline in professionalism is a major factor behind this disappointing reality.

At its simplest level of definition, professionalism means the competence or skill to carry out a specific activity recognised by society. A more sophisticated definition covers the qualities and characters that define a professional. The mark of professionalism defines a set of expectations that society should have on how an industry, bank or employee should operate.

Former NAB CEO Don Argus summed the situation up well:

> It is not an unreasonable expectation for customers to be dealing with employees who have the appropriate accreditation to help them achieve their goals, and I suspect a light will be shone on the adequacy or otherwise of employee development programs as the royal commission proceeds.[145]

---

145 Argus, D., 'Banks must go back to basics to regain public trust', *The Australian*, 18–19 August 2018.

The decline in professionalism can be understood by the prevailing underlying culture that has become deeply rooted within the industry where there is no professional accreditation needed to practice as a banker. In some banks the ranks within and close to the C-suite were filled with people who had no grounding in banking and sometimes no respect for its traditions, its competencies and its history. These talented mid-career hires occasionally looked at career bankers as relics of yesteryear's business model and akin to Mr Mainwaring, the fictional figure who was a bank manager in the sitcom *Dad's Army*. The new entrants enjoyed the intellectual challenge of complex organisations and the potential in the *financialisation* of the economy and the high rewards that flow. This financialisation of the economy and conglomerate nature of the banking model thus coincided with the decline in traditionally trained bankers (or what it meant to be a banker).[146] The financialisation of the sector manifested itself in many forms, including a bias towards selling and cross-selling products as bankers were charged with making sure that customers supported the economics of the conglomerate product nature of many banks.

Many of the new breed of bank executives had no technical or intuitive skill in understanding risk management apart from a familiarisation with concepts such as the Three Lines of Defence – discussed in Chapter 6. This was a factor in the breakdown in the risk culture, which when combined with the emergence of an incentive-based 'sales culture' resulted in a dangerous combination. The product of this, for example, is the alleged level of so-called 'liar loans and other evidence of irresponsible lending'.[147] Another product was the breakdown in moral and ethical standards, highlighted so vividly by the Royal Commission.

---

146 Kay, J., *Other people's money*, 2015, p. 165.

147 **UBS** equity research has estimated that this problem could be as high as approximately $500 billion in the $1.6 trillion residential mortgage market.

DECLINING STANDARDS AND ACCREDITATION

The evidence on a lack of professionalism in the banking industry is overwhelming, including some of the events highlighted in Chapter 1 such as interest rate market-rigging, the mis-selling of deficient insurance products, lying to regulators, abuse of pricing power and bribe taking by employees. The decline in standards is also evident in the many other ethical and conduct issues that have plagued the banks.[148] When the UK Parliamentary Commission on Banking Standards considered problems in that market in 2013, it identified a lack of basic standards of professionalism as being at the heart of the problem and the solution. The report challenged policy makers, regulators and bank boards to take responsibility for raising the bar on professional standards.[149] There is a strong case that the very same challenges exist in Australia. While banks can expect (and deserve) greater regulatory intrusion into the future, it is debatable whether much, or any, of it will tackle the fundamental weaknesses in the industry's culture and its lack of professionalism. This is the nature of an industry locked on a path dependent course. Ideally, it is for the banking industry to take the lead in re-establishing professional standards and bank boards must be at the forefront of this, taking a lead from the former ANZ CEO John McFarlane, who argued that banks 'must return to the philosophy that banking is a profession as well as a business, and that contribution rather than reward is its centre of gravity.'[150] These are profound words of guidance to bank boards post the Royal Commission. The open question is,

---

148 'ASIC accuses banks' financial advisers of working against customers interests', *The Guardian*, 24 January 2018, <https://www.the guardian.com; 'Australian banks accused of rate rigging', *Bloomberg*, 22 October 2017, <https://www.bloomberg.com>; 'Probe exposes Australian banks' abuse of customers', *Financial Times*, 1 May 2018.

149 Barber, B., 'Bankers need higher professional standards to regain trust', *Financial Times*, 12 March 2018, p. 29.

150 Boyd, T., 'Former ANZ CEO John McFarlane calls for rethink of banking philosophy', *Australian Financial Review*, 3 August 2016, p. 48.

are bank boards up to the task?

In an industry that many believe has lost its risk and moral compass, there are few bankers with the courage of Benny Higgins, who headed the retail bank at HBOS until he was fired. Benny took HBOS out of 'equity release' mortgages, clamped down on brokers with a track record of introducing high-risk loans, tightened credit standards on credit card marketing and limits and re-priced mortgages to higher-risk borrowers. As a result, HBOS lost market share and Benny was asked to leave. He left RBS for similar reasons before joining HBOS. Fast forward a few years to after the meltdown at HBOS, when one board director commented, 'Benny was a hero. He called it right in the mortgage market, but the executive and the rest of the board did not have the courage to back him' (Perman & Darling, 2012, p. 335). Benny was a highly credentialed banker when few of the management team at RBS or HBOS were. Prudent, professional bankers did not thrive or survive in banks that had become consumed by the desire for market share growth and sales targets.

There is nothing nostalgic in considering the skills that modern bankers should have, particularly in the business banking market. Given the salaries that are paid to bankers, it should be a reasonable expectation, as Don Argus suggests, that they have the breadth of skills to understand the banks products, conduct both quantitative and qualitative analysis of the customer and evaluate the Four C's of credit – character (reputation and track record), capacity (cash flow), capital (equity) and collateral (security), discussed in Chapters 5 and 6. Those that argue this would be an expensive operating model compared to the more industrialised model of specialisation, are focusing on what is *counted* and losing sight of what *counts*. The emphasis on deep specialisation has helped with the industrialisation of bank operating models, helped drive continued cost cutting and helped meet financial targets, including ROE goals. However, this has come at a cost in the service offered to customers and this is particularly the case in the SME market, which is discussed in Chapter 5.

CHANGING CULTURE

Why has banking developed such a poor reputation? While culture is a big part of the reason why this has happened, so too is the decline in professionalism. These issues are of course linked, but what can be readily addressed is professionalism and then gradually culture. The establishment of professional standards can accelerate cultural transformation. One thing that is quite clear is the relative paucity of the kind of professional qualifications that are demanded of say doctors, lawyers or accountants. Given the role banks and bankers play in the economy, the case for viewing banking as a profession and demanding professional standards and competence is a strong one. As the financialisation of the industry took hold, instead of being prudent allocators of capital across the economy, bankers became the retailers of money with sales targets in the same way that car salesmen and sales within electrical appliance retailers work.

This cultural change in the industry that swept both the Australian and the UK market is illustrated in the case of HBOS. Management consultant trained Andy Hornby, HBOS CEO, believed that management was a generic skill that could be applied in any industry, and banking was no different. In the UK, almost two decades ago, banks stopped encouraging staff to undertake the Institute of Bankers course and an MBA became the desired qualification for ambitious bankers. The MBA training often encouraged views consistent with the industrialisation of the business model – credit scoring, centralisation, divisionalisation, specialisation, standardisation and rigid policies and procedures. The logic was that this represents a more profitable operating model given the industry structure — it focused on what is *counted* (profit) and lost sight of what *counts* (service and reputation) and supported the goal of profit maximisation. The MBA training also encouraged broader thinking on the scope of the banking industry, often into adjacent but competency distinct sectors. In contrast to the Institute of Bankers training and qualification, most MBA programs treated ethics as a discretionary elective, if at all.[151] Hornby had built a strong reputation for his marketing and selling genius, with slick PowerPoint presentations. The HBOS directors came to believe 'that he could do anything'. The Northern Rock CEO, Adam Applegarth, had a lot in common with Hornby. Both were strong on hubris, both became CEOs at around age 40 and both where slick presenters and aggressive sale-driven leaders. Both ended up destroying two institutions with long and proud histories (Perman & Darling, 2012, p. 266).

THE CURSE OF THE SALES CULTURE

The story of HBOS is hugely illustrative of how a CEO drives a culture and how leadership and culture are deeply entwined. It is also illustrative of a truth: you cannot be a great leader in a bank that has a broken culture. A CEO may be the master of presentations and of corporate spin, but the test of a great leader is defined by the culture of the bank. Perman and Darling (2012) describe how the HBOS employees were not prepared for the sales-driven culture that Andy Hornby wanted to drive. Using his retail and consulting experience, he drove the need to sell products rather than provide a service. Staff were sent on training programs on how to achieve this. Supersalesman Hornby always ended his monthly newsletter to staff with the message, 'Keep smiling, keep

---

[151] Bolton, R., 'Business schools part of banking's problems', *Australian Financial Review*, 10 March 2019, p. 32.

selling'. One HBOS director commented, 'The impression was, "never mind the quality, feel the bonus".' Experienced bankers know that the easiest thing to sell is money, but getting it back is quite another thing. Hornby and others of his ilk confused the selling of loans as if they were an electrical white good. This philosophy was to also become endemic in the Australian and New Zealand banking industry.

At the end of 2018, in Paul Volcker's memoirs (Volcker was the chairman of the US Federal Reserve between 1979 and 1987), he referenced an unnamed senior Chase Manhattan banker, who in 1984 observed that 'creating an "incentive" compensation plan for individuals, that is bonuses, would be the end of responsible commercial banking, and that the understanding of the customer always should be first.'[152] Prophetic and wise words by a banker who understood banking, its purpose and its social licence. Words that were echoed by Sir Brian Pitman during the post-mortem on the GFC. In 2010, the former Lloyds Bank chairman and CEO said that 'incentives for sales targets have been a large part of the problem … It's a little short of crazy to incentivise people to maximise the number of loans they are going to grant.'[153] The astute readers will note the word 'grant' in Brain Pitman's comment, instead of 'sell'. The language is careful and responsible. It is not suggesting a return to the days of credit rationing, when the customer would ask the bank manager 'How do I stand in terms of getting a loan?' only to hear back from the bank manager 'Stand! You should kneel!' Thankfully, those days are gone; so should the days and the attitude of 'selling a loan'.

Business practices at CBA, particularly in its Retail Banking Division, were underpinned by the US imported Cohen Brown sales culture framework, which was implemented to increase

---

152 See also Wolf, M., 'Keeping at it, by Paul Volcker', *Financial Times*, 29 October 2018.
153 Pitman, B., 'Evidence to the future of Banking Commission', June 2010, <http://www.which.co.uk/documents/pdf/future-of-banking-commission-report>.

product sales and cross-selling of products. One former employee said, 'It was all about the sale, not about the customer, and all about targets and statistics and increasing revenue.'[154] This was also evidently the case at Westpac, when it was reported that a friend of a journalist went to the bank looking for a loan for an investment property. The bank manager tried to convince the customer to borrow for six properties rather than the one.[155] Then there was a Westpac advisor's inappropriate advice that cost nurse Jacqueline McDowall her home. ANZ charged one client $3300 upfront and $3790 annually to save her $238 a year. Banks need to have a fiduciary responsibility. Debt can become addictive for some people. When an individual comes to a bank to borrow $5000 to pay for an annual holiday, it should not be acceptable that the bank encourages the individuals to borrow $10,000 instead as many people, some vulnerable, would take the additional debt. Excessive debt might meet sales targets, but it can destroy lives and businesses.

The incentive fuelled 'animal spirits' in banking, combined with a lack of historical perspective as to what can go wrong ('this time is different'), leads to excessive confidence about the future and, consequently, under-pricing of risk and overpricing of assets. This leads in turn to excessive levels of debt ('if you over pay, you over borrow'), which is the story of the Australian housing market at the time of writing, creating the conditions that can cause economic harm. Readers might well ask: is this the banks acting responsibly; acting professionally?

Lending six or seven times a borrower's income, and often not verifying that income and rarely sitting down and interviewing a borrower (banks sometimes ask for and receive pay slips, which could be fake, and rarely contact the employer to double check),

---

154 Ferguson, A., 'Meddling with kids' accounts not on', *Sydney Morning Herald*, 19 May 2018.
155 Gottliebsen, R., 'Banks' credit squeeze set to worsen', *The Australian*, 25 September 2018, p. 29.

is hardly responsible lending. The cost of doing so is deemed too high – the cost of not doing so may in future prove even higher. As the Royal Commission highlighted, Australian banks were as active as HBOS was in 'bumping up the income' on a customer's application in order to get it through the credit criteria and in the use of the highly suspect HEM formula for assessing income and expenses. An extract from Perman and Darling's (2013, p. 516) account of an employee recollection of events at HBOS is illustrative of the corrupting nature of sales practices in banks, a reality that applies equally to some Australian banks:

> I visited branches across the south-east and staff were usually happy to talk about how the branch bonus was progressing and what they were having to do to keep earning it. I was in a banking hall when a customer came in and in very poor English asked for an envelope to be handed to an interviewer. I was going into the staff room when the envelope was brought in to the staff member. The envelope was opened, and she said to her colleague 'It's a credit card application with CCRC' [credit card repayment cover]. She asked of her boss: 'This woman speaks hardly any English, I could hardly understand her, how did you manage to sell the CCRC?' The answer was 'Tough, if they don't understand English, they get the cover.'

WHAT DO WE MEAN BY PROFESSIONALISM IN BANKING?

Should society look to bankers to have the same standard of training that they would expect from doctors, lawyers and accountants? Given the unique and highly privileged position that banks hold and the social licence they have been granted, there is a strong argument that they should. Through having the skills to really know their customers, banks and bankers can be a force for good in supporting economic growth and creating greater societal prosperity. If professionalism is allowed to decline, it can also be a cause of destruction, as we saw in the GFC, particularly in Ireland, the UK, many other parts of Europe and the US.

The question of professionalism in banking was explored by Kingsford-Smith, Clarke and Rogers (2017), who concluded that despite the demands for more professionalism, banking had not been a profession since the 1980s and that, in their view, there are limits of professionalism for banking given the complexity and diversity of its activities. Their scepticism is that banking as a heavily regulated industry is unlike most professions, where there is greater self-regulation. The existence of greater self-regulation in industries such as accounting does not mean however that such industries are not subject to scandals or low public esteem.[156] Kingsford-Smith et al.'s (2017) rationale for not considering banking as being subject to professional standards and accreditation is unsatisfactory. The difference to other professions from a community perspective is that most people can get through life without having to deal with an accounting firm or a legal firm, whereas banking is pervasive. The idea that lawyers, dentists and doctors would never 'cross-sell' other services beyond those legitimately needed by the customer is a truth that society holds, in the main, for those professions, albeit misplaced at times. Banking however has developed a reputation that it 'sells' products and services that the customer does not need and therefore is not a profession in a sense of *trust*. In other words, society does not believe that banks operate in the public or societal interest in the way that medicine does or (bizarrely) the way that some believe lawyers and accountants do.

In a similar vein to Kingsford-Smith et al. (2017), APRA chairman Wayne Byres, speaking at the Financial Services Institute of Australasia (FINSIA) forum argued that part of the problem revealed by the Royal Commission was a lack of professionalism

---

156 Cornish, C., & Hollinger, P., 'Accounting scandals put the Big Four on the spot', *Financial Times*, 4 May 2017.

across all the industries APRA regulates – banks, superannuation funds and insurance companies: 'Put simply, professions typically have a commitment to quality, ethical principles and the public good.' He said that while medicine, law, teaching, engineering and accounting could be defined as professional, the finance sector could not. 'There is no defined body of knowledge or high entry standards for those who perform key roles,' Mr Byres said, adding that the sector's spurning of professional standards can be traced back to deregulation in the 1980s. At that time, he added:

> Even though the lifting of regulatory shackles may well have been the perfect time for the establishment of stronger professional standards, the liberal ethos of the time meant that the development of greater professionalism, and corresponding corporate and personal restraint that come with it, was a tough ask – akin to swimming against the tide.[157]

One precondition for greater professionalism within the industry is simpler business models that are easier to apply professional standards to and to govern, the so-called 'narrow banking' concept discussed in Chapter 9. Greater clarity around industry boundaries would allow the development of relevant professional standards. So, banks that have commercial bankers, market traders, M&A specialists, private equity investors, wealth management specialists, etc. reflect a financial conglomerate that transcends several industries, as described in Chapter 1. Each of these specialisations involve different tribes, where often there is little understanding of and suspicion towards each other. In the UK, the separation of investment and commercial banking following the Vickers report is an example of how to address this problem. Thus, activities that might be remote to the real economy, such as proprietary trading, should be kept separate from those activities that involve

---

157 APRA release, Chairman Wayne Byres' speech on professionalism in financial services, <https://www.apra.gov.au>.

direct customer facing engagement and are funded by deposits. Banking needs to become simpler as a precondition to becoming professional. We return to this theme in Chapter 9.

THE BANKING AND FINANCE OATH

The introduction of the Banking and Finance Oath (BFO) in 2012 was an important initiative aimed at restoring trust and encouraging greater emphasis on ethical behaviour in the banking and financial services sector. This BFO was a step in the right direction, with many senior bankers having committed to this oath (and as a policy at Judo Bank, all staff are encouraged to take the oath).[158]

Signatories to the oath declare that:
Trust is the foundation of my profession
I will serve all interests in good faith
I will compete with honour
I will pursue my ends with ethical restraint
I will help create a sustainable future
I will help create a more just society
I will speak out against wrongdoing and support others who do the same
I will accept responsibility for my actions
In these and all other matters:
My word is my bond

The BFO provides an important ethical framework, which is administered by the Banking and Finance Ethics Panel. There is scope for strengthening the oath and, as is the case in Holland, making it compulsory for all those employed in banking. To strengthen the standing of the oath two things should be reconsidered: first, it is easy to sign up to; there are no professional

---
158 <https://www.thebfo.org>.

standards or tests to satisfy; and second, it is important to ensure that there are real consequences for those who violate the oath. Some of the offending individuals highlighted by the Royal Commission are signatories to the oath, suggesting that the individual commitment to the oath is not always taken seriously. The whole senior team at one bank, for example, made much publicity about signing the oath in 2015.[159] That same bank was subject to strong criticism in the final Royal Commission report: 'Overall, my fear – that there may be a wide gap between the public face NAB seeks to show and what it does in practice – remains.'[160] Such a criticism goes to the heart of ethics.

In the UK, the banking regulators have taken an important step by establishing a senior managers and certification regime. It requires practitioners to act competently and with integrity. If they do not, they may lose their licence to operate, in the same way that a doctor may lose their licence to practice. The argument against a professional accreditation is that banking brings together different skills, disciplines and knowledge – from the law, accountancy and management consultancy – many of which are governed by qualifications from other professional bodies. This might be true but banking has so much to do to address trust and reputation that at the least it must define minimum standards of what it means to be a banker.

BANKING EXECUTIVE ACCOUNTABILITY REGIME

In Australia, the BEAR was introduced to establish clear statements of accountability for directors and senior executives within banks.

---

159 Durie, J., 'NAB executive team signs up to Banking and Finance Oath', *The Australian*, 10 December 2015, p. 23.

160 Thomson, J., 'NAB singled out for most Hayne pain', *Australian Financial Review*, 5 February 2019, p. 1.

A goal of this new regulatory requirement is 'to ensure there are clear consequences in the event of a material failure to meet expectations'. BEAR 'imposes explicit accountability obligations on both an ADI [authorised deposit-taking institution] and on individuals who are registered as "accountable persons".'[161] Time will tell if the 'bear' has more growl than bite, if it is a cuddly bear or one that is to be respected for fear of the consequences.

To their great credit, the APRA requirements are spelt out in very clear language and cover all directors and senior executives:

> Clear accountability is the necessary foundation for any institution in establishing and promoting good governance and a strong risk culture, and requires:
> - a clear, transparent and common understanding within an institution of where accountability lies within the senior executive team for any particular part or aspect of the institution's business;
> - a clear, transparent and common understanding within an institution of how a given individual meets their obligations as the accountable individual, including for example, by making decisions, serving as a point of review or challenge, or escalating as appropriate; and
> - for those accountable individuals, direct and proportional consequences of failure to meet their obligations, whether by inappropriate action or failure to act within their area of accountability. [162]

That the regulator felt it necessary to issue these regulations will cause the reflective reader to ask, 'What were the bank boards doing?' Aren't these basic hygiene factors that all well-run businesses, not just banks, should exhibit? While BEAR is an important development, it does not go far enough. Individual

---
161 APRA, *Information Paper: Implementing the Banking Executive Accountability Regime*, 17 October 2018, <https://www.apra.gov.au>
162 Ibid.

professional accreditation through study and exams is essential.

PROFESSIONAL TRAINING

The case for industry-wide professional accreditation along the lines of the Chartered Institute of Bankers in the UK, is compelling and arguably essential. Such training should be aimed at providing bankers with extensive and essential knowledge, cognitive skills of critical thinking, and the analysis and synthesis required to make informed ethical and professional judgements. They would also learn about what the social licence and noble purpose of banking really means.

To earn the right to be regarded as a professional, bankers and the banks that employ them must adhere to generally accepted standards of behaviour as enshrined in a code of conduct, but a code that must have 'teeth'. The BFO should form an integral part of any accreditation. A professional banker must also demonstrate a competency that serves as a barrier to entry to those outside the profession. This requires demonstrating threshold knowledge and specific skills. Bankers that breach professional standards are then subject to sanction or discipline, which ultimately could mean being barred from the profession. Broadly based on the UK Chartered Institute of Bankers program (which is being promoted in Australia by FINSIA), but going further, bankers would be required to study and pass the following courses:

- The Role of Banks in the Economy
- History of Financial Crises
- Social Licence and Societal Expectations of Banks
- Introduction to Financial Analysis
- Risk Management in Banking
- Credit Risk Management
- Banking SMEs – Four C's Risk Assessment

- Legal Framework for Banking
- The Role of Regulation
- Ethics in Banking
- The Fundamentals of Psychology.

Acting ethically always has to be seen as a threshold or foundation requirement, hence the importance of the BFO. Acting ethically implies acting in a manner that is right in relation to the undisputed values held by society. Ethical behaviour is at the heart of many behavioural challenges that have plagued the banks, so it is worth going over what the core principles of ethical behaviour are.[163]

INTEGRITY

Integrity refers to having high moral standards, that is to say behaviours that are regarded as virtuous by society. Integrity is a foundation quality in a banker because laws, policies and codes cannot identify every situation or dilemma that a banker will face. When NAB used a privacy loophole to ensure that it was tipped off each time a business bank customer sought a quote from a competing bank, it was arguably breaching both privacy laws, or standards of good practice, and acting in an anti-competitive manner.[164] One customer received an email saying that the bank's 'smarter' systems alerted it to the fact she was 'seeking or inquiring for finance elsewhere'. The customer 'felt violated' by what she saw as an invasion of privacy. Legal arguments aside, such conduct lacked integrity and thus breached a principle of ethical behaviour. When bankers from several banks rigged the interbank lending rate to boost their profits, ultimately at the expense of their customers, they at the very least violated an ethical principle.

---

163 Framework adapted from the training material from the Chartered Banker MBA program at Bangor University.

164 Han, E., 'NAB using Veda to track disloyal business customers going to rival banks', *Sydney Morning Herald*, 20 June 2016.

FAIRNESS

Fairness means dealing with people, both inside and outside the bank, in a balanced, even-handed manner and free from bias and conflict, which could impact personal judgement. The Royal Commission highlighted numerous examples of how the banking industry violated this principle of ethical behaviour including charging fees for no services or using out-of-date medical definitions and dubious claims refusals at CBA's insurance arm. In dealing with customer complaints or problems, both ANZ and NAB considered customer remediation as 'a distraction' and together with CBA would take on average a year to start paying compensation for customers who had been wronged.

OBJECTIVITY

Objectivity means to view a situation from an unbiased standpoint and to deal consistently from that position. The various scandals linked to sales-based bonuses highlighted in Chapter 1 show just how widespread the violation of this principle of ethical behaviour is.

PROBITY

Probity refers to a willingness to consider an entire situation, that is, all the relevant facts, in an objective manner, in order to arrive at a well-informed view. The financial advice scandals that plagued CBA are an example of where integrity and probity have been missing and the principles of ethical behaviour absent.

OPENNESS AND TRANSPARENCY

A willingness to reveal all relevant facts and information. Transparency relates to not clouding an issue or concealing relevant details. When NAB decided not to disclose to the regulator the full scale of the compensation payable to superannuation clients they had over charged so that it would be viewed as 'just one in the pack, rather than an outlier', they were consciously breaching a principle of ethical behaviour. The judge presiding over the Royal Commission accused the NAB executive of 'saying a whole lot of other things – in order to justify your position – that are not an answer to the question'.[165] A similar criticism was made of CBA, who were accused of being too 'legalistic' and 'adversarial' in dealings with the regulator. A damning assessment of CBA's risk team, then headed by a former in-house lawyer, found the bank 'slow, legalistic and reactive' and 'at times dismissive'. These traits marked a culture of arrogance and lacking in respect for regulators.[166]

JUDGEMENT

Judgement refers to arriving at decisions or opinions having full regard for the facts, and applying appropriate knowledge, skills and experience to arrive at an outcome. The reported lending of $500 billion of 'liar loans' and the allegations made against Westpac of irresponsible lending illustrate this point.

RESPONSIBILITY

This means taking responsibility for the obligations and duties that you are charged with. When the Royal Commission claimed that employees were encouraged to 'prioritise the sale of loans over the bank's responsible lending obligations',[167] there was evidence of a leadership endorsed acceptance of conduct that was both unethical and possibly illegal. Responsibility and accountability are closely linked, as discussed in Chapter 7.

---

165 Butler, B. & Roddan, M., 'NAB hid compo from ASIC', *The Australian*, 14 August 2018, p. 17.

166 Han, M., 'Inquiry puts CBA in-house lawyers under spotlight', *Australian Financial Review*, 2 May 2018, p. 13.

167 Gluyas, R., 'Old habits of banking system about to be broken up', *The Australian*, 14 August 2018, p. 18.

ACCOUNTABILITY

Accountability means taking ultimate responsibility for a duty, obligation or burden. The responsibility and accountability for a bank's ethical position lies with the board of directors. This was illustrated in the resignations that followed the APRA report into culture and governance at CBA, as well as the resignations that followed at AMP when the firm admitted a habitual pattern of lying to the regulator. The resignation of NAB's chairman and CEO in 2019 in the face of scathing criticism from the Royal Commission is another example. Accountability must always be a societal expectation of the board of directors and there must also be a recognition that in many banks there has been a weak accountability culture, a fact that APRA called out in their investigation into CBA: 'It was extremely rare for the CEO and other group executives of CBA to have their remuneration reduced on risk grounds.'[168] Poor accountability was acknowledged by the ANZ CEO, Shayne Elliott: 'In the past, ANZ has not focused sufficiently in formally holding executives to account for failures that harm customers.'[169] When NAB staff were found to have forged witness signatures on superannuation documents relating to who should receive payment in the event of the death of the insured person, those implicated in the wrongdoings had 25 per cent of their bonus docked. The executives in charge of the division lost 10 per cent of their bonus and the divisional executive had $60,000 shaved from his bonus leaving him with $960,000. Incidents such as these speak volumes about culture and accountability and leave employees throughout the organisation bewildered by the example set from the top.

---

168 Mather, J., '"Little sting" in CBA pay structure and reward for customer calamity', *Australian Financial Review*, 2 May 2018, p. 13.

169 Ryan, P., 'ANZ boss Shayne Elliott urges disgruntled customers to email him directly', *ABC News*, 12 October 2018, <https://www.abc.news.com.au>.

LIFELONG LEARNING

In a fast-changing world, true professionals commit to updating and expanding their knowledge base in order to stay relevant. Many professions and business schools offer alumni access to updated programs and information to keep their knowledge current. For a professional body responsible for the education of its members, it is important that it stays relevant and adds value to its members throughout their careers. Qualifying 20 years ago with an MBA or banking diploma does not mean that someone's current knowledge base remains relevant. The commitment to continuous professional development is an essential quality of the professional accreditation body and of the individual. Indeed, in a fast-changing world, there is an argument that professional qualifications should have a time limit attached to them, requiring a renewal of that qualification on a periodic basis.

TRAINING PROGRAMS

Banks will argue that they provide an extensive range of in-house training, often with the support of external consultants. The reality, too often, is that as training budgets have been cut (they are an easy place to go when looking for cost savings), the emphasis on training has moved to compulsory and often mind-numbing compliance training. Beyond compliance, banks have developed or sourced a range of online self-help training covering a broad range of topics. This approach is rarely effective, for several reasons. People learn in different ways, and a class or lecture room environment with a highly skilled presenter is a very different learning experience to online or through other forms of distance learning (which has come a very long way over the years). Engagement and relevance are important in effective education and it must be supported by senior leadership, who should make time to be involved. It does not have to be a requirement of a job description, but a values-based belief that educating bankers on how to take a different lens to thinking about the bank's customers is a potential source of competitive advantage in the market.

Citibank was excellent at this (it still may be). Its in-house, residential training programs were outstanding – rigorous and challenging. The emphasis placed on developing its human capital was the benchmark; it was never seen as an expense, always as an enterprise investment – an investment also in its cultural capital. Citi had some of its rising stars spend a year of their career running the in-house training programs, including John McFarlane.

John Stewart, Peter Thodey and Cameron Clyne put a huge effort into this at NAB, with the development of a high-quality Enterprise Leadership Program (ELP). This was a well thought through program on leadership that involved the impressive INSEAD-based Manfred F. R. Kets de Vries.

Academies, or in-house training centres, opened in good times, are quickly closed when the search for cost savings is on. This is done even when such moves say much about the bank's real commitment to human capital development. When you operate in a highly profitable oligopoly industry structure, why would you make such an investment? Such a philosophy is a serious miscalculation, of course, particularly in an era where there is now almost a compulsion on lifelong learning if skills and capabilities are to stay relevant. Moreover, when you consider the fines and penalties that banks are likely to pay due to breakdowns in professional and cultural standards, a figure that in 2018–20 could easily reach $2 billion, this short-sighted approach needs no further comment. If a bank believes that its human and cultural capital can be a source of comparative advantage, then this is an area of urgent attention. It is an area that regulators might also want to focus on; it is an area that bank boards should prioritise.

CONCLUDING REMARKS

The debate over whether banking is a profession or not is yesterday's debate and it is associated with the conglomerate of competencies that have made up conglomerate banks and the so-called 'financial services industry'. The ethical standards evidenced in the findings of the Royal Commission are deplorable. As Don Argus commented, society expects commercial bankers to act 'professionally'; therefore, they must be professional and be accredited through a standard setting body. To be professional requires meeting a minimum set of standards, which must be independently assessed and in a consistent way, as it is with lawyers, accountants and doctors. The risk of losing that accreditation and therefore being engaged in the industry will be a major motivation in changing culture. Initiatives such as the BFO have an important role to play in promoting ethical standards as an integral and defining part of professionalism in the industry.

Absent concrete steps, society will continue to be sceptical that the banking industry's statements on professionalising are long on rhetoric and short on serious intent. Society is right to ask where were the professional standards and duty of care in the way that the banks have conducted themselves? These deficiencies are evident in so many examples. Society should expect, regardless of commercial imperatives, bankers to act in a professional manner, in the same way that doctors, dentists and lawyers do, and that they should never allow professional standards to be subordinated to self-interest. A major factor in the decline of professional standards in the UK, evident at HBOS, Barclays and RBS, was the de-emphasis that management placed on the Institute of Bankers qualification. The MBA replaced the Institute's training, and banks stopped insisting that bankers obtain a qualification that had been the hallmark of professionalism in the industry for over a century. A qualification that placed ethics at the centre of what it meant to be a banker.

Individuals must take some responsibility for their own development, but banks also have a major role to play in creating a cultural environment where professional standards are expected and encouraged. Regulators also have a role to play. Most importantly, this expectation must be set by the bank board. In any bank, any firm, people look to the leadership. How important are professional standards to the board? Boards are ultimately accountable and they must set the standards by insisting on compliance with a set of professional standards that emphasise core capabilities, the social licence that the banks hold and the overriding importance of ethical standards. As John McFarlane said, 'banks must return to the philosophy that banking is a profession as well as a business, and that contribution rather than reward is its centre of gravity.'[170] Boards must insist on a budget allocation to formal professional development and regulators must review this. Boards must also insist that future promotions at general manager level and above are subject to professional qualifications. Boards can also insist that some of the emerging leaders within the bank run the training and development programs, as Citibank used to do (and may still do). It is through measures such as these, much more than through new codes of conduct, that society will take notice and feel that the commitment from the banking industry goes beyond the rhetoric; it is real. Such a development would be an important step, including in a symbolic way, in addressing the cultural issues within the industry.

For banks to achieve their goal of becoming more trustworthy and 'customer centric', professionalism is the key. One of the core planks of professionalism in much of banking is the risk culture, which is the focus of Chapter 6. In the next chapter, the sector of the economy that has suffered most from the changing nature of

---

170 Boyd, T., 'Former ANZ CEO John McFarlane calls for rethink of banking philosophy', *Australian Financial Review*, 3 August 2016, p. 48.

banking and the decline in professional skills, the SME market, is reviewed.

4

THE DEMISE OF THE CRAFT IN SME BANKING

WHY the banking system has moved from being an impartial allocator of capital across the economy to acting in an ROE maximising manner, driven by a strong sales culture and a bias for household lending was described in Chapter 2. This has had a consequence for SMEs who have, to a large extent, been left behind, feeling that they suffer from the triple 'U' virus – unloved, unwanted and undervalued. This chapter looks in more depth at why this has happened, looking beyond the Basel II capital risk weighting distortion and exploring some practical research on SME attitudes towards banks. Figure 4 (Chapter 2) shows when the shift away from business lending took place, so that in 2000, every $1000 of home lending was matched by $1000 in SME lending. By 2017, every $1000 in home lending was matched by $130 in SME lending. At the beginning of 2019, household lending by banks was at $1.8 trillion, of which $1.67 trillion was in mortgage lending, and SME lending by banks was at approximately $300 billion out of total business banking lending by banks of $760 billion (excluding lending to other financial institutions). The bias to household lending by the banks is evident by these facts. This has been a significant change in how banks have discharged their responsibilities to efficiently allocate capital across the economy.

The SME sector is often described as the engine room of the economy. There are 1.32 million SMEs in Australia, which account for 56 per cent of GDP, employing 7 million people (67 per cent of the workforce) and paying 40 per cent of total company tax revenue. In New Zealand, the SME sector accounts for 97 per cent of businesses, employs 30 per cent of the workforce and contributes 27 per cent of GDP. By any definition, the health and prospects for the SME sector are critical to the economy and the descriptor of 'engine room of the economy' is justified by the facts.

However, the evidence on lending to SMEs would suggest that the banking industry no longer sees its role as an allocator of capital across the economy consistent with its social licence, but instead sees the maximisation of ROE as its driving purpose. If banks were purely private sector actors without any social licence obligations, then this would be a legitimate choice in a market economy. Absent barriers to entrance, the neglect of the SME sector would allow new entrants such as Judo Bank to enter the market to address the gap and the market failure that has been created, which is estimated at $83 billion of unsatisfied SME demand for credit in Australia.[171] That there is a *market failure* problem in financing SMEs is a widely accepted truth. In late 2018, the Australian Government acknowledged this with the announcement of a $2 billion small business securitisation fund to support lending to SMEs. In announcing this initiative, the Treasurer noted that 'small businesses find it difficult to obtain finance other than on a secured basis – typically against real estate. Even when small businesses can access finance, funding costs are higher than they need to be.'[172]

---

171 East Partners, *SME banking insights report*, September 2018.
172 <https://jaf.ministers.treasury.gov.au/media-release/2018/>.

INDUSTRIALISATION

While Basel II played a major role, the demise of SME banking has as much to do with the emphasis that banks have placed on industrialising the way they operate, primarily aimed at standardisation and cost efficiencies. They have also progressively dehumanised their approach to customer engagement, with an ongoing reduction in the number of bankers covering SMEs, and a progressive push to move more SMEs to a call centre service proposition. Many SMEs, once looked after by a relationship banker, received letters along the following lines:

> *Dear Joe,*
> *We know focusing on your business leaves little time for banking conversations that could help it grow. That's why we've introduced our Small Business Contact. A service team of banking experts with diverse professional experience.*
>
> *From this month, you'll no longer liaise with your current Relationship Manager. Instead, our Small Business Contact is available by phone or email to connect you with the business specialist best suited to answer your specific query. You can speak to the same or a different expert each time you call. And because every call is noted in detail, any specialist can pick up right where you left off simply by reviewing past information. All you need to do is call 15 17 16.*
>
> *This is just one of many new improvements we're making to better support your business needs.*
> *Kind regards,*
> ***ABC Bank**[173]*

This well-crafted but disingenuous letter of course contains one important message – you no longer have a relationship banker

---

[173] This is an actual letter sent by a bank to an SME customer with appropriate name changes made to protect privacy and embarrassment to the bank.

and here is the call centre number. Good luck! This abandonment of many SME customers to call centres of 'pools of excellence' is an illustration of how the banks are both industrialising and dehumanising their relationship service to the sector. Anyone who has had any dealings with call centres will know that, while occasionally things can run smoothly, invariably it is a highly unsatisfactory experience, particularly if there is a complex issue to be discussed. Banks are industrialising their operating model, not to improve the service to SMEs like 'Joe' but to cut costs in order to grow profits and ROE. Period. The Friedman Doctrine is a powerful invisible hand guiding decision making, and any sense of social licence is for the annual report and marketing campaigns. What John Kay (2015) described as 'obliquity', the idea that making money was a consequence of serving customers well and building a trusting relationship that underpins business sustainability, has largely become a relic of yesteryear. This should not be the case.

As banking ceased to be about customer service and became more about product sales, cross-selling, cost-to-serve, cost-to-income, profits and ROE, banks began to be staffed by people who stretched the meaning of the term 'banker' and who, as discussed in Chapter 4, had little professional training in the craft and science of banking. The mantra within most banks was that centralisation of processes would not only enable the bank to cut costs (mainly through shedding staff) and eliminate mistakes, it would 'free up' bankers to sell more products. This then allowed the banks to put in place sales incentive arrangements linked to the number of products sold to customers, including an incentive to ensure that customers sometimes borrowed beyond their means.

Another consequence of this industrialisation process was that foundation banking skills were no longer being developed. Associate level bankers, working closely with an experienced banker, were moved, in some banks, into centralised teams, and the spreading of financial statements was automated or sent offshore, in the interest of cutting costs. Thus, a generation of bankers lost the art and science of fundamental financial analysis – spotting trends and problems in financial spreadsheets; understanding the sensitivity around margin changes; the impact on working capital management of expanding the business; the link between the profit and loss, balance sheet and cash flow statements; when earnings before interest, tax, depreciation and amortisation (EBITDA) is and when it is not a good proxy for free cash flow; and so on. This was a miscalculation that prioritised what is counted (money saved) and lost sight of what *counts* (the development of core skills critical to the craft of SME banking).

The practical reality of these changes is captured in this quote from a senior banker:

> Bankers have lost their entrepreneurial edge in an environment where the burden of compliance supersedes the importance of customer service. Too often phone calls are not returned, and bankers are 'too busy' dealing with the internal bureaucracy. Reorganisation after reorganisation has resulted in much of the core support around the banker being removed and centralised in 'pools of excellence'. All this has achieved, reduced costs aside, is a diminution in customer service. The frequent turnover of bankers means that customer knowledge is weakened, and a few bankers are able to assess credit risk and effectively communicate with the customer to manage expectations. Too often the refrain is 'I'm happy to take this to Credit and let's see how they feel; I can't be certain how long it will take however, they may want additional information. I will do my best.' Unfortunately, bankers have lost their aura and they, as with the bank's customers, have been the losers in the constant drive to squeeze costs, centralise and standardise everything.

THE RETAILISATION OF BANKING

Thus the collapse in professionalism, the replacement of 'bankers' by sales people, managing their 'sales funnel' and a period of customer neglect set in. This was not banking but the aggressive retailing of financial products, hence the characterisation of Australia's *financialisation* as *retailisation* or *productisation*. More conservative grey-haired bankers who would urge caution and who saw the dangers in an aggressive market share race, were viewed as 'Luddites' belonging to an era long gone, and many of them nearing the age of 50 were forced to leave. The paradox in all this is that as the banking system grew, banking skills and experience diminished, with the irony that many of the bankers that were forced out of the banks established broking businesses, which in turn disintermediated the bank relationship with SME customers. A miscalculation with longer-term value-destroying implications for the bank franchise.

The broker market in residential mortgages, as discussed in Chapter 2, has been strong for a decade thanks to the pioneering work of people such as John Symonds from Aussie Home Loans. Since 2005, the broker market in SME lending has taken off and close to 30 per cent of all new SME lending is originated by brokers. This figure, as has happened with residential mortgages, is likely to grow to 50 per cent in the near future, such is the paucity of the quality of the relationship service provided by the banks to SMEs. Brokers are fulfilling the role once held by banks, and so the relationship between the SME and the bank has weakened.

With the weakening of the relationship management proposition, SMEs have fallen between the cracks of the more informationally efficient consumer and large corporate markets. They have become less of a priority to the banks, beyond their willingness to accept a service proposition that is all about the bank's needs rather than the customer's needs. This is a natural consequence of an oligopoly industry structure.

Many banks are promoting algorithm driven decisioning tools including credit scoring, property security and call centres as *their* approach to dealing with the cost of serving SMEs. This can work for some SMEs in dealing with routine matters, but not for all, and it is hopeless when an SME wants to invest or seek advice on funding and risk management. Hence, the path that the banks have been on for some time misses the point and the result is a market failure and the demise in the craft of SME banking. Kay (2015) summed up the problem that SMEs face in dealing with the banks:

> The financing of small businesses is not only, or primarily, a matter of judging the numbers, as J. P. Morgan recognised. The success or failure of a new business depends very largely on the personality and capabilities of the individuals who run it, and these are difficult for a computer to assess ... SME funding cannot be effectively rated by a computer. (p. 166)

We come back to the importance of judgement and the limitations of digital decisioning later in this chapter. First however it is worth reflecting on the how SMEs feel about banks given the way that they have been treated and how the erosion of the relationship proposition provided by banks has impacted trust.

A survey of 2687 SMEs by East & Partners segmented into two turnover categories ($1–10 million and $10–20 million) found Australian SMEs rate their banks a mere 2.5 out of 10 when it comes to trust (Figure 12). These findings correlate with earlier trust indices in Figures 2 and 3.

FIGURE 12: SME BANK TRUST INDEX
Average rating reported

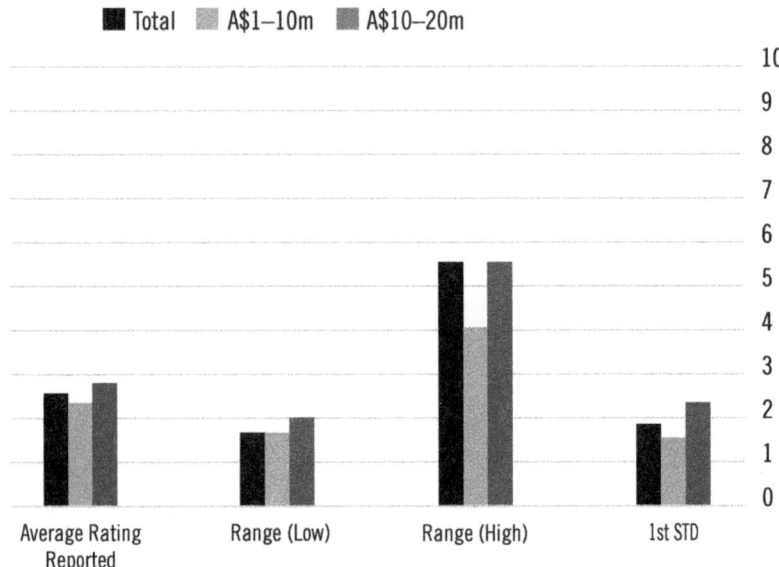

Source: East & Partners, SME banking insights report, September 2018

THE CRAFT OF SME BANKING

Linked to the belief that there has been a market failure, almost in a cause and effect sense, is the demise in the *craft* of SME banking, a competency that has been progressively lost to the Australian economy. This is a loss of a craft central to how a nation's SMEs flourish. By craft, we mean a skill in analysing both quantitative and qualitative information and forming a judgement, which benefits from the experience and knowledge of the banker exercising that craft. To develop this craft a banker needs to be steeped in SME-specific credit risk management and to have undertaken at least 10,000 hours of credit training and experience (to borrow from Malcolm Gladwell's *Outliers – the story of success* (2008)). The craft of SME banking is a different competency from relying solely on collateral (security) or heavily on quantitative data, though it never ignores such data. SME banking is an experience-based capability built on the foundation of technical knowledge, but one that understands how to interpret imperfect information in a way that an algorithm or a credit scoring system simply cannot. In SME banking, this craft is fundamental if banks are to serve the needs of SMEs, as their social licence requires. In developing this craft, to borrow again from Malcolm Gladwell (*Blink: the power of thinking without thinking* (2005)), the best bankers develop a 'blink' instinct in credit risk management, a highly attuned, experienced-based judgement for what could go wrong, or why a risk is acceptable or not. They know how to use their 'head, heart and gut instincts' in judging risk. The assessment of the character of a borrower is critical, as is discussed later.

The progressive loss of this craft is akin in many ways to the loss of local general practitioners (GPs) to online self-help medical advice, which may diagnose routine symptoms but lacks personal knowledge to diagnose emerging serious issues, or to take early steps if things deteriorate. When you visit your GP, not only will they have detailed knowledge about you, but also of people with similar profiles to you. The difference between your GP and an online driven AI is that your GP will have a relationship with you and be able to make well-informed judgement decisions based on that knowledge. Evidence suggests that people who sustain a long-term relationship with the same GP are likely to live longer than people who frequently change their GP.[174] Extending this analogy, many SMEs suffer from the frequency of changes in their dealings with banks. They often decide not to seek finance because of a lack of trust in the impersonal approach and frustration with a credit process that can feel slow and cumbersome, as it has become increasingly removed from the customer. When it is difficult to do

---

174 Birkinshaw, J., 'The future of firms in an AI world', *London Business School Review*, vol. 29, no. 3, 2018.

business with an institution, the natural preference is not to do business. This is where the broker market has been highly valuable and has an important role to play. They act as a bridge between what the bank used to do and what SMEs want the bank to do – understand their business.

All these factors result in an erosion in relationship banking from the days of strong community engagement. Consequently, research shows that nine out of ten SMEs are being left to consult their friends and colleagues for specific business strategy advice, not their bank, see Figure 13.

FIGURE 13: PRIMARY BUSINESS ADVISOR
% OF TOTAL

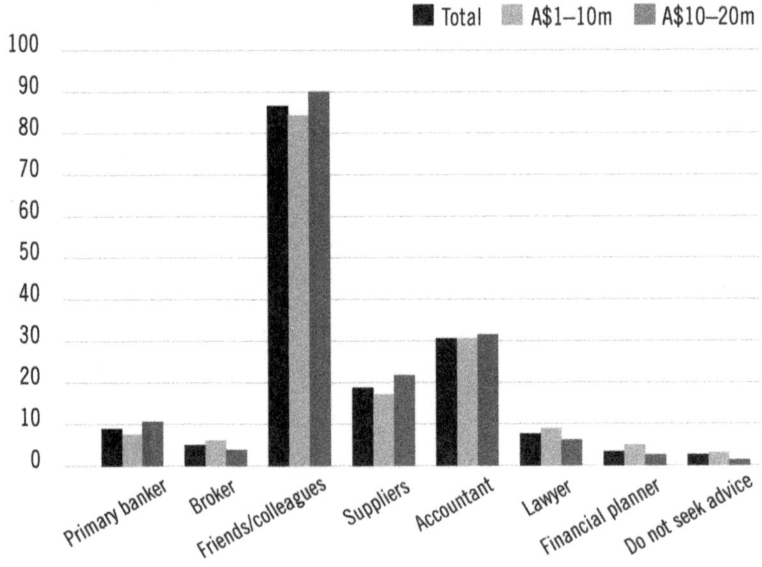

Source: East & Partners, SME banking insights report, September 2018

Among the 90 per cent of businesses that did not nominate their bank as a key source of business strategy advice, 65 per cent reported that they are simply not close enough to have an appropriate working relationship.

FIGURE 14: REASONS TO NOT CHOOSE A BANKER

% OF NON-BANK SELECTORS

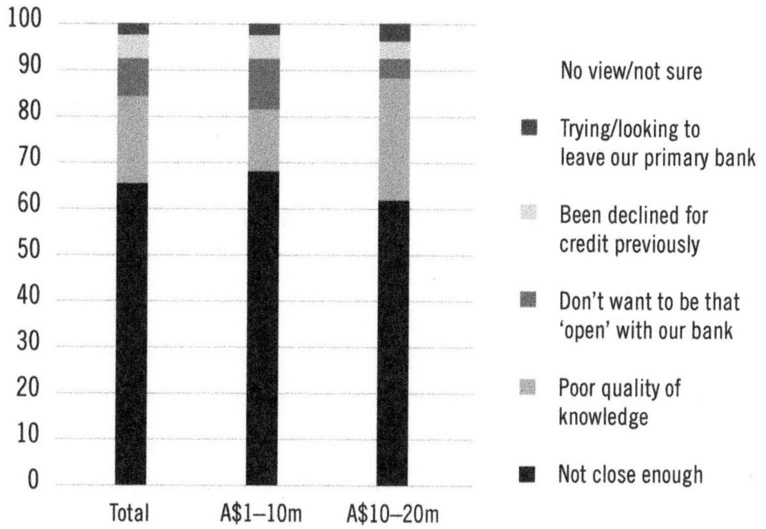
100
90
80
70
60
50
40
30
20
10
0
Total
A$1–10m
A$10–20m
No view/not sure
Trying/looking to leave our primary bank
Been declined for credit previously
Don't want to be that 'open' with our bank
Poor quality of knowledge
Not close enough

Source: East & Partners, SME banking insights report, September 2018

A major factor in this unfortunate outcome has been the consequence of a highly consolidated and profitable banking system, focused on scale and scope economies. Thus, SMEs that do not readily fit into the one-size-fits-all industrialised model are left behind. They are, after all, more complex and informationally opaque, requiring more time and more cost to deal with.

SMEs have become stuck in no-man's-land as banks argue the 'cost of acquisition' is too high. In the same way, banks have left rural communities because the branch, which had been at the centre of the local community for decades, is no longer profitable on a standalone basis, so it is with much of SME banking that does not fit the cookie-cutter, one-size-fits-all model of property secured lending. While banks always acknowledging the importance of SMEs to the economy, there is no sense of social licence considerations in attempting to accommodate their sometimes unique needs. Such a philosophy conflicts with the pursuit of greater profitability. In fairness, this problem is not unique to Australia as banking models everywhere have been industrialising. Berger, Molyneux and Wilson (2010), summarise the situation well:

> Research shows that distances between small businesses and their lending institutions has generally increased overtime and the method of contact between the firm and its institutions has become more impersonal overtime, consistent with a greater use of hard information in lending.

Absent the provision of property as security, SMEs face significant challenges in accessing funding for positive net present value projects as the Productivity Commission report highlighted. The issues faced by SMEs are illustrative of a material shift from relationship lending to transactional lending. Transactional lending is where the bank looks at lending as a standalone product and applies a standard, almost one-size-fits-all approach to SMEs, often resulting in an algorithm driven credit assessment accompanied by property-based security (much of SME lending is a mortgage in disguise, with a bit of gloss to justify a higher margin than pure residential mortgage lending).

Figure 15 summarises the issues that SMEs face, particularly those in the $1–10 million turnover category. The insistence of collateral and the 'All too hard' (banks are not easy to do business with for many SMEs) categories are noteworthy.

The genesis of this shift away from SME lending dates back a few decades, and went largely unnoticed when economic growth was strong. The problem is that these trends can take decades to reveal their full cost. An economy absent a recession for close to 30 years and a housing market that has allowed the banks (and their borrowers) to binge, can disguise many underlying problems and can cause a significant underinvestment in competencies that could be critical to the future.

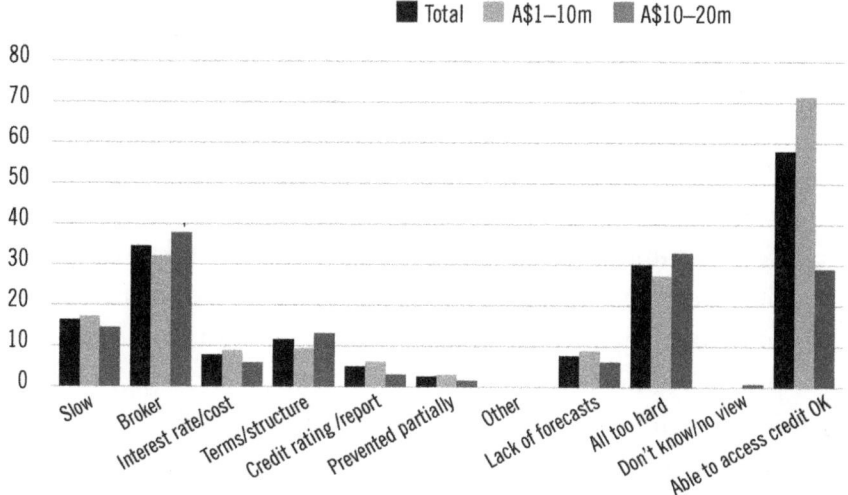

Source: East & Partners, SME banking insights report, September 2018

THE DEMISE OF RELATIONSHIP BANKING

A related factor is the constant turnover of bankers. All too many SMEs complain about the frequency that 'their' banker has moved and left them with the challenge of retraining another banker on the dynamics of their business. This lack of continuity in the role, either through banker choice or bank restructuring, is the antithesis of relationship banking and a major cause in its demise.

From time to time, particularly with the appointment of new CEOs and C-suite executives, banks will declare that they 'want to get closer to their customers'. This declaration is made even though the bank has been in business for over a hundred years and the Australian economy is largely concentrated in a few cities. The irony of these statements is not lost on staff and customers given that:

- Banks are prone to internal restructuring every few years, which always impacts customers.
- Bankers change their roles on a frequent basis, some to climb the internal hierarchy and some to join another bank.
- In some banks, frequent moving of senior executives impacts all levels below and ultimately the customer.
- Bankers are rarely given decisioning rights and delegated authorities that work in practice, so decision making can be slow and remote from the customer (banks will argue that they give delegated authority in SME banking, but in practice they have limited use given attached conditions and policy overlay).
- Some banks change their strategies every few years and sectors or industries can be either 'in' or 'out', until the next change is made. It is a hokey pokey strategy – 'in-out, in-out'.

Any business that genuinely wants to 'get close to its customer', knows that consistency is critical and in a relationship business the continuity of personnel is an essential condition of success. The Swedish bank Handelsbanken demonstrates how this can be done, as discussed later.

SME banking is largely a domestic banking business. John Reed, the then CEO at Citibank, talked about 'middle market banking' (SME banking) and how it was not a major focus for Citi outside New York. He said:

> We are not a major player in middle market banking, particularly outside New York or overseas. The requirements for success in that business seem to be out of whack with the requirements of our culture. It requires long-term continuity of people who are part of the local community. We do not attract people who want to go to Kenosha, Wisconsin, and live there for 25 years. So, we tend not to be in the middle market.

What John Reed was saying is that SME banking is the domain of domestic banks, who have the knowledge of and commitment to local communities. That commitment and the skills of bankers in looking after SMEs is at the core of how the economy works and grows over time. SME banking is relationship banking, and a big part of the social licence that large domestic banks have is to provide this capability and service. This local presence is a necessary condition of relationship banking and relationship lending.

SMEs looking at the major banks see little differentiation. John Dahlsen, a former ANZ director, noted that 'there is a huge sameness about our banks … you could switch the brand names, and no one would know the difference, it's very incestuous'. Nearly 90 per cent of small businesses think that banks are either or mostly the same (Figure 16).

FIGURE 16: BANK SIMILARITY PERCEPTION
% OF TOTAL

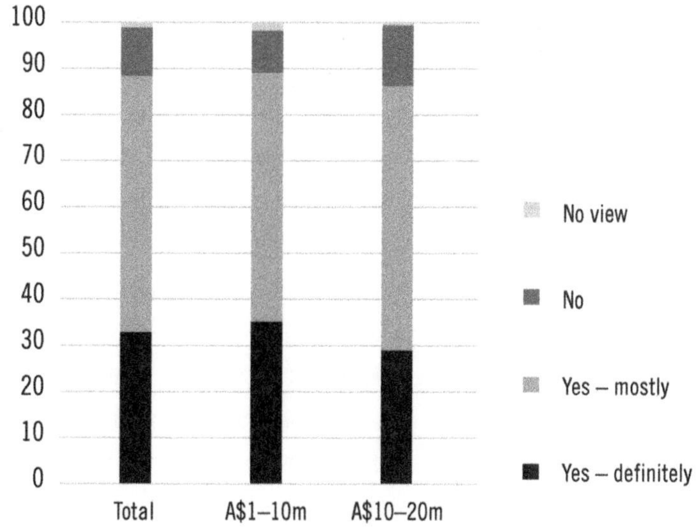

Source: East & Partners, SME banking insights report, September 2018

Relationship lending looks at the SME as a whole and considers the scope of the bank's history with the business. It applies the Four C's of relationship lending, which are critical in determining access to credit.

In relationship lending, weighting is applied to 'soft' (qualitative) information as well as 'hard' (quantitative) information; as John Kay describes earlier in this chapter, judgement matters on the capabilities of the business owner. The relationship banking model only works if the relationship banker and credit executive are skilled in the interpretation of soft information and apply judgement, which compensates for the weakness or absence of hard information. Soft information largely addresses the first of the Four C's – character – which is judgement on the business skills, reputation, honesty and integrity of the business owner. This is what the great banker J. P. Morgan referred to over a century ago. The founder of JP Morgan, in giving testimony to the US House of Representatives and responding to a question, summed up the importance of character in a way that should be a core lending principle of a banker today:

> 'Is not commercial credit based primarily upon money or property?'
>
> 'No sir. The first thing is character ... Because a man I do not trust could not get money from me on all the bonds in Christendom.' (Kay, 2015, p. 165)

Soft information alone is not enough, and it only works where there is a skilled and experienced relationship banker involved. Hard information, which relies on financial accounts, bank statements, credit reports and credit scoring technologies, together with access to security has become the dominant way in which banks assess SME credit. The sometimes opaque and often incomplete nature of some of the 'hard' information results in a default position of placing a heavy reliance on collateral, or property-based security, to underpin the credit risk decision and reduce monitoring costs. The approach to the Four C's varies between a relationship approach and a more transactional approach. The transactional approach places greater emphasis on the fourth C – collateral – and discounts the first three C's. The simple example illustrates this, as outlined in Tables 6 and 7.

> *Using a scale of 1 to 5, where 1 = very poor, 2 = poor, 3 = satisfactory, 4 = strong and 5 = very strong. Where an SME scores an overall rating of 3, they are prima facie an acceptable credit risk.*

With the demise in the craft of relationship banking, the transactional approach, with its emphasis on hard data and reliance on property as security, tends to dominate the way the banks operate (Table 6).

TABLE 6: FRAMEWORK FOR EVALUATING FOUR C'S – TRANSACTIONAL MODEL

Category	Rating (1–5)	Weighting	Rating
Character	3	5%	0.15
Capacity (cash flow)	3	20%	0.6
Capital	4	15%	0.6
Collateral	5	60%	3.0
Overall rating		100%	4.35

If there is no collateral, in the transactional approach the 4.35 score becomes 1.35 and the loan is rejected as the pass rate is 3.0. In the *relationship approach*, because of the different weightings, the 4.55 becomes 3.30 if there is no property as collateral, and the loan is granted (Table 7).

TABLE 7: FRAMEWORK FOR EVALUATING FOUR C'S – RELATIONSHIP MODEL

Category	Rating (1–5)	Weighting	Rating
Character	3	20%	0.6
Capacity (cash flow)	3	30%	0.9
Capital	4	25%	1.8
Collateral	5	25%	1.25
Overall rating		100%	4.55

This simple example highlights an important point and reason why there is a market failure; absent collateral, it is difficult for an SME to get a loan. That was not always the case.

THE DEMISE OF SME BANKING SKILLS

There is a growing body of research around the world suggesting that as banks have got bigger the fundamentals have shifted. The move for local credit decisioning to become centralised or regionalised, an emphasis on credit scoring decisioning tools, an increasing application of technology, which has depersonalised service, and the introduction of one-size-fits-all policies in the quest for standardisation, are all fundamentally aimed at achieving economies of scale, improving operating efficiency and delivering a lower cost-to-income. However, the result has been a diminution in the core skills that once defined the traditional banker, where judgement or 'soft information' has been replaced by a strong emphasis on 'hard information' (quantitative data) such as credit scoring outcomes, audited financial statements and the value of available security. Evidence of this is found in the weakening understanding of SMEs' financial accounts, where bankers fail to grasp rudimentary financial analysis. This is even though, on average, today's bankers are more academically credentialed. At Judo Bank, we put bankers that have passed at least three interviews through a three-hour credit skills competency test with a pass rate of around 40 per cent as at the time of writing (see Appendix II for an example of the test).

This low pass rate is largely because banks have lost the skills to think through basic financial analysis given that this is all largely automated and few bankers spend time spreading potential borrowers' financials and understanding the links and sensitivities between the profit and loss account, balance sheet and cash flow statements. Some banks send all financial analysis offshore, because it is cheaper and because it can 'free up the bankers'. A classic miscalculation of focusing on what *counted* (cost saves) and missing what *counts* (bankers trained in financial and credit analysis – in the Four C's). The painstaking hours bankers traditionally spent early in their careers compiling and then analysing financial statements and building forward-looking forecast models with appropriate sensitivity analyses, using frameworks such as Michael Porter's Five Forces (1980) to understand how industry, product and market structure can impact the business and the market for a borrower's products, is essential to being a professional banker. This is what Malcolm Gladwell had in mind when he talked about the 10,000 hours that helps build skill and expertise. There is no substitute for this hard work if a competency is to be mastered, be that in business, sport, entertainment or in other pursuits.

The internal process and efficiency drive within banks have made it more difficult to provide credit facilities where credit information is more 'informationally opaque' (i.e. not based on clear, quantitative data). The emphasis on 'hard information' has weakened the weighting given to judgement and thus, in the SME space, has weakened the essence of relationship banking. This issue is exacerbated by the lack of professional training and qualifications in what it means to be a banker, as discussed in Chapter 4.

Once upon a time, the banks were more attuned to SMEs, with the empowerment the local branch manager used to have and the role the local branch manager used to play in the heartland of local communities. This local connection meant that bankers had access to 'soft information' such as reputation, a sense of character and the knowledge that comes from being close to your customer and to their customers. In other words, bankers had a good sense for what *counts* as well as what is *counted*. When an experienced banker says 'this doesn't feel right', they are bringing to bear extensive experience that, as with Gladwell's *Blink*, highlights a concern that is much deeper than a simple gut feeling.

Recognising the importance of 'soft information' is a core reason why local service is important. This is one of the reasons why the success of Sweden's Svenska Handelsbanken in the UK has been so notable since the GFC. Handelsbanken's approach to risk management (which is discussed in Chapter 6) is what they call the 'church-tower principle', namely, that you should do business only as far you can see from the local church tower. Their model gives strong autonomy on credit decisioning to their local bankers, but with that goes accountability and tenure in role. They believe that effective risk management is about having deep customer relationships and strong local knowledge. They also recognise that the skills, competencies and experience of their staff are fundamental to making this work.

SME RISK MANAGEMENT

Traditionally, well-trained bankers had a good sense for what *counts* (qualitative measures such as reputation, track record, integrity) and what is *counted* (hard information). Credit assessment was based around the Four Cs of credit – character, capacity (or cash flow), capital and collateral. The first criteria, character, was always viewed as pre-eminent, with an experienced banker assessing the business acumen, management skills and integrity of the business owner. For SMEs without substantial real estate backing, this assessment of the Four C's of credit is pivotal to risk assessment.[175]

The emphasis that experienced bankers place on character is at the foundation of banking, yet it is a quality that attracts less and less evaluation today and, as a result, banks can find themselves lending to people of unsavoury character and sometimes for unsavoury purposes, just because of the reliance and comfort they take on having property as security, as illustrated in Table 6. An age-old principle of banking is *look at the borrower, not the asset*. The internal process and efficiency drive within banks have made it more difficult to provide credit facilities where credit information is more 'informationally opaque'. The emphasis on 'hard information' has weakened the weighting given to judgement and, in doing so, has weakened the essence of relationship banking, particularly in the SME sector. This has been exacerbated by the de-skilling, loss of experience and lack of professional training and qualifications (particularly around credit risk management) in what it means to be a 'banker'.

There are several consequences of this. First, the banker does not have the judgement to assess the risk profile of the customer. Second, the banker is rarely capable of providing sound advice and adding value to the customer in assessing business and financial risks. Third, if the banker is any good they are often encouraged to move on into more senior roles to develop 'their

---

175 For more context on this, see Healy, J., 'Banking on SMEs', Dun & Bradstreet *'Giving Small Business Credit' Conference*, 12 May 2011 and Healy, J., 'Business banking: current picture and future trends', *AB+F Randstad Leader's Lectures*, 12 July 2011.

people management capabilities', which can often gravitate further and further away from the customers. Who loses out here? In all of this, the customer is left feeling that they have wasted time with a banker who is not positioned to make decisions, and they must start all over again. This whole cycle of how the banks engage with their customers is the antithesis of relationship banking.

ALGORITHMS, BIG DATA VERSUS JUDGEMENT

Consistent with a view that the FinTech model and big data hold the solution to this market failure, much is made of digitalisation and AI in the way banks should think about SME banking. This perspective was underpinned in a survey of senior executives in the US by EY,[176] where 81 per cent of executives said that 'data should be at the heart of all decision-making', which led the authors to proclaim that 'big data can eliminate the reliance on "gut feel" decision-making'. This emphasis on quantitative data prevails in the minds of many bank executives as they think about the cost to deliver SME banking. What this scientific approach fails to capture is the quality of character, ambitions, concerns, need for advice, succession planning and plans to acquire, innovate and grow. What happens, absent any informed human intervention (relationship banking), when the SME hits a difficult patch or requires understanding and support in navigating major transitional events? A science-driven approach to SME banking has its role but it also has its limitations. Behavioural science has taught us much in the field of financial economics, enough to know that human judgement matters, particularly in information inefficient markets where asymmetry problems can be the norm rather than the exception.

---

176 Martin, R. & Golby-Smith, T., 'Management is much more than a science', *Harvard Business Review*, September–October 2017, pp 129–135.

UNMET CREDIT DEMAND: EVIDENCE OF MARKET FAILURE

While this approach to SME banking has served the banks well, it has failed their customers and the economy; hence the hypothesis of market failure. It has resulted in a significant credit gap in the SME sector, which Macquarie Bank has estimated to be between $50 and $70 billion.[177] Separate research conducted in 2018 by East & Partners of 2678 SMEs placed the funding gap at $83 billion. This could be viewed as a form of market failure, which is one reason why some experts believe SME financing should be a public policy matter and has resulted in others suggesting that a state-sponsored business bank be established, as has happened in the UK.[178]

The economic opportunity cost of how the banks allocate capital is difficult to estimate but the relationship between economic growth and SME access to finance is well established.[179] That there is an issue in financing Australian SMEs and that there are associated economic costs has been acknowledged by the RBA.[180]

Statistics from MoneyQuest Finance Specialists (Figure 17) on the experience of SMEs seeking finance found that 46 per cent of enquiries do not go further than an initial conversation and of the 54 per cent that are considered, only 41 per cent are approved. This leaves just under 22.5 per cent of enquiries resulting in an extension of credit. The rate of early rejection reflects the conservative credit appetite of the banks, the preference for a one-size-fits-all approach and the insistence for real estate security.

---

177 Macquarie Bank Research, 'The computer says yes', March 2015.

178 Australian Small Business and Family Enterprise Ombudsman, *Affordable capital for SME growth: inquiry report*, 29 June 2018, <https://www.asbfeo.gov.au/inquiries/affordable-capital-sme-growth>.

179 Lindgren, E., 'Access to finance: Small and medium enterprises effect on economic growth', Lund University, 2015, <https://www.lup.lub.lu.se>.

180 Debble, G., 'Business investment in Australia', UBS Australasia conference, 2018.

What these statistics do not measure is the decision by SMEs not to pursue credit for investment purposes given their perception of the challenges involved.[181] A similar picture is evident in the UK. Data on loan application rates shows a continuing decline in the share of SMEs seeking new loans. Only 43 per cent of UK SMEs are confident that they will get a bank loan, and attitudes against borrowing are becoming entrenched.[182]

FIGURE 17: SURVEY RESULTS OF SME FINANCE ENQUIRIES

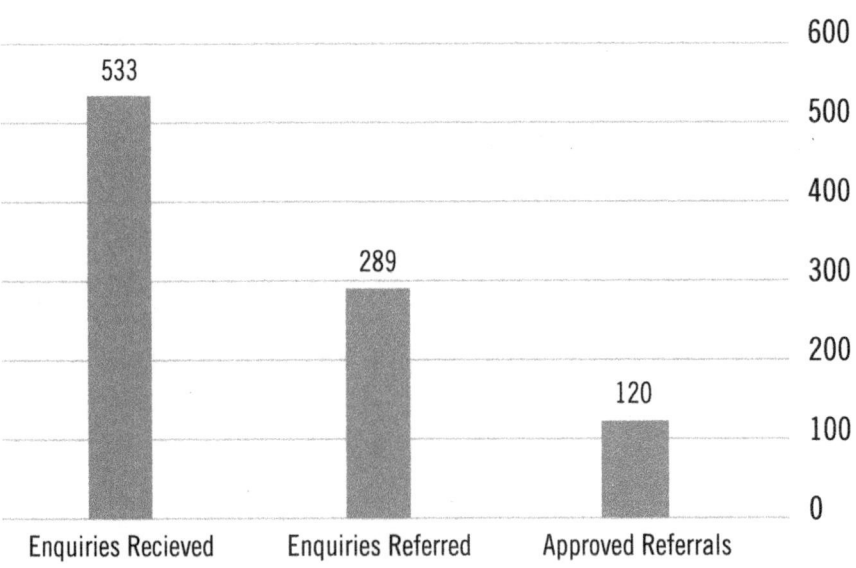

Source: *MoneyQuest Finance Specialist, SME Survey, 1 July 2017 – 20 June 2018*

---

181 This problem has been extensively discussed in the academic literature. See Myer & Maljuf, 'Corporate financing and investment decisions when firms have information that investors do not have', *Journal of Financial Economics*, vol. 13, no. 2, 1984, pp. 187–221.

182 'SME banking: lessons from history', *Euromoney*, 6 March 2108, <https://www.euromoney.com>.

CONCLUDING REMARKS

It is necessary to recognise that SME banking is different. The quality of 'hard information' and market information on SMEs is not as robust and efficient as it is for larger businesses or for personal customers. SMEs operate in an information inefficient market, which, given the emphasis banks have placed on industrialising and dehumanising their operating model, has resulted in a market failure estimated at $83 billion of unmet SME demand for finance. This is material; the total stock of SME lending in the banking system at the time of writing is estimated at $300 billion. The approach to SME banking needs to be fundamentally different from that needed for larger businesses.

To do SME banking well, the bank must be attuned, culturally, to harnessing and using 'soft information' and to do this you need bankers who are willing to commit significant parts of their career to working with the same customers. It also requires, to quote McKinsey & Company (2018), 'bespoke approaches and highly experienced talent, with the key value proposition centred on relationships, trust, reputation, and experience'.[183] These are the values that are the foundation of Judo Bank, which has many similarities to Sweden's Handelsbanken, particularly in its approach to aspects of credit risk management, as discussed in Chapter 6.

The 'dehumanisation' of SME banking is further underscored by the decision of several banks to remove relationship management coverage for SME exposures less than $3 million and centralise the 'management' of these customers through call centre style platforms. Many SMEs have received letters similar to the one to 'Joe'. Even with SMEs that remain part of the relationship management proposition, they tend to be covered by a banker

---

[183] McKinsey & Company, 'New rules for an old game: banks in the changing world of financial intermediation', *McKinsey Global Banking Annual Review*, 2019.

with a portfolio of as many as 200 customers – double the level pre-GFC – and the quality of that relationship proposition suffers accordingly.

To succeed at SME banking, the credit policies and procedures framework within banks needs to reflect the unique nature of SME banking. Today, almost all SME lending by the banks is nothing more than a mortgage in disguise, but with interest margins that are excessive given the risk assumed.[184]

As banks have industrialised their operating model and placed greater emphasis on a one-size-fits-all approach intended to optimise RWAs, SMEs have suffered more than any other customer segment. They face numerous hurdles in being able to do business with the bank, including often inflexible credit risk management policies, products that are not fit for purpose and staff that have largely lost the authority to make common sense decisions. Indeed, the constant movement of staff has meant that there is very little relationship continuity and knowledge of the customer. A frequent criticism made by SMEs is the constant need to 'retrain' their new banker, only to see them leave – the average duration of an SME relationship banker in a role is now approximately 18 months.

RWA attraction aside, another reason banks rely on collateral as the basis for lending to SMEs is because it reduces monitoring costs and the information asymmetry problem at the inception of the loan. The lender can look to the security offered and place less emphasis on the other Four C's.

There is strong evidence of market failure, despite some banks arguing that this is not the case (just as there are those who are climate change deniers and those that believe that the Earth is flat). This market failure has resulted in the Australian Government announcing the establishment of a $2 billion SME securitisation fund and the intention to establish an Australian Business Growth

---

[184] Roddan, M., 'SMEs "slugged with higher interest rates"', *The Australian*, 16 March 2019, p. 23.

Fund, modelled on the Canadian SME Growth Fund and the UK's Business Growth Fund, to provide equity finance to SMEs. Since its inception in 2011, the UK Fund has invested £2.7 billion in a range of SMEs across the economy. The symbolism alone of the government's initiative is powerful. The government acknowledged, as Sir Robert Menzies had done some 70 years earlier, that Australia's SMEs have become the forgotten people, yet they are the backbone of the country.[185]

The market failure problem represents a material cost to the economy and it is linked back to the discussion in Chapter 3 on the social licence obligations of the banks to operate in the wider interests of society rather in their narrow private self-interest of ROE maximisation.

Another significant factor that helps explain the demise of SME banking has been the decline in the risk management skills of bankers, some of which has been discussed in this chapter. A broader look at the demise of risk management skills in banking is the focus of the next chapter.

---

185 Frydenberg, J., '$2bn securitisation fund to back our "strivers"', *The Australian*, 15 November 2018.

5
THE DEMISE OF RISK MANAGEMENT IN BANKING

WHAT distinguishes banks from other firms is their role in risk transfer and risk management. As the former Citibank chairman Walter Wriston famously said, 'managing risk … is the business of banking'.[186]

To properly understand the role that banks play in society, it is essential to understand the risks that banks take on and why the strength of a bank and the banking system is critical to an economy. Martin Taylor, then CEO of Barclays (1994–98), having attended an international banker conference in Washington DC, said that being in the room with so many bankers was like being at a haemophiliac gathering; bumping into anyone could have been fatal. His point was that banking is a very risky business, as we saw during the GFC, and, of course, in Australia in the early 1990s when two major banks – Westpac and ANZ – were in difficulty and the State Bank of South Australia and the State Bank of Victoria collapsed.

Since those days and particularly post-GFC, regulators all over

---

186 Attributed to Walter Wriston, ex-CEO and chairman of Citibank by the *Euromoney* magazine in 1993, though other sources also attribute the quote to J. P. Morgan (see Salz, 2013, p. 150).

the world have done much to strengthen the financial profile of banks, including by insisting, as a result of Basel III, that they hold more equity capital and extend the duration of their own funding so they are less exposed to liquidity risk. As described in Chapter 2, equity in a bank's capital structure (as in any business) is like an airbag in a car. It is rarely needed and in the hands of a safe driver (i.e. a good manager), it may never be needed, but when there is a crash, the bigger the airbag the better, and the bigger the car (bank) and the faster it is driven, then the bigger the airbag needs to be to ensure survival. Equity capital can cushion the blow in the event of crash. A liquidity crisis can be almost certainly fatal for a bank regardless of its capital position.

As Walter Wriston implies, the primary expertise in banking is to assess and monitor risk. The accurate measurement of risk is an essential first step in managing risk. Banks are exposed to at least eight major risks:

- *Credit risk*: as lending is the major asset class on a bank's balance sheet, banks face the risk of customers defaulting.
- *Balance sheet and market risk*: this largely takes the form of interest rate funding and capital risk. If a bank's cost of funds increases and it is unable to reprice its loan assets, then its margins are reduced and with it profitability and the equity value of the bank. Capital risk is where the bank does not hold enough capital to cover losses (i.e. the airbag is too weak).
- *Liquidity risk*: as the GFC so graphically illustrated, banks can face a liquidity crisis when their liabilities, particularly deposits and short-term wholesale debt (including securitisation), become payable when the majority of bank lending assets are highly illiquid. This asset–liability mismatch could cause the bank to go under in the event of a crisis such as the GFC, as was the case with Northern Rock and potentially could have been the case with St George Bank.

- *Operational risk*: this category of risk covers a range of activities such as poor IT infrastructure, the risk of fraud (internal and external), money laundering, human error in transmitting payments, business disruption and system failures.
- *Technology risk* (including cyber risk): closely linked to operational risk, this category is of growing significance to banks. Cyber risk relates to the ability of a bank's system to be 'attacked'. Weak technology platforms can have significant ramifications for banks as is publicly evident when there is a collapse in ATMs or when payment systems do not work.
- *Compliance risk*: a growing risk category that covers compliance with laws and regulations, as well as general conduct. This category is closely aligned to operational risk.
- *Reputation risk*: this is an increasingly important category that is linked to scandals, customer satisfaction, regulatory relations and community standing. The GFC showed how banks such as RBS, Lloyds/HBOS, Citibank, UBS, Merrill Lynch and Deutsche Bank, to name only a few, had their reputations damaged. Equally, the Royal Commission and related scandals showed how conduct issues can seriously damage the reputation and standing of banks in Australia.
- *Strategic risk*: the risk of being unable to meet the strategic objectives set for the business.

While many of these risks have grown in profile and relevance over recent years, credit risk remains the single biggest risk category for most banks, with liquidity risk, which was a dominant feature of the GFC, always a critical focus. Operational risk, particularly given legacy technology and complexity of business operations, has become increasingly prominent. Linked to operational risk is the growing risk linked to technology, including cybersecurity and compliance risk.

In this chapter, the focus is on *credit risk* and a sense that there has been a serious decline in the credit risk management within banks; this is most apparent when it comes to SME banking. In thinking about credit risk, it is worth reflecting on the wisdom of Adam Smith (1776):

> Though the principles of the banking trade may appear somewhat abstruse, the practice is capable of being reduced to strict rules. To depart upon any occasion from these rules, in consequence of some flattering speculation of extraordinary gain, is almost always extremely dangerous, and frequently fatal to the banking company which attempts it.

What Smith alludes to is the importance of a bank having a clear set of rules or principles against which it will assess risk; the importance of discipline in adhering to these principles is at the heart of a bank's risk culture.

KEY PRINCIPLES OF A CREDIT RISK CULTURE

There are 10 key principles for establishing a credit risk culture in a bank:
1. *The credit culture must be set by the CEO* and the executive committee (including the CRO) and approved by the board: the bank's value system is set and enforced by the CEO, the executive committee and the board, which must always be capable of challenging what is proposed. The CEO has final responsibility for credit quality, and their commitment to sensible credit principles and disciplines must stand out clearly and be unquestioned. The CEO must take a role in risk strategy to ensure that it informs the business strategy, the risk appetite statement and the strength of the Three Lines of Defence. The CEO must also ensure that the risk management resources in the second line of defence are

adequate in number and expertise.
2. *Risk appetite statement* (RAS): in a banking business, the RAS is the most important policy document; it sets the foundation and parameters around which the business strategy is formulated. It is critical that the interdependencies between the RAS and the business strategy are clearly evident.
3. *The board must set realistic goals* and proper incentives: a bank's credit culture can be overwhelmed by incentives related to unrealistic earnings and growth goals, as was the case at HBOS and RBS.
4. *Credit success requires credit discipline.*
5. *There must be accountability* throughout the ranks: managers must be accountable for their own credit performance and that of their staff. Personal responsibility is important to a credit culture, as the BEAR legislation spells out.
6. *Fundamentals are important*: bankers succeed by sticking to the basics and picking their risks with care. Disciplined and skilled adherence to the Four C's should be non-negotiable. A cardinal principle of banking is to look at the borrower, not the asset or collateral.
7. *Bankers need to remember the past*: poor recollection of the bank's experience with past lending mistakes can create future mistakes. A 'this time is different' mentality is a sure sign that mistakes are likely to be repeated.
8. *Marketing pitfalls* should be avoided: marketing success does not necessarily translate into credit success, as HBOS so vividly illustrated. They set themselves a goal of a 15–20 per cent market share in all key markets and succeeded, just before they blew up. Plans to aggressively grow a lending book, spurred on by marketing and advertising, can, if not managed well, end up in tears with problems being stored for a future date.
9. *Boards and managers* should consider the opportunities for

human weakness and conflicts of interest: conflicts and optimism can cause credit tenets to be forgotten, rules to be broken or trading limits to be violated. Also, in banks where incentives are largely influenced by lending, there is the potential for an agency problem as bankers look to lend more, knowing that credit risk is unlikely to translate in the short-term and that if losses do occur, there is a reasonable assumption that the banker will have moved on into another role or to another bank.

10. *Risk administration is a vital function* in the risk management process: banks must monitor their exposure through regular information flows and reviews to ensure that the borrower's financial and operating conditions are in order. Monitoring total exposure limits both at the borrower and the industry level is important to ensure that the level of risk taken by the bank is reasonable and in line with agreed risk appetite policy.

The risk management culture in a bank is set from the top and it is for this reason that risk management should be a core competency of a bank CEO, many of the C-suite team and a significant number of directors. This is not however the case for most CEOs and senior executives that have graced the top of Australian banks (and many Anglo-Saxon banks) for well over a decade. Sir Win Bischoff, former chairman of Citigroup and veteran of many banking crises, commented just after the commencement of the GFC:

> If you look back at history, there is a commonality to practically all the major banking crises: leverage and real estate! Gut feel and experience may or may not be essential, but this time the lessons of history didn't sink in. When you're making lots of money it may be too good to last. I don't believe the risk processes were wrong, but the judgements based on them were. Looking at the performance of the major banks recently,

the relatively more successful ones were those who had several people at the top who had risk management experience and lots of gut feel; that arguably is better than technical competence. (Davis, 2009, p. 13)

'HEAD, HEART AND GUT' INSTINCTS

Good bankers as *first line* risk managers know how the 'head, heart and gut' instincts are used in assessing risk. When an experienced banker says, 'this deal doesn't feel right', they are not expressing a vague notion of disapproval; what they are doing is drawing on years of experience that informs them that there is something that does not stack up. Gut feel has its limitations including biases, but it is never to be ignored. One example was at the time of the commencement of the GFC.[187] Feeling very uncomfortable with assurances provided by the leasing group Allco, which owed the bank in excess of $100 million, gut instinct was allowed to be overridden by the reassurances offered by the company on how it would remedy the problem. The strong gut instinct was not to trust the assurances, but the head listened to the credible remedy that was being presented. The CEO of the borrower also sought to enlist the support of the CEO of the bank's Australian division. The bank ended up taking a material loss. Instincts were ignored. Never, ever again. Instinct or gut feel should always guide decisions on risk. In litigation against Allco's auditors, KPMG, it was revealed that the company had not disclosed $1.9 billion in interest-bearing loans in its 2007 accounts.[188] One thing that experienced bank CEOs know and do well is to not allow themselves to become embroiled in dealing with credit risk issues when they have been approached by the borrower, as is often the case. When the CEO of Centro Properties tried to pressure the then ANZ CEO, John

---

[187] This is a case study that the writer was directly involved in.
[188] Tadros, E., 'Deloitte fails to strike out Dick Smith class action claims', *Australian Financial Review*, 8 May 2019, p. 12.

McFarlane, to become involved in a dispute with the bank over a facility that was running into difficulty, McFarlane made it clear to Centro that this was a matter for the Head of Institutional Banking and that there was 'no right of appeal to the centre', that is, the decision was for the appropriate executive responsible for the bank's relationship with Centro. In 2011, in a landmark legal decision, the Federal Court of Australia found that eight executives and directors of Centro had breached the Corporations Act by signing off on financial reports that failed to disclose billions of dollars of short-term debt.[189]

Another case that still rankles was the reported $48 million loss ANZ incurred to Sydney-based group TJF-EBC in 2004.[190] The company was in the scaffolding and crane business and were provided with finance in the form of equipment leasing (asset finance). When the company collapsed, there were liabilities of $100 million and realisable assets of $12 million. When the bank went to find the assets it had financed, they were either missing or had never existed – fake invoices had been submitted. The principal behind the company was a flamboyant businessman. His other business interests included restaurants, one of which was where he regularly entertained bankers and clients, and was better known for pole dancers than for its menu. Putting the error on *character* assessment to one side, another never to be forgotten lesson was the fact that at least two ANZ employees, who had been involved in the initial decision to lend to TJF-EBC, went to work for the company, including (reportedly) the executive responsible for risk oversight of the bank's exposure.

There were several lessons in the Allco, Centro and TJF-EBC losses, mainly around the character of the company CEOs –

---

189 Akerman, P., 'Federal Court finds Centro executives broke Corporations Act', *The Australian*, 27 June 2011, p. 15.

190 'ANZ's horror loan – the scandal behind the missing $100m', *BRW*, 25 November 2004, pp. 13–16.

dominant, egotistical individuals. This characteristic was evident in other losses to firms such as ABC Learning and Babcock & Brown. Bankers with longer experience in Australia will also relate to Skase, Connell and Spalvins. The risk associated with colourful, egotistical and dominant CEOs is an important character lesson never to be forgotten.

In the mortgage market, a potential blind spot is the comfort that bankers take on the level of the LMI. Bankers would take comfort on their higher LVR loans by assuming that they were 'low risk' because of the existence of third-party insurance to cover a portion of the loan. In a market with evidence of 'liar loans' and other types of irresponsible lending, a good risk manager would know that the prospects of being able to claim under an insurance policy based on incomplete or fraudulent documentation, including where the bank is proven to have been negligent in its documentation and information verification, are weakened.

These and other lessons expanding on the 15 credit principles are summarised in Appendix III.

RISK CULTURE

As discussed in Chapter 2, there is evidence that the lengths banks have gone to to grow their share in mortgage lending has no resemblance to a sensible risk culture. NAB's 'Introducer Program' involved bribes, fraud and corruption. Then there was the allegation of irresponsible lending levelled at Westpac, which is the most aggressive bank in the investor home loan market. ANZ admitted that staff were inclined to 'short-cut the process' in assessing loan applications.[191] UBS, largely based on Westpac samples, estimated that there were some $500 billion of 'liar loans'

---

191 Chung, F., '"It's fair to say we haven't asked enough questions": ANZ says "shortcuts" taken in loan approvals', *news.com.au*, 29 November 2018, <https://www.news.com.au>.

in the market, that is loans obtained by falsely declaring income or expenses. CBA admitted that its risk controls over broker introduced loans were 'unsatisfactory' in ensuring compliance with responsible lending guidelines and in detecting fraud.[192] CBA was also heavily criticised by the Royal Commission for being 'reactive' in dealing with risk and for having a culture that was 'at times dismissive' of APRA: 'This adversarial approach appeared to put strict legal interpretations above risk or customer outcomes.' The CRO at CBA at that time was the former in-house lawyer, who had no operating experience in the bank and his first job in risk management was that of Group CRO.[193] Appointing executives with no risk management background into senior risk roles within the bank was not unique to CBA. CEOs and boards with little intuitive feel or experience in risk management had no sense of the signal that such appointments sent to the rest of the bank. Absent deep relevant experience, risk management in many banks has become 'risk bureaucracy', producing volumes of turgid policy devoid of commercial judgement.

The APRA inquiry into culture and governance at CBA shone a light on the emphasis on risk process over risk judgement. In a staff survey of 10,000 employees compiled by the investigative team of John Laker, Jillian Broadbent and Graeme Samuel, completed responses were received from an impressive 6000 employees. Employees reported a 'box-ticking' attitude to risk and a 'lack of ownership of outcomes in favour of following the process'. The report said that 'People are a lot more focused on risk management processes than outcomes in this organisation' and that 'risk management was steeped in bureaucracy'. Relatively few respondents supported the statement: 'in my experience, people

---

192 Frost, J., 'CBA finds risk controls "unsatisfactory"', *Australian Financial Review*, 17–18 March 2018, p. 25.

193 Han, M., 'Inquiry puts CBA in-house lawyers under spotlight', *Australian Financial Review*, 2 May 2018, p. 13.

in this organisation are good at dealing with issues before they become a major problem'.[194] In fairness to CBA, that same report could have been written about other banks. The risk culture and professionalism at NAB, for example, was made visible in a 2016 document presented to the Royal Commission titled *Risk culture and conduct within personal banking*.

This 2016 internal paper expresses concern about the:

> current risk culture within the Personal Bank following a review of thirty high performing retail bankers, who earned their recognition through 'the prioritisation of sales at the expense of sound risk management ... While these sales practices occur, not only do they increase the credit risk but also the potential risk of facilitating terrorism financing, money laundering or other criminal activities through false or misleading applications.

The paper goes on to explain that business leaders' 'responses lacked curiosity and sound risk judgement' with a 'lack of regard for Credit and shows that sales is the focus at the expense of prudent lending'. There are numerous lessons in these examples that talk to culture, professionalism, leadership and accountability.

Despite the severity of the allegations made and proven, there is often little accountability evident at a senior level. Even when senior executives do leave, 'for other reasons', their compensation and other arrangements often do not reflect the severity of their mismanagement. That severity is often left for more junior staff to bear. Many departing executives, who fundamentally failed in their stewardship, are rewarded with generous exit payments, and sometimes even courses paid for at leading business schools such as Harvard. For these reasons and noting that boards have demonstrated time and time again their inability to address

---

194 Gardner, J., 'Bank's staff tell it like it is in the realm of ticks', *Australian Financial Review*, 2 May 2018, p. 13.

this agency problem, the introduction of the BEAR regime, as discussed in Chapter 4, is both welcome and necessary; an example of regulation stepping in to compensate for weak corporate governance on matters of risk culture and accountability.

When it comes to lessons on the problems that a lack of risk management skills at the top of the bank can cause, it is difficult to go past the case of HBOS, RBS and Deutsche Bank. HBOS and RBS are relevant examples for Australian banks. HBOS was created in 2001 through the merger of the Bank of Scotland and the Halifax Building Society. At that time the combined group had a market capitalisation of £28 billion, by the end of 2006 the market capitalisation had grown to £42.6 billion. This growth was achieved largely through old-fashioned lending. Unlike RBS, HBOS stuck to its knitting, avoiding the racier investment banking activities that had enticed others. According to the joint review of HBOS by the UK Prudential Regulation Authority (PRA) and the FCA:

> HBOS was at root a simple bank that none the less managed to create big problems. The bank grew its loan book from £312 billion at the end of 2002, to £705 billion before its collapse in 2008. This was achieved by developing a sales culture, driven from the CEO, of growing lending market share at a rate higher than any of its competitors. From 2008 to 2011, HBOS recognised impairments on bad loans amounting to £52.6 billion.[195]

According to the regulatory report, the core issue was a weak risk management culture, with a key failing being the fact that the bank was full of senior executives and directors with little or no practical knowledge of risk management. The report also found

---

195 Bank of England, *The failure of HBOS plc (HBOS): a report by the Financial Conduct Authority (FCA) and the Prudential Regulation Authority (PRA)*, November 2015, <https://www.bankofengland.co.uk/-/media/boe/files/prudential-regulation/publication/hbos-complete-report>.

the bank board had little experience of banking, having just one non-executive with banking experience and he was only appointed in May 2007 when all the damage had been done. Meanwhile the bank appointed group risk directors with little experience in risk. The two CEOs during that period also had little relevant experience. Mr Crosby was an actuary by training rising through Halifax Life rather than its banking division, while Mr Hornby's background was first in management consulting then in retailing. The UK Commission on Banking Standards reported that 'Inside HBOS, the culture was brash, underpinned by a belief that the growing market share was due to a special set of skills which HBOS possessed and which its competitors lacked.'[196] Nemesis follows hubris. As with RBS, Barclays and Deutsche Bank, risk management was operating in a 'federal model' within business divisions, where dominant business leaders would exert influence over second line risk judgement. The Commission on Banking Standards described the risk functions at these banks as 'a cardinal area of weakness'.

Very similar issues were evident at RBS under Fred Goodwin. The risk management culture collapsed as the bank pursued growth. In 2013, the then chairman of RBS, Sir Philip Hampton, commented that 'we were lending to anyone with a pulse … We were taking clients that other banks rejected' (Fraser, 2014). RBS was hell-bent on keeping pace with an equally cavalier HBOS in the race for market share. This high-risk, highly competitive herding behaviour was, in many ways, as Ross Gittins described of the Australian banks in Chapter 1.

As with the major Australian banks, both RBS and HBOS had developed from the top down a deeply ingrained sales culture and no regard for risk management expertise, with little banking experience at CEO and board level. Davis (2009, p. 15) highlighted

---

[196] Thompson, J. & Jenkins, P., 'Bank built on flawed business model', *Financial Times*, 5 April 2013.

the wider management issue in his research:

> Risk models aren't the problem; they throw off numbers. All the top management of banks want is growth! In banking, there hasn't been real risk management since 2001 at the top banks ... in speaking to investors, perhaps the most frequent and powerful response relates to the need for relevant [especially risk management] experience and wisdom at the top of the bank.

Similarly, Jorion (2009), emphasised that a risk management system or processes cannot and should never be designed to take the place of judgement and business expertise of senior management. Traditional risk measures are backward looking and assume that distributions are stable and relevant for the future. Thus 25 years of rising house prices with historically low levels of losses given default can create a sense that housing is safe even when there have been significant shifts in leverage, pricing and affordability. Housing in Australia in 2019, for example, on any metric, looks overvalued and high risk, as discussed in Chapter 2. The huge losses incurred by **HBOS** and **RBS** were largely due to poor lending, particularly into real estate. Stephen Hester, who replaced Fred Goodwin as CEO at **RBS**, commented that 'somehow, every single generation, people forget and there is another real estate boom followed by a bust' (Martin, 2013, p. 540). 'This time is different' – the four most dangerous words in banking.

The GFC threw up numerous examples of how banks had lost their risk culture. In many banks risk management had become about risk process and policies, ostensibly compliant with the Three Lines of Defence. Algorithm based models were given far too much weight in decision making. Banks had lost sight of the reality that risk management is as much about judgement as it is about modelling – banks were seduced by the view that data could do away with gut instinct and human judgement. If financial markets followed the normal bell-shaped distribution curve, in which meltdowns are very rare, the stock market crash of 1987, the interest rate turmoil in the UK in 1991–2, the high-tech crash of the early 2000s and the GFC would each be expected only once in a lifetime. As *The Economist* noted:

> Models should be seen as metaphors that can enlighten but do not describe the world perfectly ... the quants that drive most of the models can provide overly complex rather than sensible, commercial outcomes – you may need a plumber, but you get a professor of fluid dynamics.[197]

The unquestioned conviction in big data and quantitative information is consistent with how management consultants are trained and therefore the fact that hard data was to replace instinct and judgement is not surprising. This was particularly evident in the way Andy Hornby ran HBOS.

The calibre and experience of senior executives ensures the rigour of the debate on risk management issues. This is a key test of a well-managed bank and goes to the heart of risk culture. Many banks substitute management expertise with an array of committees and fall into the trap of group thinking and volumes of policies and procedures. The sociology of committees can get in the way of debate and probing questions as dissidents can be made to feel as 'outliers' and under pressure to toe the party line. In some bank cultures, dissident views are seen as destructive team behaviour and thus the bank is exposed to moral hazard risk processes and a consenting culture crowding out important opinions. The classic example of this being the demotion and then firing of the CRO at Lehman Brothers when she expressed concerns on the level of subprime risk held by the bank. The same happened to Benny Higgins, first at RBS and then HBOS. The consensus driven and

---

[197] 'A special report on financial risk', *The Economist*, 13 February 2010, p. 13.

unchallenging culture was also a criticism levelled at CBA by the APRA investigation into culture and governance at the bank. Like HBOS before its demise, under CEO Ian Narev, CBA had sector-leading financial returns, but a series of miscalculations left a disappointing legacy. Part of this was culture, which is discussed in Chapter 7, but part of it was also, according to a CBA insider, that the then CEO was:

> unable or unwilling to hold his executives accountable, preferring to see the best in people. Any failure to make people accountable for behavioural or performance issues is a big problem that can trickle down in large organisations. Also, Ian is not a career banker and did not have an intuitive feel for the business, or for risk.[198]

The Royal Commission and the APRA investigation into culture and governance at CBA highlighted just how weak the Three Lines of Defence model was in practice, despite volume upon volume of policy documents and board papers, as many banks had become devoid of risk management competencies. The former NAB CEO Don Argus gave his views on this when he wrote:

> A catastrophic breakdown in the industry's risk practices which has led to an aggressive sales-driven culture with a profit at-all-costs attitude leading to scandal after scandal ... there has been a breakdown in risk disciplines, and in some instances, questions raised as to whether a risk framework actually exists.[199]

In the most part this can be attributed to the culture shifts within banks and the nature of senior hiring from outside the industry,

---

[198] Gluyas, R., 'Narev's legacy: big returns and big problems', *The Australian*, 7 April 2018, p. 26.

[199] Argus, D., 'Banks must go back to basics to regain public trust', *The Australian*, 18–19 August 2018, p. 28.

but it can also be attributed to the complacency that was allowed to creep in as banks thought themselves well managed in coming through the GFC relatively unscathed.

Avoiding the shock of the GFC meant that the culture that had permeated the industry since the 1990s was not reassessed as had been done in other parts of the world, in particular 'the conflict at the heart of banking: the fair treatment of customers and the maximisation of profit'.[200] Risk management is however, as every banking expert will attest, an instinctive and intuitive skill just as much as it is a science. If board directors have not been steeped in this, they cannot be properly equipped to 'form a view of the risk culture', as APRA requires. What directors will do is look to policies and systems to satisfy themselves and take comfort from the bureaucracy of risk rather than its substance. The FSA inquiry into HBOS found that the board lacked banking knowledge and did not have the experience or expertise to identify the core risks that the bank was running (Perman & Darling, 2013, p. 551).

There is a real moral hazard risk caused by the flaws in the Three Lines of Defence model, *as it is implemented*, not as it is intended. These are discussed later.

BIG PICTURE

The inability to see the wood for the trees when assessing risk, particularly when others do not want to hear any negative sentiment, can affect the brightest and most independent of thinkers. Following the crash of the property market in the US, the then chairman of the Federal Reserve, Ben Bernanke, said that rising house prices reflected strong economic fundamentals. In a narrative that will ring true with what many have said about the

---

200 Eyres, J., 'Banks complacent on risk culture', *Australian Financial Review*, 11 April 2016, p. 28.

Australian market, Bernanke said, in explaining why he and others had missed all the signs of the property bubble:

> I think it's important to point out that house prices are being supported in very large part by very strong fundamentals ... We have lots of jobs, employment, high incomes, very low mortgage rates, growing population, and shortages of land and housing in many areas. (Cassidy, 2009, p. 72)

A more reflective view of reality, which has stood the test of time, was offered by the great economist Hyman Minsky, who had as a core assumption of his financial instability theory that bankers' appetite for credit risk depends on recent experiences:

> Acceptable financing techniques are not technologically constrained: they depend upon the subjective preferences and views of bankers and businessmen about prospects ... Success breeds a disregard of the possibility of failure; the absence of serious financial difficulties over a substantial period leads to the development of a euphoric economy in which increasing short-term financing of long positions becomes a normal way of life. (Minsky, 1986, p. 237)

The lack of risk expertise within the C-suite at both RBS and HBOS meant that the ageless insights from Minsky, Bischoff and others were lost in a culture that agreed 'this time is different'. As a result, the risk cultures in these banks fell into a state of disrepair. In the lead-up to the GFC, both banks were aggressively pursuing market share and taking on bigger risks; they were competing on risk appetite, which is a sure sign of trouble ahead. When banks start adjusting their risk appetite on the run – moving up the risk curve – or seeing numerous exceptions, then this is a sure sign of a weak and failing risk culture.

The strength of personalities at RBS and HBOS and the

absence of credible challenge meant that credit committees became perfunctory, with pressure to ensure a 'faster committee process' to support lending volumes. Internally, the first and second lines of defences were taking comfort from portfolio averages (readers will remember the warning on averages from Chapter 4). RBS's vast commercial real estate loan book was viewed as safe and sound with an LVR of 60 per cent and only 2 per cent of total advances going towards speculative developments. Goodwin said, 'It does feel as if we are quite conservative'. He may have believed that at the time, but approximately £68.5 billion of RBS's commercial real estate loans were of such poor quality that they ended up having to be put in the government's asset protection scheme. (Fraser, 2015, p. 321). Internal optimism on credit quality is endemic in the banking industry and it is one of the reasons why it is so important that there is strong, credible Three Lines of Defence. In the case of HBOS, the culture of optimism blinded sensible judgement and that optimism was not challenged by the group risk function. Dealmakers were motivated by transaction volumes and risk assessment was the responsibility of the risk department, 'who were regarded within the bank as a lesser form of life'. Senior bankers promoting transactions 'had no problem in brow-beating the risk department' (Perman & Darling, 2013, p. 521).

INSTITUTIONAL MEMORY

An important part of a bank's risk culture is its 'institutional memory'. A big part of that memory is having executives who have been with the bank over several business cycles. Yet this is in stark contrast to what so often happens in banks, where senior people and structures change on a regular basis, particularly at executive levels. This risk is exaggerated when senior executives with no experience in banking are placed in important roles, or senior executives move roles on a regular basis (the average in-role tenure of a bank C-suite executive is three years in Australia). The bank loses its institutional memory. As the former governor of the Bank of England commented in a speech in 2009: 'Disasters happen when the last man who can remember what happened in the last crises, retires' (King, 2016, p. 144). It is not unusual to find a new generation of executives, particularly when they come with little banking training, seeking to prosecute strategies that are likely to fail based on previous experience. The experienced banker would have been able to point to the last time that movie was shown and what happened in the end, but the new generation believe that 'this time is different'. This time is rarely different when it comes to risk management in banking. A healthy bank risk culture must keep memories of the last crises and individual credit losses, like the examples of Allco, Centro, TJF-EBC and others, fresh in the institutional memory.

THREE LINES OF DEFENCE

It is common practice that banks develop their risk management framework (policy, strategy and controls) on the widely known Three Lines of Defence Risk Management and Assurance Model. This is a powerful and effective framework if properly applied and followed; however, it is a dangerous framework, fraught with moral hazard risks if not applied properly. It depends on all three lines functioning effectively; failure with one line weakens the whole framework, particularly the first line.

In the collapse of HBOS, there was no absence of detail on the bank's Three Lines of Defence. In their 2007 annual report the word 'risk' appeared more than 500 times and it was easy to get the impression that the bank was obsessed by risk. In the investigation into HBOS, the FSA uncovered significant failings in all three lines of defence (Perman & Darling, 2013, p. 446).

The *first line of defence* comprises the business management responsible for originating the risk and dealing with customers. It also includes key operational and technology staff. In many banks, the relationship manager is the first line of defence. The first line of defence is the risk owner and is accountable, in the first instance, for the risk assumed by the bank. How the first line and the second line work is fundamental. In some cases, the first line has delegated authority to both originate and approve the risk. In most cases, risk approval will require a sign-off from a risk specialist sitting in the second line. It is here that in practice the role of the first line and the second line can become blurred. The first line of defence is responsible for:

> Effective implementation of the risk management framework, including reporting and escalation of relevant information to responsible senior management, the second line of defence or as far as the board committees or the Board of Directors; and managing risk in a way that is consistent and integrated with the risk management framework.[201]

Making sure that risk ownership is clearly defined is an important management and regulatory requirement and the responsibility of the *second line* of defence. The second line of defence comprises a specialist risk management function, which is independent of the first line of defence. The second line of defence supports the board and its committees. The responsibilities of the second line of defence are to:

> Develop risk management policies, systems and processes to facilitate a consistent approach to the identification, assessment and management of risks; provide specialist advice and training to the Board, board committees and first-line of defence on risk-related matters; objectively re-

---

201 APRA, CPG 220 – *Risk Management*, January 2015, <https://www.apra.gov.au>.

view and challenge the consistent and effective implementation of the risk management framework throughout the APRA-regulated institution ... oversight of the level of risk in the institution and its relationship to the risk appetite, and any necessary reporting and escalation to the Board or its committees.[202]

For the second line of defence to work effectively, a good risk culture is essential. At HBOS, with its culture that valued sales above all else, risk management was regarded as a constraint on the business rather an integral part of it. HBOS executives were heavily incentivised on revenue rather than risk. This culture was allowed to flourish despite a well-documented third line of defence.

The *third line* of defence comprises those functions such as internal audit, including those externally provided, that are tasked with providing the board with assurances on the effectiveness and appropriateness of the risk management framework.[203] How the second line and third line work is critical. Evidence from the Royal Commission on management controls at CBA showed how senior management failed to listen to the concerns expressed by internal audit, whose warnings were repeatedly ignored. Giving evidence at the Royal Commission, the CBA chair, Catherine Livingston, revealed that the bank board was too willing to accept management assurances and did little to penalise executives when things went wrong. She gave the impression that despite there being little evidence in board minutes of discussions, she was the main voice holding management accountable, a recollection that was challenged by other directors. She added that minute taking had improved since she had become chair.[204] The Head

---

202 Ibid.
203 Judo Bank has commissioned EY to provide its Board Audit Committee with assurance on identified risks, a function that complements the separate role of Judo's external auditors, PwC.
204 Yeats, C. & Danckert, S., 'CBA's fall from grace: no more apologies, plenty of finger pointing', *Sydney Morning Herald*, 24 November 2018.

of Retail Bank Compliance at CBA commented that the APRA report into governance at the bank made her feel 'relieved and vindicated, because the voice of risk was not being heard' and senior executives were not challenging what was going on.[205] A not dissimilar sentiment on the effectiveness of the third line of defence was expressed by the then NAB chairman, Dr Ken Henry, during the Royal Commission and in NAB's self-assessment, which was made public.

The story of Gordon Dickson at HBOS is illustrative of how the second and third line of defence can fail inside a bank with a domineering sales culture and led by strong personalities, particularly the CEO. Gordon rose through the ranks of the bank to become a senior risk and compliance officer:

> My responsibilities were primarily to ensure that the bank adhered to all the rules and regulations. We ran a tight ship. We would jump on anything. If there was anything untoward, we wouldn't touch it. But the whole mentality changed. We became a bank that wanted to sell to you – regardless of whether you wanted it. And the one thing it's very easy to sell is money. (Perman & Darling, 2013, p. 510)

Gordon joined the bank as a 16-year-old and worked there for over 30 years, investing in the bank's shares and options and accumulating a life changing value of over £1 million, which he saved for his retirement. He lost not just his job but all his savings when the share price collapsed and the bank was merged into Lloyds Bank.

Appendix IV provides a summary of the Three Lines of Defence framework.

---

205 Durie, J., 'All talk, no action as Comyn ignores the problem', *The Australian*, 20 November 2018, p. 17.

THE ROLE OF THE BOARD

Under regulatory requirements, the board is ultimately responsible for the risk management framework and for the oversight of its operations by management. In this task, the board is assisted by the Board Risk Committee and the Board Audit Committee. APRA is very clear on what is expected of the board in ensuring that they understand the importance of a bank's risk culture:

> APRA's view is that a sound risk culture is a core element of an effective risk management framework … An institution's risk culture is strongly influenced by the "tone at the top". APRA expects the Board and senior management to demonstrate their commitment to risk management and foster a sound risk management environment'.[206]

It is hard to imagine a clearer set of instructions. Assessing the risk management skills of the Board Risk Committee should be an important duty of the regulators. A Board Risk Committee absent relevant risk expertise should be a red flag. The fact that a board member may have worked in a bank at some stage but not in a meaningful risk assessment capacity should not be considered as qualified to meet the test of 'relevant risk expertise'.

When the numbers look good, the fact that boards can turn a tin ear to warning signs is a well-known problem within banks. When Paul Moore, Head of Group Regulatory Risk at HBOS from 2002–05, warned the board that the rapid expansion of the bank was exposing it to grave risks, he was fired by the CEO (Perman & Darling, 2013, p. 408).

---

206 APRA, *Prudential practice guide CPG 220 risk management*, April 2018, p. 9, <https://www.apra.gov.au/sites/default/files/cpg_220_april_2018_version.pdf>.

RWAS AND RISK

In Chapter 2, we looked at how the banking sector has become fixated on RWA optimisation even when it leads to a material concentration on certain asset classes and is fraught with distortions in how calculations on equivalent risks are made across banks. There seems to be an unquestionable belief in the accuracy of risk weightings derived from statistical studies of the past. In a crisis, such as a 'black swan' event as described by Nicholas Taleb (2007), history, like averages, can prove to be highly misleading. Past data suggests mortgages are a safe asset class, yet during the GFC, mortgages turned out to be the source of large losses in many parts of the world, as they did in the UK in the 1990s. As the former governor of the Bank of England Mervyn King noted: 'The appropriate risk weighting can change abruptly and suddenly, especially in a crisis, and are an example of radical uncertainty, not risk, despite the words of regulators' (2016, p. 138).

King argues that in the case of bank risk management and regulation, it is better to use a measure of leverage rather than a ratio of capital to RWAs, as discussed in Chapter 2. Leverage ratios measure capital relative to total (unweighted) assets. A Bank of England study of 116 large global banks during the GFC (of which 74 survived and 42 failed), found that the simple but robust leverage ratio was better at predicting which bank would fail than the more sophisticated risk-weighted measure of capital (King, 2016, p. 138). This reality was implicitly the reason why the RBNZ moved its minimum Tier 1 capital ratio for banks from 10.5 per cent to 15 per cent of RWAs (equivalent to a common Tier 1 equity of 18 per cent), which results in the need for an estimated NZ$12 billion of additional equity into the New Zealand subsidiaries of the major Australian banks.[207] The RBNZ's scepticism of RWA methodology

---

207 Turner, S., 'RBNZ could end big four's NZ super profits', *Australian Financial Review*, 1 March 2019, p. 21.

and the variances between different banks, as discussed in Chapter 2, was reflected in the following statement: 'Where there are multiple methods for determining capital requirements, outcomes should not vary unduly between methods. In essence, there should be as level a playing field as possible.'[208] Bravo to the RBNZ.

AN ALTERNATIVE PARADIGM FOR RISK MANAGEMENT: THE CASE OF HANDELSBANKEN

One of the most successful banks over the past 20 years is the Swedish bank, Svenska Handelsbanken. They first came to Judo Bank's attention when exploring the emergence of challenger banks in the UK. Numerous experts in London, having had the Judo Bank philosophy on relationship banking and risk management described to them, pointed to Handelsbanken as the benchmark. Their model is described by Niels Kroner in his book *A blue print for better banking* (2011). The Handelsbanken model, which has been successfully imported into the UK, is very much 'Banking as it used to be, banking as it should be'. One of the standout features of the bank is the low level of credit losses, including when the Swedish banking system collapsed in the early 1990s. In contrast, they have produced a respectful, sustainable but not spectacular financial performance over decades.

At the centre of their business philosophy is a culture of staff stability, branch/business centre accountability and a very strong emphasis on the Four C's of credit risk management. Contrary to industry norms, however, they are not committed to the principle of industry portfolio limits and diversification. Instead they believe that local business banking centres should only take on risk that they understand and will be held accountable for (the 'church-

---

208 Creighton, A., 'Kiwis show the way on regulation', *The Australian*, 28 December 2018.

tower principle'). Their implicit belief is that selecting individual credit risks on merit is a better approach to risk management than assessing loans with industry limits and diversification objectives. In a banking model where relationship bankers know the borrower and can assess the Four C's, this is a safer approach to banking than setting arbitrary limits, which could involve lending to certain businesses with a less than strong credit profile in order to operate within industry limits. Their core belief is the importance of picking the right customers regardless of industry and less about sector allocation and diversification limits. The evidence from the GFC and earlier banking crises is that industry diversification limits do not protect banks in an economic downturn as the correlation, particularly in domestic markets, is always greater than the model assumes. Having a strong credit risk management culture however, where judgement and accountability count along with models and limits, is a much more effective way of protecting the bank in times of stress. To make this work however, as Handelsbanken have, it requires a strong value-driven culture. It also requires experienced bankers operating with some autonomy but within a framework of non-negotiable controls, including a strong risk culture deeply ingrained in the Four C's principles, where character matters, as do other forms of qualitative judgement-based criteria. This would be very challenging, if not impossible, to make work inside a large bank, as was evident at Wells Fargo. Wells Fargo had an entrepreneurial culture, in which business units and managers had discretion to pursue growth based on local conditions. A strong culture of credit risk management underpinned this decentralised model; however, that was offset by 'precious little culture of operational risk management'.[209] It was poor operational risk management and an arrogant culture that brought Wells Fargo to its knees, even though it had a strong credit risk culture.

---
209 Armstrong, R. & Noonan, L., 'Wells Fargo: repairing a damaged brand', *Financial Times*, 14 January 2019.

PARADOX OF RISK MANAGEMENT

As many examples in this book have highlighted, banks still have a problem with risk management despite the significant investment that has been made in the function and with the elevation of the CRO to the C-suite. In significantly strengthening the risk management function, banks were sending a message to the regulator that they were taking seriously the regulator's desire that risk is an important control within the bank and that risk culture is critical.

This puzzle or paradox is explained in three parts; first, there has been the promotion into the CEO and senior executive role of too many people without an instinctive knowledge for risk, as described several time in this book; second, too many CROs have weak business and operational experience; and third, risk management as a professional competency of a banker has been allowed to fall into decline as banks have separated 'sales' from 'risk'. A set of serious miscalculations.

This third explanation was a significant miscalculation as it has created almost a generation of customer facing bankers who lack essential risk management competencies, and this has had a negative effect on the relationship with the customer and with the quality of risk decision making. Bankers came to think that risk management was someone else's job, even though most banks reinforce (at least symbolically) the role of the first line of defence. The outcome of this problem, which is widespread, is that instead of strengthening the risk management culture within a bank, which the regulators intended to do, it has weakened it substantially, with flow-on effects particularly into the SME market, as discussed in Chapter 5.

As banks decoupled risk management from the banker and created separated risk management functions inside the organisation based on 'independence', an internal culture evolved of 'them' and 'us'. The 'sales' team versus the 'risk' team. A consequence of this is that customer facing bankers are no longer steeped in risk management and the risk team can regard what is presented to them with a high degree of suspicion. The unintended consequence of this is that the senior management supervising the 'sales force' reduce their oversight of credit risk management, feeling that the specialist risk function would act independently in their decision making. Moral hazard risk is thus created. This then opens up a gulf between bankers and risk executives who sees it as their job to 'keep the bank safe' or to 'keep the CEO out of jail', implicitly mistrusting the judgement and motivation of their banking colleagues. This mistrust in the competencies and motivation of the bankers became self-fulfilling and the demise of risk management as a core competency of a banker is set on a path dependent course. Power struggles emerge between the different groups, which weakens the internal cohesion and culture within the bank. As many CEOs had no substantial credentials in risk, they were poorly placed to manage this tension and set the right tone. CROs were given and encouraged to use a direct line to the chair of the Board Risk Committee, which can be done in a way that undermines the authority of the CEO and other senior executives.

Newly empowered CROs saw it as 'their job' to keep the bank safe. Some even claimed to have the ability to keep executives out of jail. The CRO at GE Capital said:

> On an individual level, perhaps the most compelling benefit of risk management is that it promotes job and financial security for senior managers.... Senior executives involved in corporate frauds and accounting scandals have appeared on national television being led away in handcuffs and face the potential of severe criminal sentences. (Pernell, Jung & Dobbin, 2017, p. 513)

This theme was further explored in Pernell et al. (2017), when they argued that moral hazard risk is created when risk management authority becomes independent from the risk-taking activities of the business, as senior managers assume that risk management specialists have responsibility, whereas once upon a time, that would be a core responsibility and accountability of the senior business manager. If allowed by the CEO, CROs tend to want to centralise their control over risk for fear that their underlings might be 'captured' or unduly influenced by other senior executives, as they were at RBS, HBOS and Barclays (and other banks) in the period up to the GFC. This centralisation and creation of 'enterprise risk management' (ERM) further cements risk management as a separate function within a bank, rather than a common, shared competency, with a strong risk specialisation acting as a second line of defence. This paradox of risk management is unfortunate because it weakens not strengthens the risk management culture in a bank. It also creates power plays and internal politics, which can weaken the overall culture in the bank.

Risk management should be democratised throughout the bank if a risk culture is to be embedded and effective, with the specialist risk team there as a true second line of defence, ensuring policy adherence, coaching, mentoring and advising of a new generation of bankers committed to professional standards, that can be summed up as 'banking as it used to be, banking as it should be'. For this to work, however, a strong professional ethos is a prerequisite, one steeped in risk management and ethics, as discussed in Chapter 4.

It is important that inside every bank there is absolute clarity on credit risk appetite and how that ties into the business strategy. The RAS should shape the business strategy, not be shaped by it. It is also vitally important that the credit risk appetite is based on a foundation of clear credit risk management principles that define the credit culture of the bank.

CONCLUDING REMARKS

A bank's business is to take risks and manage them. It succeeds when the risks are commensurate with the bank's resources and competence. Ultimately a bank's quality is defined by the sum of its risk-taking decisions. Bank services and products have varying risks and embody features that in enough mass could nudge a bank into trouble. Given the centrality of risk to banking, a sound risk culture is essential. The most important document written in a bank is the RAS. This should inform the strategy of the bank, not the other way around. Serious miscalculations are made when banks treat the RAS as a subordinate document to the strategic plan.

One of the biggest risks a bank takes is in the appointment of a CEO who has no, limited, or narrow banking experience. Both HBOS and RBS have shown that a lack of banking qualifications and experience at the top is not compensated for by intellectual genius in marketing, consulting or any other professions, nor by slick PowerPoint presentations. Boards equally should not confuse financial services expertise with banking expertise. It is akin to confusing a heart specialist with a neurologist. Very different competencies, even though both are medical professionals.

A risk culture forms the bedrock for risk taking. In part it is values based, but clear policies and procedures are critical. History affirms that a risk culture can be established only with the leadership of senior management and the CEO. Its currency is defined by the senior leadership's actions, words, directions and tone. Banks with a weak risk culture are disasters waiting to happen! A good risk culture is evident in a well-functioning Three Lines of Defence framework, with all three lines equipped to perform their responsibilities and accept accountability. As the Royal Commission findings and the APRA investigation into CBA clearly illustrate, the Three Lines of Defence model, though valid in theory, is fundamentally broken in practice, notwithstanding volume upon volume of policies and Board Risk Committee papers.

So, although ostensibly formal risk frameworks and controls have increased significantly, the practical application of the Three Lines of Defence and the risk management culture that permeates many banks has weakened the effectiveness of risk management. This is particularly true of judgement. Risk management capabilities and instincts that once defined senior bankers no longer do so. The tone from the top has been weakened. In its place, as evident in the APRA review of CBA, are layers of bureaucracy. Bureaucracy is like cholesterol; there is good cholesterol and there is bad cholesterol. The latter, if allowed to go unchecked over time, can be very damaging, to the bank as well as to the body. The risk management culture and framework in far too many banks is clogged by bad cholesterol.

The concentration of risk on housing assets in Australia feels more like bankers betting on asset prices, in contrast to investing in businesses and prudently allocating capital across the economy to facilitate life cycle consumption smoothing. It feels like casino banking. It also feels as far away from the public interest as banking could be and it is potentially exposing the economy to a huge shock: it highlights how there can be a fundamental conflict – what is good for bankers privately may turn out damaging for the broader economy. It is as far removed from prudent risk management as you could imagine and it is currently predicated on the economy holding it together in terms of employment and interest rates. What a gamble. Veteran bankers and regulators know that while system shocks can strike like a bolt from the blue, they almost always have a long gestation period.

Banks are by nature too optimistic in good times and too pessimistic in bad times, often exaggerating the impact of risk on both the upside and the downside. The irony is that bank boards can become fixated on how the economy might impact the bank, yet it is rare for boards to think about how the banking system could affect the economy, as it did in the US and the UK as a result of the GFC. For this reason, regulators and government have a legitimate interest in a bank's risk culture and how well versed the bank board is on this. This is highly relevant, as Nicholas Taleb (2007) points out, echoing the sentiment of Keynes:

> 'Banks have the ingrained habit of plunging headlong into mistakes together where blame-minimising managers appear to feel comfortable making blunders so long as their competitors are making the same ones ... It can be safely pronounced charlatanism.'

In the UK, the author of an earlier review into the banking sector, Don Cruikshank, points to Basel II as the catalyst for lighting the fire that became the GFC and that this was a dereliction of duty by politicians for allowing the 'banks (to) decide what risk meant' through the use of their internal risk weighting models and creating a race to optimise RWAs, which meant reducing RWAs and thus capital requirements.

Following the Friedman Doctrine because of investor greed for higher ROE lending is not an acceptable excuse for management to pursue such a strategy, nor is the observation by Keynes that all bankers fail together, so no one can blame an individual. Bank CEOs and C-suite executives are paid a lot of money and they should 'own' their risk management judgement and not seek comfort and sanctuary sitting in the middle of the pack.

They should also 'own' the culture within the banks they have responsibility for, which is critical to risk management. The cultural capital of a bank is a fundamental measure of leadership quality, and these are the themes of the next chapter.

6
THE ROLE OF LEADERSHIP AND CULTURE

CULTURE in banking is widely seen as the root cause of weak risk management and of major conduct failings. Some have described the culture in the industry as 'broken' and even 'rotten to the core'.[210] While we should hesitate to simply say that there is an 'industry culture' when each bank has some differences, largely defined by its leadership, human resources (HR) practices and history, it is fair to say that in the cocoon of the Australian banking industry, particularly its concentration around Melbourne and Sydney and the mobility of staff between banks, together with the ever-gentle nudge from regulators towards standardisation, that there is a high level of similarity among the banks. Enough similarity to talk generally about culture while not suggesting that 'one-size-perfectly-fits-all'. That said, customers, as shown in Chapter 5, largely see the banks as very much alike.

If banks are ever to rebuild trust, then they must first address culture, and with it, accountability. Too often damaging events are put down to rogues, bad apples and rotten eggs, as descriptors of individuals who have caused harm to the bank. These labels are

---

210 Ferguson, A., 'Disregard, lack of respect: NAB leads poorly behaved pack,' *Sydney Morning Herald*, 25 August 2018, p. 26.

then followed by statements that '99.9 per cent of our people do the right things day in, day out'. While there is little doubt that '99.9 per cent' of the people working in the banks are fundamentally good, honest and well-intended, this response misses the point. Research outlined in *Designing trustworthy organisations* (2013), published by the MIT Sloan Management Review, shows that major violations of trust are almost never the result of rogue actors.[211] When they repeat themselves over time, there must be an acceptance that there is a systemic problem. The MIT research concludes:

> Companies often blame trust violations on 'rogue employees,' but these violations are predictable in organisations that allow dysfunctional, conflicting or incongruent activities to take root.

The findings from the Royal Commission and other scandals referenced throughout this book provide overwhelming evidence that there is a deep-rooted cultural problem within the banking industry and not facing this serves only to further entrench that culture. It does not get much worse for a bank, wrote Adele Ferguson, when it is told that it has 'a total disregard for laws and regulations' and when the Royal Commission comments that the violations of laws 'may be attributed, at least in part, to the culture and governance practices within the NAB Group'.[212] In the final report, the Commissioner added:

> NAB also stands apart from the three major banks. Having heard from both the CEO, Mr Thorburn, and the Chair, Dr Henry, I am not as confident as I would wish to be that the lessons of the past have been learned. More particularly, I was not persuaded that NAB is willing to accept the necessary responsibility for deciding, for itself, what is the

---

211 Gittins, R., 'Not one rotten apple, it's the whole barrel: crunch time for banks', *Sydney Morning Herald*, 17 November 2018.

212 Ferguson, A., 'Disregard, lack of respect: NAB leads poorly behaved pack', *Sydney Morning Herald*, 25 August 2018.

right thing to do, and then having its staff act accordingly ... overall, my fear – that there may be a wide gap between the public face NAB seeks to show and what it does in practice – remains.[213]

It is hard to think of a more damning indictment of culture within an organisation. This perspective on culture was reinforced by the scandal of the alleged fraud carried out by the CEO's executive assistant. While the bank was in one way the victim, the lack of controls and oversight that allowed such excesses to occur over an extended period reflects poorly on the management of the bank, including the apparent absence of the second and third lines of defence.[214]

WHAT IS CULTURE?

What do we mean when we use the term culture? There is a proliferation of definitions, but Barney (1986) provides a neat definition that captures the essence of most others: 'An organisational culture refers to the norms, values, and practices that are manifested in how employees think and behave.' Cultural norms therefore define what is encouraged and what is discouraged within a bank; what is accepted behaviour and performance and what is rejected. While a business strategy can be clearly defined, culture is more elusive, but no less real. The cultural capital of a bank can be a source of competitive advantage, in the same way as its human and financial capital can be; it is an important intangible asset, yet the evidence from the banking industry is that the banks have failed to invest in it (Stiroh, 2018). In fact, many banks have

---

213 Gluyas, R., 'How a single page destroyed a chairman and his CEO', *The Australian*, 9–10 February 2019, p. 25.

214 Cormack, L., 'From a private jet to a police cell: Rosemary Rogers charged over alleged NAB fraud', *Sydney Morning Herald*, 5 March 2019, p. 4.

underinvested and sweated their cultural capital, as an oligopolist is inclined to do. If a bank's structure and systems represent its 'hardware', to use an IT analogy, it is human capital and cultural capital that represent its 'software'. The difference between one bank and another is all down to its 'software', as 'hardware' is easily replicable.

There are many once great banking institutions that were defined by a strong, unique culture. Think about Citibank, JP Morgan, Goldman Sachs and Wells Fargo. In his bestselling book *Built to last* (1994), Jim Collins wrote that one of the things that successful companies have in common is a 'cult-like culture' and traditions that are unique to the institution. Wells Fargo, as discussed in Chapter 8, fell from grace not because of any major credit or trading losses, but because it turned out that its arrogant culture was a root cause of the scandals that engulfed the bank, much in the same way as happened at CBA.

That 'success is toxic' arrogance was evident at NAB in the 1990s, where according to Fraser:

> Fred Goodwin had made a conscious decision to emulate the approach of his mentor, Don Argus, former chief executive officer of NAB, believing that NAB possesses a unique set of skills and intellectual property, Argus feared these 'state secrets' would be diluted if shared. (2014, p. 151)

Changing culture is not easy; in fact, absent a crisis, it can be very hard as, so often in institutions such as banks that are locked on a path dependent course, the cultural concrete has set. Moreover, asking the same senior executives responsible for the current culture to reform that culture, is a leap of faith not supported by many precedents. After two years of limited progress under an internally appointed CEO following the fake account scandal, Wells Fargo accepted the resignation of their CEO, who commented: 'It has become apparent to me that our ability to successfully move Wells Fargo forward from here will benefit from a new CEO and fresh perspective.' The bank confirmed that it would search for a new CEO from outside the company.[215] When Westpac needed radical reform it went overseas for Bob Joss. When ANZ was determined to address its culture in 1998, it went overseas and appointed an outsider in John McFarlane, who spearheaded the internally popular cultural transformation program called 'Breakout'. That transformational program was based on the 'right' to grow and was predicated on performing first and growing second, which provided the licence to breakout and differentiate. The bank aspired to position itself as 'the bank with the human face' by its commitment to:

- Put our customers first.
- Perform and grow to create value for our shareholders.
- Lead and inspire each other.
- Earn the trust of the community.
- Breakout, be bold and have the courage to be different.

The breakout program, launched in 2001, transformed ANZ under its highly visible CEO, John McFarlane, who among other things invested all his salary (except for $44 to pay his social club membership fee) in ANZ equity. The symbolism of this is very powerful in many ways, and in a way that is consistent with a 'founder centrism'. Sacrificing discretionary salary for equity to the extent that McFarlane did is unprecedented among bank CEOs. Research published by the University of Oxford characterised the leadership style of JP Morgan Chase CEO, Jamie Dimon, as pragmatic 'founder centrism' — a founder's mindset, an ethical disposition towards shareholders and an intense focus

---

215 Ensign, R. L., 'Wells Fargo chief throws in the towel', *The Australian*, 30–31 March 2019, p. 31.

on exponential value creation.[216] The idea of 'founder centrism' is powerful. It transforms the mindset from an employee to an 'owner', which can be a powerful determinant of culture. The team at Judo Bank knows this in a deeply ingrained way.

The critical role of leadership in addressing culture was highlighted by Lou Gerstner, who was hired to turn around a failing IBM in the 1990s. The IBM culture was deeply ingrained, and Gerstner later wrote:

> Transformation of an enterprise begins with a sense of crisis or urgency. No institution will go through fundamental change unless it believes it is in deep trouble and needs to do something different to survive ... the thing I learned at IBM is the culture is everything.[217]

Management guru Peter Drucker is purported to have said that 'culture eats strategy for breakfast'. What Drucker meant was the power of company's culture will be defining regardless of the elegance of its strategy, a belief echoed in Gerstner's words. The existence of a healthy corporate culture is a core responsibility of the board, but it is not something the evidence would suggest that boards pay anywhere near enough attention to, beyond annual employee engagement surveys, which can be deeply flawed, as discussed later. The board can be more important than the CEO and C-suite executives in driving cultural change given that most boards will go through at least two CEO cycles and can protect the bank from the sometimes unnecessary revisionist tendency of the new CEO.

---

216 Rojas, C., *Eclipse of the public corporation revisited: concentrated equity ownership theory*, University of Oxford, 2017.

217 Lagace, M., 'Gerstner: changing culture at IBM – Lou Gerstner discusses changing the culture at IBM', *Harvard Business School*, 12 September 2002, <https://www.hbswk.edu>. See also, Gerstner, L. V., *Who says elephants can't dance? Inside IBM's historic turnaround*, HarperBusiness, 2002.

EVIDENCE OF CULTURAL PROBLEMS

There are many tell-tale signs on how the company's culture is viewed both internally and by external stakeholders. These signs include:
- dominant CEO/C-suite executives
- leadership arrogance
- instability within the senior leadership team
- weak senior management team (including limited industry knowledge)
- poor communication at all levels
- lack of openness to challenge
- subcultures (e.g. dealing room culture at some banks)
- casual attitude towards regulators and compliance
- weak diversity
- poor employee engagement
- flawed executive remuneration design
- high employee turnover
- exit interviews
- customer complaints
- customer losses
- persistent market gossip.

Another window into culture, which vigilant board members can detect from the market and occasional 'mystery shopping', was succinctly stated by the chairman and CEO of advisory firm Seawick when he wrote:

> Surprisingly, the markers of declining culture are often in plain sight: not returning phone or email messages, cancelling meetings without explanation, promises to arrange meetings or to respond to requests that never eventuate, unilateral changing of trading terms and treating stakeholders with disdain or contempt, just to name a few of these, all

signify a culture of arrogance, self-importance and standing, and deluding themselves into believing that they can exercise those attributes indiscriminately.[218]

Leadership values and culture are most obviously evident in how and what people are paid. As the chairman of APRA, Wayne Byres commented that a key focus for the regulator is the risk culture within a bank as defined by the formal and informal incentives that individuals face and their accountability (or lack thereof) shown when outcomes are below what was expected. What is rewarded is condoned. Thus, when APRA investigated into rewards and consequence management at banks and other financial institutions, a clear finding was that senior executives seemed insulated from the consequences of poor outcomes. Byres said that:

> if incentives are the carrot used by companies to boost staff performance, accountability mechanisms are the stick ... there has to be clear consequences for adverse outcomes. The perception in the community is that in the financial services sector, particularly at senior executive level, the carrots are large, and the sticks are brittle.[219]

Others might have replaced 'brittle' with 'feather'. There is actually very little in the way of consequences and some would say that this tells all you need to know about culture and corporate governance. The theme of remuneration is explored in Chapter 8.

All the banks investigated by APRA had the well-documented frameworks, policies and procedures in place, but they had a culture of gaming them and did so with the implicit if not explicit consent of their boards. The policy frameworks were there in form but not in substance. Boards did not fully understand that this lack of leadership accountability spoke volumes about the real culture

---

218 Fast, J., 'How to stop the rot within: fix your culture', *The Australian*, 26 July 2018, p. 25.
219 Byres, W., 'Incentives to fly safely', *Australian Financial Review*, 5 April 2018, pp. 48–49.

within a bank and sent a clear message to both employees and to the public. Equally, the APRA investigation into CBA, together with separate whistleblower testimonies, highlighted the way in which warnings from front-line staff into suspicious conduct and potential illegal money transmissions were ignored by senior staff. The first line of defence was doing its job, the second and third lines failed badly. There were examples of instances where concerned staff alerted management, only to find that the issues got 'lost' in a head office culture that prioritised profits over compliance and staff concerns. In fairness to the third line of defence at CBA, as discussed in Chapter 8, they – particularly internal audit – were highlighting many problems that the senior management team and the board chose to ignore.

Root cause analysis suggests that misconduct occurs in organisations where poor behaviours are ignored or sometimes even tacitly encouraged. That is because people look to cues from the behaviour of people around them to determine how to behave. In Chapter 4, the internal report into conduct within NAB's Retail/Personal Bank highlighted instances where senior management had turned a blind eye to serious breaches of policy and potentially of the law, because of the positive sales figures. The then NAB CEO failed to act on widespread concerns, including findings from KPMG, who discovered a litany of control issues and, although not confirmed, concerns that the program could have been linked to organised crime and terrorist financing.[220] The same bank, as evident in the Royal Commission, chose to engage with its regulators in a highly disrespectful and somewhat arrogant manner, lacking in transparency and blaming what are deep-rooted cultural problems on systems and technology. In operating in this way, the leadership was sending a clear statement about what was culturally acceptable.

---

220 Frost, J., 'NAB kills scandal-plagued home-loan referral program', *Australian Financial Review*, 25 March 2019.

Eyebrows were raised when CBA appointed Matt Comyn as CEO following the scandals that had engulfed the bank under his predecessor.[221] The market reaction was based on the fact that many of these scandals had occurred in the division that the new CEO had responsibility for. Question marks over accountability were naturally raised.[222] In justifying the appointment of the new CEO, the CBA chair noted, 'He had led a team which delivered strong profit growth for shareholders with NPAT in retail banking increasing 60 per cent over the period since 2012.'[223] Based on the scandals that engulfed the division he was responsible for, that endorsement could equally have been read as: 'His team demonstrated how to use the bank's pricing power in retail banking to maximise profits, using whatever means necessary, thereby confirming his credentials to be CEO.' Given the scandals that plagued the retail bank at CBA, and the reputation of the industry in the way that they abused customers, the ability to maximise profits in this way is a questionable endorsement of credentials for becoming the CEO. Australians love winners, but as with ball tampering in cricket, it is not a case of winning at all costs; doing whatever it takes.

The case of the once iconic Wells Fargo is one where there was evidence of cultural problems that their board failed to detect. For example, senior management gave the Wells Fargo bankers a goal of selling eight products to each customer. Why eight? Because 'eight' rhymed with 'great'. Bonuses and promotions were tied to bankers hitting eight products per customer and many customers were 'sold' products they had not asked for nor knew about. Given the focus on hitting the target and the coercive pressure applied,

---

221 Clarke, C., 'Why boss of scandal-plagued CBA got top job', *ABC News*, 29 January 2018, <https://www.abc.news.au>; Thompson, S. & Moullakia, J., 'CBA CEO appointment may surprise: Goldman', *Australian Financial Review*, 29 January 2018.

222 'CBA chair defends Comyn appointment as CEO', *SBS News*, 21 November 2018, <https://www.sbs.com.au.cba>.

223 <https://www.commbank.com.au>.

employees failed to check their ethical values in opening accounts customers had not asked for; everyone was doing it and senior management encouraged and rewarded it (Moore, 2018). Wells Fargo admitted that employees had opened 3.5 million phantom accounts in customers' names to meet sales targets.[224]

Leaders need to be very careful about how they frame expectations and goals. When the Business Bank at NAB during 2008–10 pushed for growth in a market that others were being cautious about for fear of GFC spillover, the management team went to great lengths to communicate that the strategic formula was market share growth *and* margin growth *and* risk management discipline. There was no option to go for two of the three, it had to be all three and particularly no compromise on risk. At that time, this was an appropriate strategy given market conditions, as other banks were reducing their risk appetite and funding costs and risks were rising. The NAB management team knew that absent constant communication, the bias would have been to compromise on risk or margin.

Product cross-selling without a deep understanding of customer needs and benefits analysis is professionally abhorrent. In some professions, 'selling' has a negative connotation, particularly where there is a relationship based on trust. Would you want your dentist or doctor, for example, to 'sell' you more treatment than you need? The retail emphasis in banking has created a deeply ingrained sales culture, which creates the conditions for the scandals that have plagued NAB and CBA in their Retail/Personal Bank and Wealth Management businesses. At HBOS, the sales culture rewarded staff for opening new current accounts, so when a customer had a mortgage from the bank, a current account was also opened, and staff would credit 1 pence into the account, unbeknown to the customer, so as to meet the criteria for a 'new account'. The same

---

[224] Flitter, E. & Cowley, S., 'Wells Fargo says its culture has changed. some employees disagree', *New York Times*, 9 March 2019.

happened at Wells Fargo, suggesting that this kind of conduct was endemic across the banking industry. Ethically this is abhorrent behaviour, akin to identity fraud.

Stiroh (2018, p. 52) underlines the importance of culture as a top management and board responsibility, when he talks about the adverse selection risk that banks face when they ignore or underinvest in their cultural capital:

> Adverse selection is another type of market failure than can lead to underinvestment in cultural capital. Firms with relatively low cultural capital may attract and retain employees, directors and clients more inclined to take imprudent risks and exceed internal limits and controls. High-quality employees or directors may leave such firms or decline to join them, contributing to a further deterioration of the firm's cultural capital.

The problem that Stiroh identifies is real and was evident at HBOS and RBS. The departure of Bernie Higgins is an example of a high-quality employee leaving because of an unwillingness to go along with the prevailing culture. This and other cases highlight the opportunity for regulators to insist on interviewing senior executives who resign or are nudged out of a bank, and not be constrained in doing so by confidentiality deeds that departing executives are often coerced into signing.

The Wells Fargo case illustrated just how a bank's carefully cultivated cultural capital can evaporate within a short period (arrives on the back of a tortoise and leaves on the back of a galloping horse). That '99.9 per cent of employees' in most banks are genuinely good, honest people is not in dispute, but just as the people at Wells Fargo lost their ethical compass in the face of coercion, so can employees at other banks, and this clearly happened within some of Australia's major banks. As psychologists Stanley Milgram, Philip Zimbardo and Solomon Asch suggest in their research, 'good' people will do 'bad' things if their group has a coercive culture to which they conform (Levilee, 2011). In other words, people of otherwise good character, working in a culture of fear, are more likely to conduct themselves badly and do the wrong thing (Steare, 2018). This fear factor of not making the numbers is pervasive in the banking industry given the short-term pressure of revenue, profit and ROE growth. While the threat of repercussions if someone fails is rarely explicit, it can be subtle and part of the industry folklore ('Charlie is behind on plan and Mary is not happy as she may miss her numbers … he won't be here for long and there goes our bonus'). Linked to this is the dreaded performance and appraisal framework, which is discussed below.

The challenge for banks in recrafting their culture is the bureaucratic and policy-bound environment that defines most banks. This is vividly described in Chapter 6 in the context of CBA. The highly prescriptive and rigid nature of internal frameworks make it difficult to build positive cultures as there are consequences of not following the policy, even if the policy has negative, intended or unintended, customer consequences. Most bankers feel obligated, for fear of the consequences, to follow policies that are inflexible, 'one-size-fits-all' in nature and often designed to deal with the lowest common denominator problem. In many cases, and sometimes out of sheer frustration, bankers looking to meet reasonable customer needs, will bend or 'game' the rules. This is hugely unfair pressure on staff who want to do the right thing. This is arguably another form of coercion, where people are not able to exercise common sense solutions to customer needs because of the overly rigid and often complex design of systems and policies. This is not to argue that there should be a cavalier attitude towards policies; it is to argue that senior management have a responsibility to make sure that policies are appropriate, simple and clear.

ETHICAL LEADERSHIP

The Wells Fargo case is a vivid reminder of what happens when leadership lacks ethics. It was common practice in that bank for branch employees, operating under intense sales pressure and incentive schemes that emphasised cross-selling, to open millions of sham deposit and credit card accounts without the knowledge of customers. The bank also admitted that customers were billed for insurance they did not want and were overcharged for wealth management services.[225] There are uncanny parallels to what some of Australia's leading banks were doing.

Ethical leadership is so important in shaping culture, as is a strong sense of accountability. Good, strong ethical leaders set the tone and have no tolerance for senior executives who violate ethical standards. Good leaders know the importance of hiring people with integrity, who always accept responsibility and promote the desired culture. Prior to Shayne Elliott's appointment as CEO at ANZ, the bank had a colourful and externally well-known reputation in terms of culture, especially among its financial markets team, who were alleged to enjoy some of the more insalubrious aspects of life with their large bonuses.[226] When it came to allegations of fixing the BBSW, ASIC described ANZ as having 'unconscionable conduct and market manipulation' and its behaviour as 'absolutely appalling' as the bank sought to be 'obstructionist' during the inquiry.[227] The same obstructionist behaviour at CBA, NAB and Westpac in dealing with regulators, described elsewhere in this book, does raise the question of whether the banks have an understanding, a societal

---

225 Armstrong, R., 'Wells Fargo to pay $575m more over sales practices', *Financial Times*, 29 December 2018.

226 Fife-Yeomans, J. & Chancellor, J., 'ANZ faces $30m suit over "strippers, coke and wads of cash"', *The Daily Telegraph*, 16 January 2016, p. 4.

227 Rhodes, C., '"Command and control" banks have got ethics and culture all wrong', *The Conversation*, 18 March 2016.

understanding, on what having an ethical culture really means. Readers will form their own view.

The ethical and cultural scandals that engulfed ANZ had parallels at NAB, where the practice of falsely witnessing documents on who gets a customer's superannuation when they die was described by the NAB senior executive as 'sloppy and unprofessional'. In response, journalist Adele Ferguson said that it would be more apt to describe the conduct as 'ethically challenged and morally bankrupt'. According to the media, one former NAB employee listening to the Royal Commission testimony said, 'falsifying documents was a commonly accepted moral standard … receiving kickbacks for inflated invoices, cocaine use by foreign exchange dealers … dealing with culture like it's a cliché'.[228] In terms of cultural insights, there was also the time when the then NAB CEO was forced to apologise for charging fees to customers for no service provided, but only after the bank's lawyers had fought tooth and nail to prevent the relevant documents from becoming public.[229] As the same newspaper commented, Thorburn 'admitted the bank had "drifted" away from doing right by its customers, a fairly astonishing mea culpa for someone earning millions of dollars a year.' Criticism of culture and governance at NAB was also expressed by the Royal Commission's legal counsel Ms Rowena Orr QC when she said that the misconduct and the failure to report serious financial services licence breaches to ASIC within the required 10 days, 'may be attributable, at least in part, to the culture and governance practices at NAB as well as its risk management recruitment and remuneration practices'.[230] If this is not an indictment on a bank's culture, it is hard to imagine

---

228 Ferguson, A., 'Culling the bank culture clichés is going to need more time', *Sydney Morning Herald*, 25 April 2018, p. 24.

229 Farrer, M., 'NAB's bosses Andrew Thorburn and Ken Henry have quit – what took them so long?', *The Guardian*, 8 February 2019.

230 Eyers, J., 'Hayne may find series of wrongdoings', *Australian Financial Review*, 24–25 March 2018, p. 18.

what might be. If this is not a good reason for the CEO to depart, it is hard to imagine what would be.

The major challenge in driving cultural change in large banks, and building cultural capital, is the attitude of the employees, the majority of whom are overworked and sometimes overwhelmed by the demands that are placed on them. This is particularly true of the category within a bank that is loosely described as 'middle management'. It is unproductive to point to the role of middle management as the permafrost or immune system that rejects foreign change agents. Middle managers have seen leaders and change programs come and go and, almost to cope with the demands placed upon them, they are adept in 'playing the game' and managing to survive through yet another cultural change program. Many have seen different brand slogans and versions of values, mission and purpose statements every few years, often coinciding with the CEO, C-suite cycle, etc. They are asked to ensure the execution of the change program, often in an environment of growing demands, fewer resources and increasing uncertainty around job security let alone career development. Driving cultural change must begin with a greater appreciation of the challenges placed on middle management and the challenge of winning the hearts and minds of middle managers and recognising that they play a crucial role in influencing behaviours, that they are the real agents for cultural change.

Well Fargo provides an insightful case in the challenges of cultural change. Following the scandals that plagued the bank, management embarked on several changes including eliminating sales targets and bonuses within the branch network. Branch staff were told that their primary job was to serve customers, not to sell them products. The sense of sales pressures however did not disappear. Employees felt that senior management exhibited 'doublespeak' when it came to cultural change. A survey of 27,000 employees highlighted as a top concern the inability to raise a grievance with managers on whether 'Wells Fargo conducts its business activities with honesty and integrity'.[231]

GENDER DIVERSITY

Although the topic of gender diversity is outside the scope of this book, it is an important factor in the cultural make-up of a bank, and needs to be explored in much more depth. It is worth reflecting that all the actors in the scandals outlined in this book have been men. This is no real surprise as men dominate the upper echelons in banking and in finance more broadly. This is arguably a reason, perhaps a major reason, for the crisis the industry finds itself in. The 'glass ceiling' metaphor may sound and feel dated, but it remains real. In part this may be because a certain type of alpha personality is attracted to competitive sales cultures, and more men than women prima facie fit that crude criteria. Andrew Haldane, Chief Economist at the Bank of England, argues that 'Groupthink was the reason most banks – as well as many regulators, central banks and academics – failed in 2008.'[232] The absence of meaningful gender diversity robbed many banks of a potentially more restraining influence on the arguably riskier behaviour of men.

The gender mix at the senior ranks within banks remains a vexed issue. In the UK, the government commissioned a study into this topic in 2016, *Empowering productivity: harnessing the talents of women in financial services*, and found that only 14 per cent of executive jobs were held by women. The picture in Australia would not be much better. The report made a number of recommendations that

---

231 Flitter, E. & Cowley, S., 'Wells Fargo says its culture has changed. Some employees disagree', *New York Times*, 9 March 2019.

232 Bates, S. & Woodman, C., 'Women in finance: beyond the glass ceiling', *London Business School Review*, vol. 29, no. 3, 2018.

became the backbone of the Women in Finance Charter, which asks for four commitments:
- Appoint a member of the executive team to be accountable and responsible for gender diversity and inclusion.
- Set and publish internal targets for gender diversity in the senior ranks.
- Publish progress annually against these targets on the firm's website.
- Have an intention to ensure that the pay of the senior executive team is linked to delivery against these targets.[233]

The report identified a 'permafrost' that mid-tier women were either failing to progress or leaving. According to a member of the review team, Clare Woodman, a senior executive at Morgan Stanley, the main reason was that '[t]hey leave when they don't think the management team supports them … Women have a tendency to be less vocal about their aspirations … Managers have always been open to thinking about different leadership styles.'[234]

Actions and priority to creating meaningful gender diversity at the top of banks, with suitably qualified candidates, is an essential ingredient in building a more sustainable and healthy corporate culture. The challenge of sourcing suitably qualified women in an industry dominated by men is a real one, and it is a challenge that must be tackled without compromising on capabilities to satisfy quotas. There is frequent debate on this topic and, from time to time, much hand-wringing at the lack of progress. It is a major cultural and skills topic that requires greater investigation than can be justly done in this book.

---

233 Ibid.
234 Ibid.

EMPLOYEE OPINION SURVEYS

In monitoring culture, there are no short cuts for senior management and directors to spending time with their finger on the pulse of the bank. Doing this enhances the understanding of the 'tone' by meeting employees, speaking to customers and suppliers, and listening to the market and investors. Directors should look for leading indicators of potential problems, not in a perfunctory manner as is sometime the case, but in a substantive way. In taking the pulse of the bank, it is important not to place exaggerated importance on what can be carefully managed employee opinion surveys. In many banks there is a huge internal public relations campaign in the lead-up to engagement surveys, with much internal competition for score rankings. This causes executives and HR professionals to undertake an election style campaign to influence outcomes, which can sometimes feel like bordering on coercing and even bullying employees to speak positively in the survey. To help remind employees how positive things are, they are often invited to morning tea or other forms of 'town hall' meetings in the days before the survey and reminded of all the great things achieved and how important it is that they 'speak truthfully' about how they feel (with the clear message being 'speak positively'). These surveys rarely highlight concerning disconnects that can exist between the executive team and the wider workforce and in an organisational environment where staff are concerned about retaining their job, there is a natural reluctance to speak out. At Barclays, for example, in the period up to 2012, the surveys showed an increasingly positive picture. The board saw the aggregate data and was encouraged. The board did not look at the more granular data, which revealed at least two important insights: first, there were wide ranging concerns about escalating ethical issues; and second, nearly 70 per cent of those polled said that they did not believe that their leadership lived and breathed Barclays' values (Salz, 2013, p.

92). Criticising your employer is not something people are prone to do even if they are assured that the survey is confidential and that the identity of the staff member is not discoverable. Insiders in many banks share the scepticism that the rank and file at RBS had towards their employee engagement survey: 'the annual survey was about as reflective of people's genuine views about the bank as a Zimbabwean election' (Fraser, 2015, p. 149).

Depending on the nature and complexity of the bank, one other insight is to understand how closely different divisions and functions cooperate and have common goals; this can be an endemic problem in large banks where internal competition for investment and silos thrive.

PERFORMANCE EVALUATION FRAMEWORK

The most invidious aspect of bank culture can reveal itself in the annual or biannual performance rating and ranking ritual. The Performance Evaluation Framework (PEF) can come in many forms across different banks. The most common approach is to do some form of rating and then rank people on a curve that highlights the top 10 per cent and the bottom 10 per cent, modelled on the famous GE approach under the legendary Jack Welch. Different banks have a variation on a theme, which rates people, for example, on a scale from 1 to 5: 1 = very poor performance, 2 = poor performance, 3 = good performance, 4 = very good performance and 5 = exceptional performance. The rating system is normally determined across a range of factors including meeting financial targets, which is normally given a high weighting, explicitly or implicitly, in any balanced scorecard. In some banks, to augment a rating is a behavioural and cultural measure, which covers just how well an individual exhibits enterprise values and leads by example – this approach however can feel more akin to what might be associated with a totalitarian state; something from George Orwell's *1984*. The system of assigning a behavioural or cultural measure works as follows: an A rating would denote exemplary behaviours, a B would be good or satisfactory behaviours and a C would identify someone as not representing the desired behaviours in a serious way. Most employees are rated 3B; outstanding, role model style individuals would be 5A and anyone with a 2 or a 1 and a behaviour rating of C is in real trouble.

The system of rating and ranking is one that is open to abuse and is disliked by the majority of people who have to use it. It can create a dysfunctional internal culture and it can drive bankers to push for a revenue target to achieve a 4 or a 5, but in doing so they create the incentive to aggressively push sales that are not consistent with customer interests. This may lead to irresponsible lending and the cross-selling of unsuitable products and services. The system can turn bankers into quasi-electrical white goods or car salespeople, and it is corrupting of moral values in a banking industry context. An example from the UK on the mis-selling of PPI is illustrative of this, with uncanny parallels to the then CBA CEO, Ian Narev, allegedly telling Matt Comyn 'to temper his sense of justice' when Comyn raised concerns about the ethics of selling flawed insurance products to unassuming and trusting customers:

> Jayne-Anne Gadhia, a retail banking executive at RBS, was dismayed when her bosses insisted on continuing to sell PPI policies even after they were aware that it was a rip-off ... She told the UK Parliamentary Commission on Banking Standards that she spoke to a senior RBS colleague 'about the need to withdraw PPI from RBS's marketing.' The reply was, 'Yes, it's clear that that should be withdrawn, but we can't be the first people to do it because we would be the ones who lose profit first.' (Fraser, 2015, p. 147)

Another concerning aspect of the rating and ranking system,

particularly the behavioural code, is that it drives group thinking. People who are viewed as being anything other than conformist are open to being labelled 'non-enterprise leaders', which is not career enhancing. The comparison to the totalitarian state is apparent. Such classifications can also expose individuals to random discrimination, sometimes on the flimsiest of evidence and occasionally on no evidence other than hearsay or a personal vendetta. It was normally the first step in 'managing people out of the bank'. This can be done to longstanding and loyal staff who are no longer wanted, sometimes to avoid proper termination payments. The rating and ranking system can be used to 'manage them out'. This is done, particularly at relatively junior staff levels, where people are not able to defend themselves. An example of how this might be done is to set someone who has been a good, consistent performer and diligent employee, aggressive performance targets – sometimes unrealistic and unattainable – and when they fail to meet them, the process begins; a 3 or a 4 rated performer becomes a 2 or a 1 and then the dreaded C is applied, sometimes without cause. This whole approach lacks dignity and decency and is also counterproductive, because other staff members can see what is happening and say to themselves, 'there but for the grace of God'.

Although the theory of culture and values should be an integral part of evaluating leadership, in practice it can be given little weighting. In the Salz review of Barclays, the report noted: 'Our review of the performance evaluation documentation revealed little emphasis on culture and values' (Salz, 2013, p. 80). Based on the evidence from the Royal Commission and on the admissions of some CEOs, it is a fair assumption that the same would hold true of some Australian banks. Yet, it is the culture that prevailed within the banks that drove the wrong behaviours. It was the dominant culture of pursuing profit above all else that saw banks lose sight of their purpose and the failure to see that the individual and collective strategies of all the banks can create systemic risk. It was the prevailing culture that weakened the fundamental principles of professionalism in banking.[235]

CORRUPTING NATURE OF PERFORMANCE TARGETS

The rich case studies from RBS also provide examples of an aggressive sales culture that has parallels in Australia. Take the case of Donald Mackenzie, an RBS manager who was hailed internally as a hero, repeatedly top-ranked in PEFs, even named the RBS business manager of the year three times. He turned out to be a crook who had embezzled £21 million from the bank and was sentenced to 10 years in jail. The QC defending Mackenzie cited the pressure that people such as his client were put under to meet sales and lending targets (Fraser, 2015, p. 146). Parallels can be seen in Australia such as in NAB's 2016 internal paper cited in Chapter 4, which admitted that the:

> current risk culture within the Personal Bank gives prioritisation of sales at the expense of sound risk management ... While these sales practices occur, not only do they increase the credit risk but also the potential risk of facilitating terrorism financing, money laundering or other criminal activities through false or misleading applications.

There are numerous other examples, which bankers reading this book will readily attest to.

Culture change has to come from the leadership of the bank, driven by the board. Regulators cannot be the principal drivers of cultural change, though they do have a voice and a role to play

---

235 See UK Banking Standards Committee: Evidence from Douglas Flint, chairman of HSBC Plc.

given the fundamental nature of culture to the way a bank is run. In the UK, the FCA clearly states that 'All firms must be able to show consistently that fair treatment of customers is at the heart of their business model'. Regulators have to find ways of testing culture in a bank that are free from board or senior executive bias. One approach, following the lead from the APRA review of culture, governance and accountability at CBA, is to conduct an annual anonymous and confidential survey of employees. As discussed in Chapter 6, the CBA survey had 6000 respondents and provided the review team with an invaluable insight into what went on 'under the bonnet' at CBA, including a strong impression that the leadership at CBA never really took APRA seriously. It repeatedly ignored or responded with legalistic defensiveness when called to account by APRA. The APRA report found:

> a widespread sense of complacency, a reactive stance in dealing with risks, being insular and not learning from experiences and mistakes, and overly collegial and collaborative working environment which lessened the opportunity for constructive criticism, timely decision-making and a focus on outcomes.[236]

While APRA focused on CBA, the cultural problems evident in that bank are not unique to it. APRA acknowledged that the banking industry is grappling with how to manage culture and accountability and has signalled intent to raise capital adequacy levels to compensate for cultural risk.[237]

---

236 Boyd, T., 'CBA facing $500m risk fix', *Australian Financial Review*, 2 May 2018, p. 48.
237 Yeates, C., 'APRA mulls cash lift over culture risks', *The Age*, 23 May 2019, p. 24.

WHISTLEBLOWERS

Banks should do more to promote whistleblowing policies, to promote a culture of ethics and integrity. The unfortunate reality is that whistleblowers are often viewed with contempt due to the negative consternation that still comes with 'blowing the whistle' and the idea that they have somehow breached the trust of their bank. In many cases this can equate to career suicide, and potentially the individual can find themselves informally blacklisted from the entire industry. In *Post-disclosure survival strategies: transforming whistleblower experiences* (2018), Professor Marianna Fotaki of the Warwick Business School and Professor Kate Kenny of Queen's University, Belfast found that 62 per cent of whistleblowers reported being demoted or given more menial tasks, almost all eventually resigned or were dismissed. It is no wonder that most people think long and hard before 'blowing the whistle'. To its credit, NAB, in its self-awareness of its corporate governance and accountability framework, reported that one in four employees were afraid of reporting unethical behaviour for fear of retribution. Banks are very wary of whistleblowers and anyone seeking to move from one bank to another with a whistleblower 'conviction' is highly likely to be 'googled out'. This is wrong, and something must be done to address this failure.

Banks should promote the fact that whistleblowing plays an important role for the greater good of the bank. Banks need to do more to encourage staff to come forward with any concerns they may have and protect them when they have done so. In the US, individuals are rewarded financially if they 'whistle blow' and a conviction occurs. Australia should do the same.

CONCLUDING REMARKS

A bank cannot choose whether to have a culture, it can only choose the type of culture it wants to develop. Values are the foundation of culture. No board wants to hear that the bank culture has fostered a 'total disregard' for the law and regulators and that it is seen as being 'rotten to the core'.[238] This is very important to the people who work inside these organisations who, particularly the case with millennials, are increasingly interested in culture and values (Deloitte, 2017). Banks must view culture in the same way they look at financial and human capital; cultural capital can be a powerful source of comparative advantage and an equally powerful source of destruction.

Perhaps the single biggest insight into the culture in banks is the clear priority given to maximising profit over customer service and the way that senior executives are rewarded but rarely held accountable when things go wrong; a big carrot when rewarding financial outcomes and a slight tickle with a feather when any transgressions are found, even when the law is broken. The consequences below senior executive level are harsher and the further down the organisation, the greater the pain. This style of leadership and the culture that it represents is hugely damaging both within the bank and in the eyes of society, yet all the evidence says it is pervasive.

In their book *In search of excellence* (1982), Tom Peters and Robert Waterman point out that 'poorer-performing companies often have strong cultures, too, but dysfunctional ones. They are often focused on internal politics and they focus on "the numbers" rather on the customer or the people' (Fraser, 2015, p. 150).

Within many of our banks, these cultural problems have been lingering for some time but they have been disguised by a benign

---

238 Ferguson, A., 'Disregard, lack of respect: NAB leads poorly behaved pack', *Sydney Morning Herald*, 25 August 2018, p. 26.

economic environment and a housing market that has kept on giving. It would have been very hard not to have done well in such circumstances and in a highly privileged industry structure. The only pressure that was really placed on the banks was that of meeting investor expectations of growing revenues, lowering expenses and a higher ROE. What occurred was that these quantitative measure of success, or what is *counted*, were achieved at the expense of what *counts*, that is, reputation, professional conduct, ethical behaviour and customer and societal trust. The success of the banks was, as *The Economist* reported, 'through a litany of abuses ... by a consumer-crushing oligopoly'.[239] The MIT study referenced earlier, emphasised that firms rarely get to the root cause of their cultural problems: 'Companies are often so concerned with appearance and damage control that they are unwilling to engage in the degree of examination required to root out the entrenched causes of trust violations.' History says that, despite numerous internal campaigns, 'town halls', training programs and surveys, this will be true of our major banks.

Transforming a bank's culture is very hard and most cultural change programs fail to stick given the powerful path dependent nature of culture in banks. This is because in part there is a lack of urgency or a burning platform for change; in part because there is little tangible evidence that culture and values influence financial rewards in the PEFs; and in part because of the so-called permafrost of the much-maligned middle management, which does not believe that the change program will stand the test of time given CEO tenure cycles, and that a new leader will set the bank on a different course. In some cases, where change is forced on the bank, say by a regulator, middle management can sense that top management is being coerced into something that it is less than enthusiastic about. In many ways culture change programs can be

---

239 'Australian banks – the charge sheet', *The Economist*, 6 October 2018, p. 58.

like asking the dog to stand on its two hind legs given the prospect of a treat. As soon as the treat is withdrawn, or senior leadership attention is diverted, the dog will revert to all four legs and only respond again to the incentive of another treat. Not a sustainable approach. Prospects of success are enhanced when new leadership is brought in. Gerstner succeeded at IBM, Joss did the same at Westpac and McFarlane at ANZ, and all came from outside. The prospect of an incumbent CEO or an internal replacement with a history within the bank achieving this is rarely evidenced. It is also unlikely that someone without deep banking experience could successfully change the culture within a bank.

People are products of the stories of their upbringing and environment. Professionally, we are greatly shaped by our early career and the beliefs that come from that culture, be it law, accounting, consulting or banking. People are influenced greatly by the leaders they see early in their career. These leaders and the culture they represent inform others of what it takes to succeed, of what values count and what do not. Hence leadership and culture cannot be separated; they go hand in glove. A bank cannot have a broken culture and great leadership; it is an oxymoron. Yet many leaders thrive and are well rewarded in banks with deep cultural problems. Why? An ineffective board of directors is the only reason this can happen.

A board has an important role to play in protecting the culture in a bank and ensuring that the culture is consistent with the stated values. In assessing the cultural health of a bank, its board must start with simple first principles or ABC – attitude, behaviour and consequences. The challenge, however, is if the boards are up to leading cultural change, when there is evidence that the core cultural problem within many banks starts with the board. The fish rots from the head. The next chapter discusses the challenging role of the board of directors.

7
THE ROLE OF THE BOARD OF DIRECTORS

AT a time of an extraordinary crisis in societal confidence in the purpose and governance of banks, the leadership demands placed on bank boards have never been so acute. Boards must re-establish the moral and ethical purpose of the banks they lead; no other priority should come close to competing with that imperative. But are bank boards up to the task? Is there a burning platform for action or will bank boards, looking to each other, do the minimum required to satisfy regulatory demands for change? Will lawyers and consultants rather than leaders shape the industry response to the demands for change?

Banks are complex organisations. Added to this complexity is the fact that BEAR, discussed in Chapter 4, covers non-executive directors (NEDs), who have personal obligations to take reasonable steps to prevent matters that can adversely affect the bank's prudential standing or reputation. Despite this, membership of a bank board is a keenly sought-after prize in the eyes of many, even though the demands and expectations placed on NEDs have never been greater. It is no longer the cosy transition from executive life to retirement. Nor should it be.

In his report into Barclays, Salz (2013, p. 99) noted that given the systemic importance of major banks, 'attracting the strongest and best qualified people to non-executive roles should be a concern to us all'. The emphasis on 'best qualified' is important, which we return to later in this chapter.

Many who have an interest in the business world believed that by following the reforms from scandals such as Enron, WorldCom and HIH, the era of poor governance had largely been addressed; there are more board committees and volume upon volume of board and annual report disclosures, all of which are visible evidence of greater transparency, and often highly descriptive policies and procedures. The paradox of this well-intended drive for greater transparency is that compliance-driven disclosures offer volume and ambiguity over brevity and clarity, and unfortunately the issues so evident back at the beginning of the twenty-first century remain prevalent two decades later, as the Royal Commission and the APRA review into CBA have so clearly highlighted. That nothing much of substance has changed is captured in a *Financial Times* feature in 2002, which summed up the situation with words that would be current today:

> At the heart of the Enron scandal is a failure of corporate governance … An audit committee that signed off on misleading accounts. A board that was ineffective in supervising senior managements actions. These failures are all too common. Similar lapses can be found in most other big corporate scandals. And they exist, too, in companies where there are no scandals, merely poor performance or entrenched mediocrity.[240]

The corporate governance at HBOS and RBS highlight how so much has changed and yet how so little has changed. Both banks had elaborate corporate governance structures designed by the leading experts in the field and both were supported by a large

---

240 Gapper, J., 'Enron lessons not unique', *Financial Times*, 19 February 2002.

department of risk and governance specialists. The annual report from both banks consumed between 40 and 50 pages on the sophistication of corporate governance. Yet despite this, corporate governance at both banks failed badly. The RBS and HBOS boards, comprising highly credentialed directors, turned out to be anything but good stewards or custodians of the business. This is what the chairman of HBOS wrote in the 2007 annual report:

> For 2008 we will continue to pay careful attention to the importance of both strong capital and strong liquidity and to size our balance sheet to the certainty of both. We are, I believe, rightly proud as a board that we have been altering the risk profile of our liquidity requirements ... purely as part of being good custodians of your business. You may be quite sure that we will continue to bring to bear the same standards of rigour and financial conservatism as the business moves forward.

Within months, the bank was a train wreck and had been revealed as running one of the riskiest funding and capital positions in the market, with close to half of its lending funded from the short-dated wholesale markets (a liquidity profile not dissimilar to several Australian banks back then). The boards at HBOS and RBS lacked the relevant banking expertise despite the considerable risk management and governance resources that were available to both boards. It is hard to escape the conclusion that the NEDs did not understand the bank and the implications of the risks it was taking. This lack of relevant banking experience at chair and director level plagues too many bank boards.

BOARD CULTURE

The theme of board culture was something that Harvard's Michael Jensen (1993) discussed when he concluded that the problem is that 'board culture is an important component of board failure'. What Jensen meant by this is that the emphasis on the 'old boy network' and courtesy at the expense of truth and frankness in boardrooms is both a symptom and a failure in the control system. Jensen's views are almost 30 years old, yet they could equally have been made today.

Corporate governance expert Bob Garratt (1997) famously said, 'the fish rots from the head' when describing the root problem of so many corporate scandals. The culture within a bank is a core responsibility of the board and an integral part of corporate governance. The Walker report commissioned by the UK government in 2009 to examine corporate governance within the banking sector, focused mainly on risk management, board composition and board effectiveness, but did not address culture. The author, Sir David Walker, later acknowledged that a major omission from the report was 'culture' and that had he been writing the report today, greater attention would have been given to how culture is at the root of much that went wrong within the banking sector in the lead-up to the GFC (Stigter & Cooper, 2018). While the Walker report did not focus on culture, the Salz review of Barclays (2013) placed much more emphasis on culture, from the boardroom to the coalface.

As discussed in several places in this book, one of the most obvious board failings has been on the culture within the banks and an absence of real accountability for poor outcomes. A whole range of early warning signs were largely discounted so long as the financial results of the bank were in line with expectations. Boards have long known that culture and conduct are heavily influenced by incentives and that those incentives are heavily weighted to financial outcomes. This is true regardless of whether a balanced scorecard exists with multiple well-diversified categories, ensuring that at least an average or satisfactory score (3B) is achieved given that many categories are subjective and easily gamed. Customer service suffers, as it has been doing in banking for many years, but the oligopoly industry structure and customer inertia mean that this abuse can go on without material financial consequences. So long as the economy does not turn, the financial outcomes, given the pricing power that the banks have, is largely locked in. Boards have to reflect on this context and dig deep, as the APRA inquiry into CBA did, into what the real culture is within the bank and, in doing so, understand if conduct and compliance problems were being merely 'relegated to a cost of doing business'. They need to know what the customer and risk management culture is as described by staff close to the coalface of the bank and not as presented by senior executives. In dealing with these issues, particularly incentives, boards may feel trapped in a 'prisoner's dilemma' of not wanting to change their position in case others choose a different course. Major bank boards like to 'stay in the pack'. No bank board has demonstrated the courage to fundamentally change senior executive remuneration in case no one else does. Therefore, the regulator must step in and do the job that the board was appointed to do. The disappointing evidence to date is that there is little courage to address problems that are hard to miss – that of culture, remuneration and accountability.

BOARDS AND SOCIAL LICENCE

Bank boards need to spend time discussing the social licence that the bank has and how the bank is conducting itself in terms of that licence. They need to ask: How does the strategy of the bank align with its social purpose? How does the culture of the bank align with its social purpose? Banks also have to understand what is meant when society says 'banks are different', and having a primarily self-serving Friedman Doctrine interpretation of shareholder focus as a measure of success is to misunderstand the importance of the social licence to operate. Lord Turner, the former FSA chairman, captured the real meaning of 'banks are different' when he said:

> Banks are different and society has an interest in bankers taking a different attitude to the balance between risk and reward to that which applies to the rest of the economy … their failure is of public concern, not just a concern for shareholder.[241]

In his review of Barclays, Salz (2013) commented, 'Banks matter. They hold a unique position in our society.' The FSA report went on to add comments regarding the RBS board, which are lessons for all bank boards: 'the board appears to have displayed inadequate sensitivity to the wholly exceptional and, compared with other companies, unique importance of customer and counterparty confidence in a bank and its chosen strategy.'[242] Very similar utterances were expressed in the final Royal Commission report.

Prior to the Royal Commission, a temptation for most Australian bank boards would be to say that when the bank is among the most profitable in the world, what is the problem? The reality is, as with HBOS and RBS, that those problems were there to be seen if the boards had been knowledgeable, curious, inquisitive and alert to questioning and had taken steps to independently verify what they were being told. A useful heuristic for NEDs is to probe with equal rigour those parts of the bank that are outperforming, just as they should for those parts that are underperforming. In other

---

241 Financial Services Authority Board, *The failure of the Royal Bank of Scotland: report*, December 2011, pp. 4–5, <https://www.fca.org.uk>.
242 Ibid, p. 229.

words, if they had their finger on the pulse and knew what to look for, NEDs would have been alerted to the problems in many banks long before they became a major problem. The APRA report into CBA outlined a deeply ingrained flawed culture, but it could easily have been a report on several other banks and their boards, as the evidence from the Royal Commission would suggest. A responsible assumption is that the dulled senses that permeated the CBA board were not specific to them; they were, in many ways, just unfortunate to be the case study. The criticism of NAB's governance culture by the Royal Commission is an example that CBA was not alone. Absent some of the scandals that plagued CBA in modern times, the failures of that board would have gone unnoticed, as they have done in some other boardrooms, given the emphasis on financial performance. The same would be true of NAB, that absent the Royal Commission's findings, not much in terms of governance or culture would have changed. The criticism by the Royal Commission that 'Overall, my fear – that there may be a wide gap between the public face NAB seeks to show and what it does in practice – remains'[243] would have gone without public scrutiny in what is one of Australia's largest and most important companies.

COMPETING PRIORITIES

Some bank directors have argued that after the GFC, the priority of bank boards has been heavily weighted towards financial risk, particularly the strength of the liability side of the balance sheet. An appropriate response, but one that does not go far enough. Given the CVs of the board members and the size of most bank boards, society would have a reasonable expectation that they

---

[243] Danckert, S., 'Hayne unleashes on NAB boss and chairman', *Sydney Morning Herald*, 4 February 2019.

were capable of the *and* not the *or*; in other words, the financial risk in the banks *and* the strategy *and* the overall risk management framework *and* the risk to the housing market *and* the culture within the bank *and* the technology risk embedded in legacy systems *and* the performance of the CEO *and* C-suite executives in managing well today *and* making the bank future proof. Isn't that what directors are supposed to do? The CBA case highlighted how ineffective boards can be and how disconnected they can be to the reasonable expectations that society has of them. The then chairman of CBA, according to a media report based on the APRA inquiry, was highly illustrative of the problem:

> The Chairman's face-to-face meetings with the CEO were not sufficiently frequent to develop a targeted agenda or understand pressing issues. The Chair of the Audit Committee regularly failed to close issues in a timely manner related to anti-money laundering and counter terrorism financing despite numerous red flags.[244]

Uncharacteristically, in Australia, the Treasury has also been critical of how bank boards have performed and the complacency that financial success has caused. The Treasury said that bank profits have been propped up by a lack of effective competition, which has led to a collective dulling of the senses of board members:

> Despite their conduct failures, many financial services firms have continued to generate strong profits assisted by a lack of effective competition. In these circumstances, boards seem to have had their 'senses dulled' to the significance of the misconduct by their firm and its employees, and shareholders have had little incentive to intervene.[245]

---

244 Boyd, T., 'CBA facing $500m risk fix', *Australian Financial Review*, 2 May 2018, p. 48.
245 Frost, J., 'Treasury lashes boards' "dulled senses"', *Australian Financial Review*, 27 July 2018, p. 4.

We return to some of the challenge's boards face in overseeing banks, but it is important to first recognise some of the real issues facing boards in exercising their stewardship responsibilities. A big part of the problem that bank boards must grapple with is the ever growing demands placed on them by the laws, regulations and codes of conduct. It is difficult, given these demands, to spend enough quality time on culture and strategy.

GETTING FROM THE DANCE FLOOR TO THE BALCONY

Today, many directors not only have to grapple with increasingly complex issues of a fast-changing environment, in particular the disruptive influence of digitalisation and cybersecurity risks, but with the ever growing and often mind-numbing 'box-ticking' compliance requirements together with the never-ending pressure of rising expectations, often in the form of short-term earnings growth. It is no surprise that boards struggle to stay on top of the range of issues that they are expected to be across, but this cannot be allowed to be an excuse for poor corporate governance. This is a harsh assessment but one that reflects the tendency for directors to be strong on regulatory compliance and delivering earnings-per-share growth while poor on bank strategy, risk management and culture.

This ever-expanding workload is what experts call a boardroom information crisis. As a general observation, it has become very difficult for even the most diligent board members to absorb, digest and reflect on all the material they are sent. This in turn creates frustration on the part of management, who are frequently left aghast at the poor recollection of the detail of board topics discussed not so long ago. The reality is that the sheer burden of largely compliance-based paperwork and range of matters that can find their way onto a board agenda leaves little time for the big strategic and cultural issues, materially hampering board effectiveness. Most directors will testify to the reality that there is little time to 'get off the dance floor and onto the balcony' to consider the major strategic, cultural and risk management themes that will shape and determine the future of the bank.

Repeating themes from Carter and Lorsch's excellent book *Back to the drawing board* (2003) – and reminding us how little has changed – in a thoughtful *Harvard Business Review* article[246] the authors highlighted the challenges that many boards face in both allocating enough time to understanding and then preparing for the future. The constraints on time and, in the case of many sectors, the increasing regulatory burden boards must manage, together with the pressure in ensuring that short-term results are delivered, means that insufficient quality time is spent on factors critical to the future success of the firm.

One of the burning questions for most boards is how long do they have to adapt the current business for the future and does the bank have the management capabilities to shape that future rather than being shaped by it? Too many boards resign their destiny to industry forces and regulatory imposts and do not believe they and management can outperform or reshape industry norms. The impulse of most management teams is to follow the herd, that way no one can single them out if things go wrong.

In most businesses, directors are simply appraising and signing off on strategy rather than playing a central role in shaping strategic thinking. A big part of the issue in banking is that too many directors have a weak appreciation of the bank's value chain, economic engine, financial sensitivities and industry dynamics, and even less knowledge about the major risks that the bank faces. It is not enough that these matters are considered the sole domain

---

[246] Hill, L. A., 'The board's new innovation imperative', *Harvard Business Review*, November–December 2017, pp. 103–109.

of the Board Risk Committee; *all* directors have to be across these issues. In banking, technology is another area of primary risk, with many banks running on antiquated systems, which are exposed to breakdown and to cyber attacks. Don Argus highlighted this and other issues in an opinion piece in a leading newspaper: 'the Royal Commission quite rightly raised questions about the knowledge of boards of Australian banks ... with legacy systems a real challenge for financial institutions when they transform from old products to new digitalised technology.'[247]

Paradoxically, a related theme is the curse of conservatism or risk aversion. The paradox of this mindset is that avoiding risk may only add to the risks facing the bank in the long term. In their excellent book *Boards that dare*, Stigter and Cooper (2018) call this courage; the courage to express views, challenge decisions and not hide behind consensus. The next time you read that important decisions were made by 'unanimous board consensus', ask yourself: has the board been captured by consensus or a groupthink mindset and is it lacking in individual courage? This is particularly acute in banking, where there is evidence that incumbents are locked into a path dependent future, a future that is a continuation of the past, while new technologically advantaged and agile challengers attack profit pools within the industry. The concern is that boards can find their agenda consumed by regulatory compliance, including satisfying the ASX Corporate Governance Principles, where the emphasis is on 'tick the box' compliance-oriented work, which research by McKinsey & Company (2018) suggests can take around 70 per cent of board time.[248] As a consequence, boards struggle to focus on strategy and/or culture, which are core to the bank's future success, to being strategically and operationally future proof.

---

247 Gottliebsen, R., 'Argus put bank directors under the microscope', *The Australian*, 21 August 2018, p. 28.

248 <https://www.mckinsey.com/business-functions/strategy-and-corporate-finance/our-insights/building-a-forward-looking-board>.

This is a very serious issue. Ironically, some management teams take comfort in the fact that boards are tied up on compliance matters as it keeps them away from meddling in strategy and operations; a classic illustration of the principal–agent problem, where owners (principals), through the board, have difficulty monitoring the activities of management (agents). The strategic agenda can be a once or twice a year deep dive, often at glamorous offsite locations, steered by management PowerPoints, which can leave many directors feeling that they are being 'managed' and their contribution is at best perfunctory, in a skilful execution by management of a highly choreographed event, where information 'dumping' is the order of the day.

Sir David Walker, in his review of corporate governance in UK banks, highlighted issues equally evident in Australian banks:

> The pressure for conformity on boards can be strong, generating corresponding difficulty for an individual board member who wishes to challenge group thinking. Such a challenge on substantive policy issues can be seen as disruptive, non-collegial and even as disloyal ... Critically relevant to success of the challenge process in any well-functioning board will be the demeanour and capability of the CEO, who is unlikely to be in the role without having displayed qualities of competence and toughness which are not dependably tolerant of challenge. Even a strong and established CEO may have a degree of concern, if not resentment, that challenge from the NEDs is unproductively time-consuming, adding little or no value, and might intrude on or constrain the ability of the executive team to implement the agreed strategy. [249]

Managing and balancing this natural tension is greatly assisted when NEDs have knowledge of the industry. The lack of board banking expertise can be even shallower when it comes

---

[249] Sir David Walker, *A Review of corporate governance in UK banks and other financial industry entities: final recommendations*, 26 November 2009, pp. 53–4, <https://webarchive.nationalarchives.gov.uk/+/www.hm-treasury.gov.uk/d/walker_review_261109.pdf>.

to considering the risks and opportunities from digitalisation or exploring the strategic options that the bank should create to position itself for growth. As Don Argus commented:

> The royal commission has quite rightly raised questions about the knowledge of boards of Australian banks and whether they understood the risks associated with products being sold by people who it appears had little knowledge of the product being sold, not to mention the technology support and how that integrated with the traditional bank system.[250]

Board members are susceptible to all the anxieties that any human can encounter, and this can include a resistance to change, where individual board members may feel that their relevance is at threat and a sense of impostor syndrome takes grip. They can feel that their capabilities are not up to the job; this can be a real dilemma as people become accustomed to the prestige of being on a bank board.

BOARD CAPABILITIES

Very much consistent with the UK, in what looks to outsiders like a very incestuous world, most Australian directors are sourced from a very narrow and shallow pool in what is often described as a 'cosy, clubbish' world. Too many consultants, lawyers and accountants dominate board position and too few directors have relevant practical banking experience – without the practical, hands-on experience of banking, judgement can be dulled regardless of the intellectual prowess of the individual. The 'blink' instinct that Malcolm Gladwell (2005) described, is absent. Bank boards need directors who are curious of and have insights into

---

250 Argus, D., 'Banks must go back to basics to regain public trust', *The Australian*, 18–19 August 2018, p. 28.

the changing nature of the global and domestic economy, of technology, of banking and a strong sense of what can go wrong if the fundamentals are not respected.

The question of relevant capabilities is a major issue. Research by Watermark showed that less than 20 per cent of the top 300 directors in Australia had direct industry experience relevant to the company on whose board they sit, while close to 50 per cent had a legal or accounting/financial background.[251] A leading newspaper captured this when it wrote: 'Australia's boardrooms have a problem. Too many people who sit on them are not up to the job because they are drawn from narrow circles, or are more interested in building their own brand than their firm's.'[252] Aligned to this, is the 2014 research by University of New South Wales (UNSW) professor of finance Peter Swan, which demonstrated, in the 200 Australian firms covered by the research, that the emphasis on 'independent boards' had cost shareholders upwards of $50 billion over the previous decade. Swan concludes that 'ASX governance guidelines, and proxy firms which push firms to appoint generalist directors, are robbing boards of vital insights and sapping shareholder returns.'[253] In reviewing corporate governance in the UK following the GFC, the Financial Stability Board (FSB) noted: 'The crisis highlighted that many boards had directors with little financial industry experience and limited understanding of the rapidly increasing complexity of the institutions they were leading.'[254]

The Basel Committee (2006) focused on what it believed to be important corporate governance principles specific to the banking industry. The principles were established as 'guidance' and not as

---

251 Evans, S., Durkin, P., Thompson, B., & LaFrenze, C. 'Too many lawyers, accountants "surfing" boards', *Australian Financial Review*, 18 May 2018.

252 'The questions that hang over our boardrooms', *Australian Financial Review*, 18 May 2018.

253 Eyers, J., 'Exposing a cosy club of corporate board box-tickers', *Australian Financial Review*, 2 August 2018, p. 47.

254 Financial Stability Board, *Thematic Review of Risk Governance*, 11 February 2013, p. 1.

a replacement of existing national legislation, regulation or codes, but nonetheless, they went someway to provide a nudge as to what capabilities and requirements should define a bank board. The Basel Principles on Corporate Governance are as follows:

1. Board members should be qualified for their positions, have a clear understanding of their role in corporate governance and be able to exercise sound judgement about the affairs of the bank.
2. The board of directors should approve and oversee the bank's strategic objectives and corporate values that are communicated throughout the bank.
3. The board of directors should set and enforce clear lines of responsibility and accountability throughout the bank.
4. The board should ensure that there is appropriate oversight by senior management consistent with board policy.
5. The board and senior management should effectively utilise the work conducted by the internal audit function, external auditors and internal control function.
6. The board should ensure that compensation policies and practices are consistent with the bank's corporate culture, long-term objectives and strategy, and control environment.
7. The bank should be governed in a transparent manner.
8. The board and senior management should understand the bank's operational structure, including where the bank operates in jurisdictions or through structures that impede transparency (i.e. 'know-your-structure').

These eight principles provide a useful framework to assess corporate governance within banks. It is productive for the reader to reflect on how the boards of major Australian banks have satisfied these principles. In addition to the examples of board failure cited throughout this book, including the shocking corporate governance failures at RBS and HBOS, several contemporary case studies involving major banks highlight that progress has been slow and that there is much work to do to ensure that boards and corporate governance are fit for purpose.

CASE STUDY: COMMONWEALTH BANK OF AUSTRALIA

CBA enjoyed stellar financial and stock market performance in the decade up to 2017/18, which saw its senior executives richly rewarded. Largely undetected through internal control systems but evident externally to competitors, an arrogant and damaging culture had taken root within the bank over many years, which prompted the banking regulator to launch a public inquiry into CBA's culture and governance. This was felt necessary after so many egregious scandals such as selling life insurance policies that were made difficult for customers to make a claim on, including evidence of doctors being bullied into rejecting legitimate claims. This coincided with the fraud in the bank's financial planning division, which management tried to cover up by sanitising files and then lying to ASIC.[255] To cap things off, there was the blind eye turned to money laundering through the bank's 'smart' ATMs and other policy and legal breaches that were highlighted by staff but ignored by management. With parallels to events at the US bank Wells Fargo, the CBA culture extended to illicit sales practices such as creating fictitious accounts in the name of children to boost a performance metric. The litany of scandals that plagued CBA was unprecedented.[256]

The APRA initiated review of CBA found that:
- There was a widespread sense of complacency throughout

---

255 Morris, J., 'I gift wrapped Commonwealth Bank for ASIC and it did nothing', *Sydney Morning Herald*, 20 April 2018.

256 Ferguson, A., 'Governance takes centre stage', *Australian Financial Review*, 30 April 2018.

the bank, starting at the top.
- The bank was reactive in dealing with risk.
- A slow, legalistic and reactive, at times dismissive, culture also characterised many of CBA's dealings with regulators.
- The bank was insular. It did not reflect on and learn from experience and mistakes, including at board and senior leadership levels.
- A remuneration framework that ... had little sting for senior managers when poor risk or customer outcomes materialised.[257]

The APRA report found that 'there was a complacent culture, dismissive of regulators, an ineffective board that lacked zeal and failed to provide oversight, a lack of accountability and ownership of key risks by senior executives, a remuneration framework that had no bite.' Quite a damning assessment on the board of one of Australia's leading firms and the country's leading bank as measured by market capitalisation.

CBA's board relied too heavily on management, leading to 'a level of complacency' and 'dulling of the sense' within the board.[258] These are gentle, diplomatic words consistent with what one would expect from regulators, which simply say that the board failed to exercise its duty of care and, perhaps by inference, that the board was not up to the job. This was also apparent when the CBA chair, Catherine Livingston, faced the Royal Commission, admitting that detailed board discussions on sensitive matters were not always subject to board minutes. A practice that has since improved under her chairmanship.

---

257 White, A., 'Complacent, reactive, insular', *The Australian*, 2 May 2018.
258 Gordon, T., 'Boards need more than accountants and lawyers', *Australian Financial Review*, 23 May 2018.

What was also apparent was the collapse of the Three Lines of Defence within CBA. One CBA manager said that her team felt 'vindicated and relieved when they read the APRA report'. An internal auditor wrote: 'Frankly there is not much in the APRA report that audit has not said before, but perhaps we need to improve in the area of articulating our views.' Highlighting just how CBA was not an outlier in facing problems, the then NAB CEO acknowledged that there was 'a culture of us not learning from issues of misconduct in the past. That's why I said we get into a period of ongoing remediation without fundamentally understanding the root cause in each of those matters.'[259]

At CBA, nemesis had followed hubris as it had done at HBOS and RBS; and as it had done at NAB, almost 15 years earlier.

CASE STUDY: NATIONAL AUSTRALIA BANK

The NAB board was plagued for more than a decade by the harrowing experiences of the foreign exchange scandal in 2004 and the board implosion that followed.[260]

Following a series of mishaps, including the disaster associated with the 1998 acquisition of US-based mortgage servicer HomeSide Lending Inc. where the bank wrote off $4 billion,[261] NAB found itself embroiled in a $360 million foreign exchange loss as a result of fraudulent behaviour in its dealing room. The board appointed PwC to investigate the losses, a move that was resisted by one of the independent directors, Catherine Walter. Ms Walter's view was that PwC was too close to many of the NAB

---

259 Pash, C., 'Senior CBA executives knew the bank's culture was failing customers', *Business Insider*, 19 November 2018.

260 'How Cathy Walter fought the brotherhood', *Sydney Morning Herald*, 1 September 2004, p. 23.

261 McConnell, P., 'National Australia Bank – 30 years of strategy failure', *The Conversation*, 23 February 2016, p. 10.

directors and that their ability to be independent was conflicted by these relationships. (NAB's association at board level with PwC alumni remains a feature some 15 years later.)[262] With parallels to the board implosion at AMP in 2018, Ms Walter also felt that the board would seek to influence the findings of the investigation to protect their own reputation:

> There I was on the board of one of the icon firms in Australia feeling that there was dodging, a fudging, of issues in a way that went to the interests of shareholders. There was no shortage of opposition to my views ... accounting firms, law firms, some sections of the media ... A friend said it looked to him as if I were not so much having a disagreement in a boardroom but rather having a disagreement with some of those old style trade unionists resisting labour market deregulation with cries that 'unity is everything' and 'solidarity forever'.

Ms Walter found that she was in battle to protect board independence ahead of collegiality, where a defensive board, not dissimilar to the Wells Fargo case cited below, was intent on protecting its own reputation rather than facing the serious concerns over independence and failure of corporate governance, in a bank that had been exposed as having a poor culture.

Readers will find it interesting to contrast APRA's 2018 investigation into CBA with their 2004 report on NAB – *Report into irregular currency option trading at the National Australia Bank*. In its report, APRA found that at NAB:

- *Line Management* turned a blind eye to known risk management concerns. Despite some worrying signals of irregular trading practices on the currency option desk, these were ignored. 'Profit is king' was an expression frequently heard in our interview with Corporate and Institutional Banking (CIB)

---

262 <https://www.nab.com.au>about-us>board>.

staff. As long as the business unit turned a profit, other shortcomings could be overlooked.
- *Executive Risk Committees* were particularly ineffective, missing or dismissing risk information pertinent to the problems that emerged and failing to escalate warnings. If the members of the Risk Management Committee had acted on warning signs before them – for example, by commissioning a targeted review of known control weaknesses by Internal Audit – the irregular trading would surely have been discovered.
- *The Principal Board (the Board)* was not sufficiently proactive on risk issues. Despite often asserting that risk issues were of such importance that they should be dealt with by the full board, the Board paid insufficient attention to risk issues.[263]

The APRA report went on to say that 'cultural issues are the heart of these failings … The culture that predominated in CIB at NAB was one in which risk management controls were seen as trip-wires to be negotiated rather than presenting any genuine constraint in risk-behaviour.'[264] APRA insisted that there had to be 'cultural change' at the bank.[265]

In comparing NAB in 2004 and CBA in 2018, and then reflecting on the regulatory findings into HBOS and RBS, readers will be excused for feeling a sense of deja vu. Bank boards do not learn the lessons from history; they constantly fall into the trap of 'this time is different'.

In NAB's case, the bank had developed an unfortunate reputation for being 'accident prone' as it stumbled through a sequence of costly errors. These events led to 20 years of underperformance.

---

263 APRA, *Report into irregular currency option trading at the National Australia Bank*, 23 March 2004, <www.apra.gov.au>.
264 Ibid.
265 Letts, S., 'NAB entrenches itself as Australia's most accident-prone bank as it sets off up a mountain', *ABC News*, 7 May 2019.

Fast forward from 2004 to 2018/19 and the Royal Commission:

> It is open to the Commissioner to find that there were a number of causes of misconduct which are attributable to the culture and governance practices at NAB as well as its risk management, recruitment and remuneration practices.[266]

In the final report, the Commissioner questioned whether NAB had learnt the lessons of the past and whether the current management and board were capable of reforming the bank's culture.[267] In all this, society is justified in asking: Where was the board? Where is the institutional memory?

CASE STUDY: WELLS FARGO

In the US, the case of one-time global banking role model Wells Fargo is an illustrative study into 'success is toxic', board hubris and the risk of regulatory intervention absent effective board leadership. In 2018, the US Federal Reserve (Fed) moved to sack four Wells Fargo directors while accusing the board of failing to prevent 'wide spread consumer abuses'.[268] The Fed went on to say that the bank's balance sheet was capped at US$2 trillion and was barred from any expansion until such time that the regulatory officials were satisfied with the bank's governance.

While the Fed stopped short of imposing individual penalties on the four fired directors, the statement of intent was clear. The Fed was putting the directors on notice, and perhaps sending

---

266 Thomson, J., 'Hayne may find series of wrongdoings', *Australian Financial Review*, 24–25 March 2018, p. 22.
267 Smyth, J., 'Australia must begin to rebuild trust in banks', *Financial Times*, 5 February 2019.
268 Gray, A. & McLannahan, B., 'Fed puts banks on notice with action against Wells Fargo', *Financial Times*, 6 February 2018, p. 19.

a textbook example to regulators in other jurisdictions that negligence in performing their duties would have consequences. As a leading financial analyst quoted in the referenced article said, 'Any finance executive thinking that getting onto a bank board would be a cushy, mail-it-in, part-time retirement hobby needs to think again.'

The Fed intervention followed months of resistance from the Wells Fargo board to market pressure for a clear-out of directors. An 'independent' report produced for the directors about the scandals that had engulfed the bank concluded that while board actions 'could have been improved', they felt that they had been 'misinformed by management'. In response, the Fed blasted the Wells Fargo board for failing to oversee the bank.[269] The Wells Fargo board finally agreed to submit a plan to the Fed within 60 days on how it would improve board oversight and risk management practices.

Wells Fargo, like CBA, had become an industry icon, a bank whose management Warren Buffet had praised as being 'brilliant', but its reputation had been built on a foundation of sand. In a very short period Wells Fargo went from being perceived as one of the world's best run banks to a horror movie in management scandals and board ineptitude. From a rooster to a duster. Erik Gordon, a professor at the University of Michigan, summed up the gravity of the situation when he said: 'The bank is lucky it is too big to shut down. A smaller bank might have lost its banking licence.'[270] The Fed criticised the bank for:

> pursuing a business strategy that prioritized its overall growth without ensuring appropriate management of all key risks. The firm did not have an effective firm-wide risk management framework in place that covered

---

269 Flitter, E., Appelbaum, B. & Cowley, S., 'Federal Reserve shackles Wells Fargo after fraud scandal', *New York Times*, 2 February 2018, p. 14.
270 Ibid.

all key risks. This prevented the proper escalation of serious compliance breakdowns to the board of directors.[271]

The parallels to the criticism of the CBA governance framework are uncanny, just as the parallels are between AMP in 2018 and NAB in 2004 and 2019. Not much has changed, despite volumes of compliance-based reporting, which if anything has served to further dull the senses. It is hard to escape the conclusion that the current modus operandi for many bank boards is simply not fit-for-purpose.

MORE ACTIVE BOARDS

When Archie Norman became chairman of Marks & Spencer he moved to replace a number of senior executives, making it clear at the early stages of his chairmanship that he would be actively involved in C-suite appointments,[272] something most boards leave solely to the CEO.

In the normal course, bank boards learn to manage what is a fine balance, by sticking to three guiding principles:

1. Ensure that the bank has the best management team possible (not just the CEO) and take (early) steps to replace them if necessary. Many boards leave this far too late by which time the damage is evident; this damage can often be sourced to poor C-suite appointments by the CEO, where personal loyalties and associations can go back a long way and cloud judgement. Cronyism in the C-suite can lead to cronyism at the levels below. This had been an endemic problem in

---

271 Gara, A., 'No slap on the wrist: Wells Fargo plunges after Federal Reserve bars lender's growth', *Forbes*, 5 February 2018, p. 6.

272 Hipwell, D., 'The retail wizard putting M&S under his spell', *The Times*, 23 April 2018, pp. 34–35.

some banks. Central to making sure that the right checks and balances are in place is to ensure that a high calibre HR executive is given the same emphasis at board level as is accorded to the CFO and CRO.

2. Ensure that the strategic direction and investment decisions of the bank are positioning the business for success tomorrow as well as for today (and in this context having a clear view on the impact of digitalisation, emerging competitors and its strategic future).

3. Ensure that the culture within the bank is healthy and sensitive to wider societal expectations on how the business should conduct its affairs, including on important matters such as gender equity in both opportunity and pay. To do this effectively a board must have its fingers on the pulse and have a clear understanding of its culture, including subcultures. In this regard, the feedback loops are critical.

These guiding principles help inform the six core responsibilities of the board:

1. Select, evaluate and, if necessary, replace the CEO. Ensure that there is a high calibre HR executive in place. Determine management compensation, ensuring that it is aligned with societal expectations and not seen as excessive rent-seeking. Review succession planning on a half-yearly basis, with a list of internal and external candidates. Watch carefully CEOs who are prone to frequent leadership restructures. Management continuity can be a key success factor. A CEO who is frequently restructuring, firing or losing key talent, is sending a signal that the board should not ignore. This was very evident at NAB between 2014 and 2018, when virtually the whole team assembled in late 2014 had left or moved roles by mid-2018.[273]

---

273 Gluyas, R., 'How a single page destroyed a chairman and his CEO', *The Australian*, 9–10 February 2019, p. 28.

2. Play an active role in all C-suite appointments, remembering that As attract As and Bs attract Bs and Cs. Boards that allow CEOs a free hand in appointing senior executives are abdicating responsibility. Many weak management teams form under a weak leader; executives who 'manage up' and present well do not always make for successful CEOs or C-suite executives. CEOs can have blind spots or be compromised by longstanding personal relationships and other forms of association.
3. Review and, where appropriate, approve financial objectives, major strategies and the business plan. Play an active not a passive role in strategy formulation. In playing an active role, this is not to undermine the authority of the CEO.
4. Provide advice and counsel to top management and stay very engaged, unlike the criticism of David Turner when he was chairman at CBA.
5. Select and recommend to shareholders for election an appropriate slate of candidates for the board, avoiding the unconscious bias of appointing like-minded and 'safe' candidates, and place priority on relevant experience and industry knowledge.
6. Actively engage the third line of defence to review the adequacy of systems to comply with all applicable laws and regulations.

BOARDS ON EXECUTIVE REMUNERATION

Success and failure in sport is visible for all to see. It is less visible in business and sometimes it can look as if incentives do not correlate with success or failure outcomes. Of all areas of governance, the one that generates antipathy in society is the level of executive remuneration and the propensity to pay high bonuses to CEOs and C-suite executives when there have been major business failings, including allegations of breaking the law. When you look at the 'bonus reductions' imposed on bank CEOs and C-suite executives following the *annus horribilis* in 2018, it is very difficult for the vast majority of people to comprehend. In a year where banks were proven to have violated so much of societal values and with allegations of criminal offences, CEO and C-suite executives had their million-dollar bonuses cut – 'cut'! And in many instances, bonuses paid in previous years were not subject to the 'claw-back' provisions that in theory exist but which few boards have the courage to enact. The fact that bank boards decided to pay bonuses is one serious miscalculation, the other was the personal values of the executives, particularly the CEOs, in accepting the award. A principle-based leadership team would have come to a different moral and ethical position, as the Lloyds Bank CEO did in 2011 when he declined his bonus given the 'tough financial circumstances that many people are facing'.[274]

Banks talk a lot about 'doing the right thing' but in practice that is not always evident at an institutional or individual level. Society is left asking 'what does it take to not get a bonus?' Shareholders, of course, made their own views known, with three of the major banks receiving a first strike rejection. In NAB's case that was an overwhelming and record setting 88 per cent. Despite a damning report from APRA in 2016, which criticised the high level of executive remuneration, combined with a scandal ridden 2018 and a share price that continued to underperform, the NAB board endorsed executive remuneration payments that were then rebutted by a record level of shareholder rejection. What does this say about the leadership and culture at board level, particularly at the bank remuneration committee?

At NAB, bonuses were paid when shareholders had seen value lost, brands trashed and embarrassing allegations of serious errors

---

[274] 'Lloyds chief Antonio Horta-Osorio declines annual bonus', *BBC News*, 13 January 2013, <hhttps://www.bbc.co.uk>news>business>.

of judgement. These errors of judgement included the case of the then CEO making the news because he accepted gifts such as a Thermomix and a heavily subsidised holiday in Fiji[275] and then his trusted assistant allegedly helped herself to millions of dollars of the bank's funds, with no internal checks and balances apparent.[276] These outcomes reinforce a sense that it is not shareholders who are prioritised over customers, but it is banker remuneration that has a priori preference over all else. Societal bewilderment and increasing resentment to high bonuses in poorly performing businesses is not restricted to banks – see for example Telstra in 2018, a significant underperformer and company once chaired by the current CBA chair[277] – but given the scandals that plagued the industry, that many banks merely shaved executives' bonuses rather than not pay them at all is an unmistakable accountability and governance failure.

So, instead of a bonus of $4 million, a CEO receives $2 million, while many in society are wondering how they retained their jobs. Shareholders who lost significant value in their investments in the banks wonder how any self-respecting executive or any sensible and responsible board could allow what can only be described as farcical outcomes. As APRA chairman Wayne Byres noted:

> Not only are rewards generous, but there are seemingly few repercussions for poor outcomes ... employees below the senior executive level often bore the brunt of bad conduct, executives were largely insulated from problems. The way bonus scorecards were designed usually averaged out differences.[278]

---

275 McKenzie, N., Danckert, S. & Baker, R., 'NAB CEO in investigation over luxury resort holiday', *Sydney Morning Herald*, 16 November 2018, p. 23.

276 Crawford, K., 'NAB executive charged over $40m fraud granted bail', *ABC News*, 5 March 2019, <https://www.abc.net.au/news>.

277 McGowan, M., 'Australia's executive pay backlash hits Telstra', *The Guardian*, 11 October 2018.

278 Bartholomeusz, S., 'BEAR will put some fear in bank boardrooms', *The Australian*, 5 April 2018.

It is hard to imagine an industry so out of touch with reality and simple standards of decency. Contrast what has become the weak accountability norm within the industry with the exemplary standard set by Israeli national Eric Ben-Artzi, who was a whistleblower on law breaches at Deutsche Bank in the US. Eric refused to accept a US$8.5 million reward from the US Securities and Exchange Commission (SEC) on principle because he felt it was wrong that shareholders who had lost value and employees who lost their jobs should bear the cost when the responsible senior executives went unpunished. Eric Ben-Artzi is a person of virtue.

The *Macquarie dictionary* defines a bonus as 'something given or paid over and above what is due'. Most people would add to this definition 'for performance over and above what was expected'. The banking industry however essentially treats bonuses as a deferred fixed payment, which can be varied at the margin, and only in extremis can it be withdrawn.

Outside the leadership position taken by the CBA board in 2017/18 and NAB in 2019 in the case of the departing CEO, there are scant examples of bank boards exercising their powers. CBA's track record on accountability was one of the poorest in the industry. The CBA chair, Catherine Livingston, noted that in 2016, the bank's remuneration committee acted 'inadequately' in considering bonuses given the scandals that had engulfed the bank, which included a $700 million fine to AUSTRAC in relation to anti-money laundering breaches. In that year, the 12 most senior executives made more than $44 million, including the value of at-risk shares.[279] Bonuses, while dressed up as a reward for outstanding results, are in practice no such thing. They appear to get paid for just turning up.

The core idea behind a bonus is that it helps align total executive remuneration with sustainable shareholder outcomes

---

279 Yeates, C. & Dankert, S., 'CBA's fall from grace: no more apologies, plenty of finger pointing', *Sydney Morning Herald*, 24 November 2018.

and stakeholder expectations. Any comparison with the share performance and TSR of the major banks in 2017/18 and bonus payments is not evident. These payments have nothing to do with true capitalism; it is elitism and rent extraction on a grand scale. There is no correlation, in fact it became a hedge for executives as the value of their equity fell; the bonus payments provided some compensation. No such deal for the shareholders who entrusted their savings to the stewardship of the bank boards and management. The global marketplace for talent, the argument often used to justify high salaries, is largely a self-serving myth. The reality is that boards have failed to exercise effective governance and have exposed themselves to increased reputational risk and greater investor and potentially legislative intervention. The Australian Council of Superannuation Investors CEO, Louise Davidson, warned on this:

> At a time when public trust in business is at a low ebb and wage growth is weak, board decisions to pay large bonuses just for hitting budget targets rather than exceptional performance are especially tone deaf. This may be a sign that boards have lost sight of the link between a company's social licence and the expectations of communities and investors. We may need legislative intervention to give shareholders a greater say – such as we have seen in other markets, like the UK.[280]

The design of bonuses must be reviewed and paid only when performance exceeds stated goals, including superior TSR. Bonuses should not be tied to loose or soft criteria or to a single criteria, and balanced scorecard weightings have no credibility. Senior executives should be assessed on an all metric basis and on an *and* basis, that is failure in one category means failure overall. This is regardless of the outcomes assessed on other categories.

---
280 O'Dowd, C., 'CEO pay: call for intervention as bosses paid "tone-deaf" bonuses', *The Australian*, 17 July 2108, p. 24.

There should be no arbitrage. They should never be paid when there are serious risk management or compliance issues.

NAB had been warned by APRA in 2016 that its risk management failed to meet standards.[281] The regulator required NAB to work on three objectives:
- A risk framework appetite including proactive management.
- A development of clearly defined responsibilities and accountabilities in risk management.
- Improved reporting and monitoring of risk at board and subcommittee level.

All this is fundamental to running a bank, and this at a time of many scandals, which have been documented throughout this book. What does it take to not get paid a bonus? What were the boards thinking?

Bonuses aside, the growing gap between CEO and employee remuneration has been an unresolved problem of modern capitalism and this is starkly illustrated in banking. In her excellent book, *Are Chief Executives overpaid?* (2018), Deborah Hargreaves argues that the answer is 'yes'. She argues that the explosion in executive pay over the past few decades overwhelmingly reflects rent extraction, not reward for performance. This is economically damaging because supposedly 'performance-related' pay encourages poor decisions and is socially destructive because it undermines the legitimacy of a market-based economy, of capitalism. The real tragedy in all this is not the abuse *by* capitalism but an abuse *of* capitalism with in too many cases, boards front and centre of cause and effect.

Bank remuneration of senior executives remains a puzzle to many in society. Being a CEO or senior executive of a major bank is a prize with excellent rewards. While these are big jobs given the size of the banks, they are not complex jobs. Given the privileged

---

281 Frost, J. & Eyres, J., 'Henry: NAB board was too soft', *Australian Financial Review*, 28 November 2018, p. 9.

position of major banks and the fundamental annuity basis for much of the profits, 95 per cent if not more of which is already in the system when the new financial year begins, people outside the industry scratch their heads at the levels of pay. The size of the remuneration can blunt any desire to strongly challenge consensus views or groupthink, for fear of losing your role and its rewards (see comments in the Epilogue). This is particularly the case in the shallow C-suite banking market in Australia, where opportunities to find equally lucrative roles are limited. Senior executives therefore can be prone to 'temper their sense of justice'. Most people will tolerate a lot when annual rewards are $2–3 million.

SKIN IN THE GAME

One important lens a shareholder might have is the degree to which directors are committed to a bank's success and nothing illustrates this more than the equity they hold in the bank: 'the skin in the game' as Nassim Nicholas Taleb (2018) writes in his book. 'Do not pay attention to what people say, only to what they do, and to how much of their neck they are putting on the line.'[282]

We return to the theme of directors having 'skin in the game' later in this chapter and address the myth that independent directors with material, in a personal sense, stakes in the bank are conflicted. In arguing that absent 'skin the in the game', directors are conflicted, it is also important to acknowledge the view that independent directors should be free from self-interest in their governance of a business and that having equity in the company can create a conflict. While respecting this view, it feels like a weak argument and that the opposite is true. When directors have little economic interest in the bank, they are not aligned with

---

282 Taleb, N. N., *Skin in the game: hidden asymmetries in daily life*, Random House, 2018.

the investors they are supposed to represent. That is a conflict. A clear enunciation of alignment is expressed by most investing institutions such as TDM Asset Management. TDM argue that directors should have invested at least five times their directors' fees in the company.[283] Perhaps the sage words of Warren Buffet best summarise this:

> Our directors are all major shareholders in Berkshire Hathaway. In the case of at least four of the five, over 50 per cent of family net worth is represented by holdings of Berkshire. We eat our own cooking.[284]

We return to this topic below.

FIT FOR THE FUTURE?

Director selection remains a burning issue at the heart of board effectiveness and corporate governance. It is an issue that has become confused and arguably distracted by the emphasis given to compliance-driven board diversity and the emphasis placed on 'independence', all of which can often result in director selection where there is no experience or knowledge of the activities of the bank or of banking.

Appendix V sets out an example of the specification and criteria for the appointment of a bank director.

It is important to acknowledge that it is easy to criticise, when the real contribution would be to formulate constructive recommendations. To do this one must first acknowledge that while the business world continues to go through transformational change, the practices of most boards have barely evolved, though they have arguably moved on from the time when Peter Drucker

---

283 Whyte, J., 'Directors need more skin in the game', *Australian Financial Review*, 17 May 2018.
284 Boyd, T., 'Qantas chair from shallow pool', *Australian Financial Review*, 29 June 2018, p. 40.

somewhat harshly described the board of directors as 'an impotent, ceremonial and legal fiction'.[285] Part of the problem is that bank board agendas have been dominated with legal, compliance and regulatory related matters, as discussed earlier. This has left limited quality time to focus on strategy. Moreover, the compliance related matters can represent personal risk to directors, thus creating an incentive to overkill on compliance. This risk is reinforced by the BEAR requirements. No director has ever faced personal liability for simply poor business judgement or inertia, even though shareholder and societal costs can be huge.

An effective assessment of a board's composition and competence has never been of greater importance, thus described in Table 8 is a simple scorecard framework that can guide investors and nomination committees in their assessment of directors against an overall fit for the future criteria.

The scorecard has an individual category rating and an overall rating. All scores are on a scale of 1 to 5: 1 = poor, 2 = weak, 3 = acceptable, 4 = good and 5 = very good. An overall weighted rating of '3' is a pass, anything below that would be a good reason for not investing in the company or appointing a director. Investors, directors and employees should naturally be attracted to companies with an overall rating of '4' or '5'. Boards might consider exiting directors who represent a drag on the overall rating, regardless of how well they are liked and what it might do to gender and other diversity metrics. Boards should also use this framework in considering new directors, not just in evaluating the individual but in assessing the impact of the appointment on the overall board composition.

---

285 As quoted in MacAvoy, P. W. & Millstein, I. M., 'The active board of directors and its effect on the performance of the large publicly traded corporation', *Journal of Applied Corporate Finance*, vol. 11, no. 4, Winter 1999, pp. 8–20.

TABLE 8: EXAMPLE FRAMEWORK FOR EVALUATING DIRECTORS AND BOARDS

Category	Rating (1 to 5)	Weighting (%)	Rating
Independence/courage	3	20	0.60
Meaningful equity stake	2	20	0.40
Banking experience	5	45	2.25
Digital expertise	1	15	0.15
Overall rating	-	100	3.40

The matrix focuses on four key categories: independence and courage, equity stake, banking experience and digital expertise.

Independence and courage of directors from management and potential conflicting loyalties has been given a 20 per cent weighting in the above hypothetical example. Shareholders want to be satisfied that directors can avoid conflicting interests that could detract from their ability to be loyal to the company and act in the best interests of the company. The emphasis on 'independent' directors means independent as a state of mind. The performance of some companies, however, could have interpreted independent as 'indifferent', as investors might feel an element of indifference is a factor in explaining poor performance and this indifference may be partly evident in the lack of an equity stake in the company. The flip side of independence can also sometimes mean poor knowledge of how the business operates. A similar conclusion is derived from the research conducted by professor Peter Swan at UNSW.[286] While conventional thinking holds that having more independent directors on a board, the better, there is little evidence that 'independence' alone is enough – in fact the evidence is to the contrary. To ensure that directors are engaged and aligned with

---

[286] Eyers, J., 'Independent directors destroy value, University of NSW study says', *Australian Financial Review*, 30 July 2014, p. 33.

external investors, they should all hold a minimum amount of equity in the bank. There is a qualifier for banks, however; banks should have a majority independent director, meaning a director who does not represent an investor holding more than 5 per cent of the equity. This is an important qualifier, but it does not excuse directors from owning a material, in a personal sense, stake in the bank.

Equity stake for directors is given a weighting of 20 per cent. The higher a director's equity stake in a personal wealth sense, the better. As a general guide an equity stake should equal at least five times the director's annual fee, although this can be built up over time (it is recognised that some very able directors may not be able to make such a financial commitment immediately). Small stakes, say less than three years' fees, are insignificant and would score low. Several thousand shares bought for cosmetic reasons is a charade. Equity ownership by directors remains a controversial topic, with academics and other high priests of corporate governance arguing that by owning equity, directors are incentivised to act in concert with management. This is a controversial view; the opposite is that directors must invest in the company if they are to demonstrate their commitment and care. If you do not believe in the company's prospects, do not join the board.

Banking experience is closely associated with track record and reputation and is weighted at 45 per cent. Many companies fail to succeed because they have too many directors (and sometimes management) with weak experience in the industry in which the company operates. Shareholders should have every right to expect that each director has experience relevant to the objectives of the company. The GFC highlighted how inept many bank boards were at understanding the business and the risks it faced, as illustrated by HBOS and RBS. Many bank directors in the US, UK and Australia were out of their depth in understanding the complexity of the institutions they had stewardship for.

Digital expertise is an important expertise for a bank board given the wave of technological change impacting the industry and the imperative to think both technically and strategically about the risks and opportunities of digitalisation, and is given a weighting of 15 per cent.

CONCLUDING REMARKS

Critics of bank boards have plenty of ammunition. While no system of corporate governance is perfect, corporate boards are among the most important institutions in capitalism as they lie at the heart of governance and are key to mitigating the principal–agent costs facing shareholders and society. The record of boards, however, can be politely described as mixed and perhaps, some would argue, one of the weakest links in the capitalist system. This is particularly evident where directors have little if any equity interest in the company. Numerous reforms have left the core role of the board largely untouched for over a century, except for adding layer upon layer of low value-add bureaucracy in the form of compliance requirements. At a fundamental level, board reform remains legalistic and regulatory driven and incredibly conservative – which is perhaps why lawyers and accountants tend to dominate boards.

Absent significant, not more perfunctory change, a reasonable conclusion is that today's boards are not future proof. Sure, board members may be more diverse today than 10 years ago, but at their core they remain a composite of part-timers, largely from the same shallow pool with little real incentive to monitor companies effectively. The majority of board members in the banking industry lack the expertise to do so. As UNSW professor Peter Swan commented, the culprits of dysfunctional and underperforming boards are the directors with no skin in the game or understanding of their companies.[287]

Legendary investor Warren Buffet summed up the situation well when he said:

> The requisites for board membership should be business savvy, interest in the job and owner-orientation. Too often, directors are selected simply because they are prominent or add diversity to the board. That practice is a mistake. Furthermore, mistakes in selecting directors are particularly serious because appointments are hard to undo: The pleasant but vacuous director need never worry about job security.[288]

Boards are, as Carter and Lorsch (2004, p. 181) described, a conundrum. Largely comprising part-time members, many, the evidence would suggest (e.g. McKinsey & Company (2018)), with little real appreciation of how the business creates wealth and manages its risks, and captive to the traditions of the past, which over time have seen some fine-tuning but never a total revamp. Yet, boards as an institution are responsible for ensuring that the major economic assets in the economy and much of our investment wealth is subject to sound stewardship. Does this sound like a satisfactory set of arrangements? Clearly it is not. Who will drive the change? It should be institutional investors, but they have a very poor track record in discharging their duties except in extremis. Absent investors, the onus falls on government through legislation.

The evidence of history is that boards cannot be relied upon to self-adjust and address the chronic problems currently evident in what passes for corporate governance. Albert Einstein reminded us that 'we cannot solve our problems with the same thinking we used when we created them'. The modern history of corporate governance demonstrates that Einstein's advice has fallen on deaf ears.

---

287 'The questions that hang over our boardrooms', *Australian Financial Review*, 18 May 2018.
288 Boyd, T., 'Qantas chair from shallow pool', *Australian Financial Review*, 29 June 2018, p. 40.

8
MOVING FORWARD AND LOOKING BACK

THIS book set itself an ambitious goal: to analyse what had caused the demise of banking in Australia, and, having done so, to then set out a course for a change agenda aimed at restoring professionalism, credibility, confidence and trust. Can the toothpaste be put back in the tube, or to mix metaphors, has the concrete set and, true to a path dependent hypothesis, is it too late to change in a meaningful way? This chapter summarises many of the topics explored throughout the book, weaving them together and in doing so forming a blueprint for change.

A strong, stable, trusted and competitive banking system is essential to a thriving, innovative and prosperous economy. The first step on the path to redemption is that the major banks should operate in accordance with a social licence, with a clear sense of purpose. Banks must exist to act as the servant to the economy, not as its master. As well as asking what the economy might do to their performance, banks should always ask what their conduct and collective strategies might do to the economy and wellbeing of society. As former ANZ CEO John McFarlane said, 'banks must return to the philosophy that banking is a profession … and that contribution rather than reward is its centre of gravity.'[289] Banks must stop making excuses. It was an indictment on the industry when *The Economist* wrote:

> A royal commission (in Australia) has exposed a litany of abuses. Its interim report paints the country's financial institutions as consumer-crushing oligopolies. The banks have tried to pin the blame on a few rogue staff. In fact, the wrongdoing was pervasive.[290]

Banks should return to the essential principles of good banking, as summarised in Appendix VI, and they must act in the public interest given the privileges that society has bestowed on them, including the implicit guarantee, for the major banks at least, that there is a call option on taxpayer funding in the event of a crisis. The taxpayer acts as the unpaid insurer in a crisis; this should never be forgotten, nor the prospect of a crisis dismissed. Very few private sector industries operate in this knowledge and for that and other reasons, banks are different. The major banks are not disciplined by the threat of failure or takeover in the way that other businesses are. Major banks may not like to think of themselves as quasi-nationalised, but, in extremis, they are. Society and government therefore have a legitimate interest in how banks conduct their affairs, discharge their responsibilities, allocate capital across the economy and practise their corporate governance, and in how the industry is structured to serve the economy. For this fundamental reason regulation is important.

---

[289] Boyd, T., 'Former ANZ CEO John McFarlane calls for rethink of banking philosophy', *Australian Financial Review*, 3 August 2016, p. 48.

[290] 'Australia's biggest banks are in the dock – the charge sheet', *The Economist*, 6 October 2018, p. 58.

PUBLIC POLICY AND REGULATION

Traditionally, governments intervene in the operations of a market economy, whether through taxation or through regulation, for two primary reasons: either to ensure that markets work efficiently or to alter outcomes to achieve social objectives. Economic theory identifies three market failures that form the justification for government or regulatory intervention:
- Monopoly or oligopoly power. This is where a few firms have the power to restrict competition and conduct themselves in a way that is contrary to consumer welfare and society interests.
- To address externalities or spillover costs. These arise when the activities of market participants indirectly affect the wellbeing of others, for example, the impact of pollution created by coal power stations.
- To deal with information imbalances or asymmetries. For example, failure by market participants to provide enough information to allow informed decisions by market participants, including customers.

Attempts by governments and regulatory agencies to address these issues, however, can be frustrated by powerful industry groups, such as the banking industry. The banking industry has cultivated strong relationships within policy and political circles, which have tended to prevent any change in the status quo. The extensive lobbying of politicians and regulators, often away from the public eye, is par for the course. An example of this was the way in which the major banks shaped the Royal Commission, limiting the scope and placing time pressures that would hinder a more extensive investigation.[291] The banking industry has also done a

---

291 Long, S., 'This letter from the big banks helped shape the royal commission', *ABC News*, 5 February 2018, <https://www.abc.net.au/news/2019-02-05/big-banks-ask-government-to-call-short-royal-commission-letter/10778928>.

masterful job in building a jargon-based barrier to make general understanding of what they do almost impenetrable. Conducting themselves in this way only reinforces the private interest agenda at the expense of the public interest.

This impenetrability helps confuse policymakers and the public, making informed debate difficult and misleading statements go by unchallenged. Banks also employ tactics such as suggesting credit restrictions and higher costs to scare off policy initiatives. As argued later in this chapter, against the backdrop of both the Royal Commission and the Productivity Commission, the case for radical reform has never been (and never will be) stronger. Bank spokespersons, and their powerful supporters, often claim (threaten) that changes in regulation or any new requirements placed on banks will 'harm the supply of credit and economic growth'.[292] These threats do influence policymakers, yet they are self-serving, often misleading and absent any substance. If what banks are saying is that new restrictions will reduce 'liar loans' and other forms of 'loose lending', then that is a good thing and should be welcomed. The idea that making banks more responsible is bad for the economy is simply untrue: fake news. To ensure banks are acting responsibly, greater regulatory intervention is needed. This is what the facts on the ground suggest and this is what history repeatedly informs us.

The argument put forward against more capital to make our banks safer is that higher capital levels will reduce lending. Not true; more capital increases the capacity of banks to lend through the leverage applied to capital. Higher capital does put some pressure on ROE, but in an industry generating lucrative economic rents, this must be put in perspective. In banking, as in driving, safety first; record speeds and excitement come second. Speeds limits are important. If banks choose to increase their capital ratios by

---

[292] Gluyas, R., 'Bankers fear redefining "small business" will restrict loan access', *The Australian*, 27 February 2019, p. 23.

reducing their appetite for 'loose' and speculative lending, then they are serving the public good.

The Royal Commission raised many points for reflection for the industry's regulators: Have they equipped themselves well or fallen victim to their own version of 'success is toxic'? Does the regulatory regime encourage new entrants and greater competition, or does it reinforce the status quo? Society will want to better understand how an industry that is so heavily regulated can conduct itself in such a disappointing manner and expose the economy to such significant systemic risk given the amount of debt in the household sector.

PROFESSIONALISM AND SOCIAL LICENCE

For banks to be successful in the future, it is critical that they employ simpler business models, be humble and trustworthy, and always work in the interests of their customers and of society. They also must be defined by professional standards earned through study and examination. This should be set at a high standard given the level of remuneration within the industry. Being a qualified 'banker' should be a prize worth striving for. Those that do not like the idea should leave the industry; those that are committed to high professional standards will thrive. Rebuilding a sense of a vocation or profession among bankers is an important step in rebuilding trust, and the regulator has an important role to play in insisting on this. Based on the UK Chartered Institute of Bankers qualification, efforts by FINSIA are encouraging and should be supported but much more needs to be done, such as boards (or regulators) making it mandatory that all staff undertake this qualification (a policy that has been adopted at Judo Bank). The BFO has an important role to play as part of the drive for greater professionalism, particularly in the promotion of ethics as an essential individual virtue. Following the example set by the Dutch authorities, consideration should be given to making it obligatory that every person working within the banking industry take the oath. There may also be a leadership role for the ABA to play in driving greater professionalism.

All who care about the banking industry must accept that social expectations have changed, and banks have a significant task in front of them to regain society's trust, knowing that it arrives on 'the back of tortoise and leaves on the back of a galloping horse' and is never inclined to return unless there is good cause to do so. Any attempt to restore trust must begin with an understanding of why it was lost. The so-called rational self-interest motives for running banks must reflect on the virtues of old, as espoused by John Reed, Don Argus, Sir Brian Pitman and others. It is vital that banks revisit the essence of their social licence and purpose. Bank boards must once again establish the moral and ethical purpose of their banks, nothing else can have greater priority. In doing this, banks have an opportunity to take a lead in promoting 'ethical capitalism' and they may want to reflect on what Adam Smith meant when he provided the intellectual foundation for capitalism. Banks are the natural leaders in the business community to do this given the central role that they play.

AUSTRALIAN FINANCIAL CRISIS

For sure, Australia and the Australian banks did not face a GFC in the way that other Western economies did. That was in part due to good luck and in part due to skilful management by the government and its agencies. It is a myth to argue, given the exposure to short-dated wholesale funding, that it was due to the strength of the banks (and by implication that they were well managed). Absent a proactive approach, St George Bank and Bankwest may well have collapsed, which would have been a major calamity and simply not worth speculating on. The Australian authorities in nudging Bankwest to CBA and in supporting St George Bank's acquisition by Westpac, were conducting their business in a superior way to that occurring in the UK, with, for example, an appallingly managed bank such as HBOS almost crippling an otherwise well-managed bank such as Lloyds Bank. In the face of a crisis, authorities need to take quick and decisive action to prevent systemic damage. Messrs Rudd, Swan, Henry, Stevens and Laker should take a bow. It was they who were the real heroes of the GFC.

With Australian banks having missed the GFC, ironically the Royal Commission has revealed an AFC; a crisis in the relationship between banks and the society that they were established to serve. This is a crisis of trust, legitimacy and purpose caused by a deeply flawed culture, which underpinned unethical and potentially illegal conduct. The AFC may prove a more challenging crisis to remedy, given how the cultural concrete within the industry has well and truly set. The regulatory developments are unlikely to differentiate between a financial crisis requiring government support and the crisis that the Royal Commission highlighted. In many ways, from a regulatory perspective, developments in the UK have been adopted in Australia, developments such as Open Banking, Senior Managers Regime (our BEAR) and the encouragement of new competition. The challenger bank and neobank developments we see emerging in Australia are modelled on developments in the UK. It is important that new entrants are well managed and governed, as a weakness in one can have a reputationally contagious effect on others. In this regard, the experience and quality of management and directors is critical, as is the commitment to sound risk management practices, and respect for regulators.[293] A legitimate concern is that new entrants

---

293 Binham, C. & Megaw, N., 'Bank of England finds UK challenger banks cut corners', *Financial Times*, 14 June 2019, p. 1.

will seek to grow by loosening risk management standards and mispricing risk.

The consequences of an AFC are still to play out, but this will happen in time, when after a decade of soul-searching and rebuilding, most banks in the West have taken their medicine, detoxed and are coming out fitter and stronger, albeit much leaner and more boring. Whether they have changed culturally, time will tell. History informs us that this is unlikely, as bankers have a deep-rooted self-belief that 'this time is different', and their DNA is more aligned to the Friedman Doctrine that the social responsibility of banking is to maximise ROE and test any and all standards of civil, ethical and moral standards in doing so. (Milton Friedman did not advocate unethical conduct, nor would he have approved of rent-seeking behaviour in uncompetitive markets.) Banks must address a culture that has created a values system that can feel to outsiders as one of 'what can I get away with?'. If caught, penalties and fines become a 'cost of doing business'. Such a philosophy, of course, is not what the banks portray, but it is what society sees and experiences. Any material change will require legal and regulatory intervention as well as the ethical and moral leadership of bank boards. The prisoner's dilemma will mean no board is likely to have the courage to take the lead. The path dependent hypothesis means change will be very difficult.

The good fortune of avoiding the GFC only stored up problems for future years, problems the Australian authorities are now facing. Australia in many ways has become a victim of a perverse form of 'winner's curse'; its banks most certainly have fallen into the 'success is toxic' trap, some more than others. Conduct issues aside, the prospect of an AFC is heightened by the potential for a major correction in a highly indebted housing market, which accounts for two-thirds of aggregate bank lending. There is already evidence of 'bad investments', 'loose lending' on interest-only loans and a considerable level of suggested 'liar loans'. Even though it has been almost 30 years since the last economic recession, they do happen, and it would be a miscalculation of some magnitude to assume that Australia is immune from this economic reality.

FINANCIAL CRISES HAPPEN: BE PREPARED

Cassidy (2009, p. 239) reminds us that while every bubble is different, all of them share three common features: 'policymakers beholden to the illusion of stability; financial innovations that make speculating easier; and New Era thinking typified by overconfidence and disaster myopia.' During a speculative bubble, the laws of demand and supply still hold true over the long term, they simply get ignored in the rush to 'get in on the action' for fear of missing out. When the banking system is accommodating and even encouraging such speculative behaviour, the ending is rarely nice and often very ugly. The level of lending, including speculative lending, in the household sector bears no resemblance to responsible lending. The banks have created a dangerous skew in capital allocation that is more akin to casino banking and it has created an unnecessary macro-economic risk, all done to maximise ROE and consequently executive incentives.

According to the Behavioural Finance and Financial Stability project at Harvard University, an average of four countries a year have faced a banking crisis between 1800 and 2016. From 1945 to 1975, when the banking system was tightly controlled and domestic, most years were free from a crisis. Post deregulation of the banking systems in most Western countries from the 1980s onwards, 13 countries have found themselves in the throes of a banking crisis each year on average.[294] There is a telling message in these facts supporting greater regulation and government interest

---

294 'The world economy, special report', *The Economist*, 13 October 2018, p. 4.

in our banking system and in particular in our major banks. There is little disputing the argument that some banks are too big to be allowed to fail; there is a compensating argument that if a bank is too big and important, it should not be allowed to exceed a certain size. Admati and Hellwig (2013, p. 89) reached a similar set of conclusions when they argued that:

> one approach to reform is therefore to find a way to break up the banks into smaller, more manageable, less complex entities. Although large banks boast that big is beautiful ... there is little to suggest that banks that grow beyond about $100 billion in assets create gains in efficiency.

There is evidence that beyond a certain size in scale and scope, diseconomies start to set in and management's capacity to manage becomes constrained. This becomes a problem that can spill over from the banks into the economy and society.

NARROW BANKING IS GOOD BANKING

The idea of Australia's own version of narrow banking carries appeal for two reasons: first, it will simplify the banking business model, which will make the re-establishment of professional values easier; and second, regulation can be more directly channelled and banks made even safer. To some extent, the Vickers report in the UK was largely aimed at achieving that, but it only went so far. The term 'narrow banking' sounds restrictive and the concept of banks as a utility, boring. John Kay (2009), who researched this concept in the UK, refutes the idea that 'boring' is a necessary outcome. In his view, such a model puts customer satisfaction, not products, sales targets, conflicts of interest and ROE-driven remuneration, as the key measure of success. At Judo Bank we call this 'banking as it used to be, banking as it should be', similar in terms of business philosophy to that of Handelsbanken, as described by Niels Kroner in this book *A blueprint for better banking* (2011). All businesses know that if customer satisfaction is strong, a range of economic outcomes flow, as John Kay's *Obliquity* reminds us.

The lack of political conviction to change the fundamental structure of banking is a concern. This is an opportunity that the Australian authorities should seize given just how concentrated our banking system is and how damaged its reputation has become. There was new legislation passed in both the UK and the US that affected the banking industry: in the UK, the *Banking Act 2009* was passed followed by the *Banking Reform Act 2013*. In the US, the *Dodd-Frank Wall Street Reform and Consumer Protection Act 2010* was passed. However, in both markets, society feels that nothing much has changed. The same banks dominate Main Street and the High Streets (King, 2016, p. 40), even though there have been a number of challenger banks, neobanks and FinTechs emerging in both markets. The conviction to face the structural changes needed in the industry has been too tough an assignment for political leaders. This is very disappointing.

Narrow banking, with strong regulatory engagement, also helps address the 'herding instinct' problem that plagues banks. Banks will follow each other, all the way over the cliff. This is an endemic problem in banking. History would suggest that banks do not learn from past mistakes and they always believe that 'this time is different'. Society needs regulatory protection from this. This amnesia risk is compounded by the fact that almost all the bankers in Australia with experience of the last economic downturn in the early 1990s will have left or will be planning on leaving the industry very soon. Indeed, in the modern era, a generation has come to mean no more than 10 to 15 years in the industry; when people go, they carry with them a wisdom that is denied to their successors, who are often better qualified academically, but poorly qualified in the instinctive skills and experience of banking – the craft of banking. Institutional memory is very short, and this represents a significant risk to individual banks.

MORE COMPETITION

The primary cause of the conduct issues plaguing the industry is that Australia does not have a competitive banking market, something the Productivity Commission report so vividly concludes. Most of the problems evident in the industry, and so emphatically highlighted by the Royal Commission, are symptoms of weak competition. A competitive market is one where well-run banks earn profits at least in line with their risk-adjusted cost of capital and poorly run banks do not, which should result in a change of CEO. A level playing field is a necessary precondition, however, and that does not exist in Australia or New Zealand. This is evident in several ways, most obviously in the determination of RWAs and thus capital. Through healthy competition, the market system promotes innovation and economic development; suppression of competitive forces ultimately damages innovation and economic progress and allows entrenched cultures to flourish, where customer interests are for marketing campaigns and little else.

Addressing the issues raised both in the Royal Commission inquiry and in the Productivity Commission report will require a commitment to competition and courageous bold policy leadership not seen in Australia since the Hawke–Keating era, or in New Zealand since Sir Roger Douglas and the 'Rogernomics' reforms of the 1980s. This can be done through demergers of existing banking groups – for example, reversing mergers that have been conducted over the last decade – and through the encouragement of new entrants. The current barriers to entry are significant. The UK has managed this transition to market entry reasonably smoothly and several banks exist in the marketplace that did not exist 10 years ago. The UK authorities failed in their attempt to carve out parts of RBS, but they compromised by forcing the bank to create an incentive for other smaller banks to take their SME customers.[295] This is an example of what might be possible in Australia and New Zealand in order to promote competition. In the US, there are over 5000 smaller banks and several larger ones. Recently the US changed its law so that the smaller banks are freed from some regulation and compliance to give them a better chance to grow and compete with larger banks. In Australia, we have a diametrically opposite state of affairs; smaller banks are handicapped, and the oligopoly structure is largely protected from material competition.[296]

Steps taken to open the bank licensing system are a move in the right direction, as is the commitment to 'open banking', but much more needs to be done to allow effective competition. Open banking alone will achieve very little based on the early experience in the UK, where it has been a feature of the market since early 2018. In the 12 months since its introduction, only 3 per cent of personal customers and 4 per cent of business customers have switched to a different bank.[297] Recognising the challenge of encouraging competition in the UK, Kay (2015, p. 172) suggests that 'perhaps the most useful initial role for government is to promote the creation of new financial institutions directed to providing the mix of loans and equity finance needed to help SMEs grow.' In this light, the decision by the government to establish a $2 billion SME securitisation fund and the intention to create an Australian equivalent to the UK Growth Fund, which was set up to hold equity stakes in SMEs, is encouraging news and

---

295 Megaw, N., 'Eleven banks gain approval to join RBS competition scheme', *Financial Times*, 19 December 2018, p. 17.
296 Ibid.
297 Deutsche Bank Research, *Australian banking sector*, 17 January 2019.

will go some way to address the $83 billion market failure gap, if properly administered. But banks should do more; they should commit to establishing equity and hybrid equity capabilities for their SME customers, capped at 10 per cent of total SME lending. These are not easy businesses for banks to run. They require specialist skills and the need to be very disciplined in focusing only on the bank's customers and only using the bank's capital. They should never invest third-party money or stray from well-known SME customers, as both these steps create conflicts of interest and increase investment risk. ANZ reportedly lost $100 million running an SME-focused private equity fund because it morphed the business into a third-party fund and moved outside its focus on the bank's SME franchise.[298] It became a fundamentally different business from the one that was established in 2000.

There is also an opportunity to do more, including looking at the scope for tax incentives to encourage equity and debt investments in SMEs. As Haskel and Westlake (2018, p. 166) argue, most Western economies create tax advantages to debt over equity. In an increasingly intangible asset rich economy, creating stronger tax incentives to encourage capital into SMEs has the potential for material economic dividends. Such a development requires vision and courage.

The Productivity Commission report into the state of competition in banking was unequivocal in highlighting that the profitability of the sector came at a cost to consumer welfare. To support this finding, John Kwoka, in his excellent book *Mergers, merger control and remedies* (2014), researched 50 studies covering more than 3000 mergers and found that when an industry has six or less significant competitors, prices rose in nearly 95 per cent of cases. The case for reversing previous mergers in the public interest and dismantling the oligopoly market structure is well worth

---

298 Butler, B., 'ANZ to close fund after $100m lost', *Sydney Morning Herald*, 6 June 2012, p. 31.

considering. But this will require courageous political leadership, not seen in Australia or New Zealand for a very long time.

REGULATORY PHILOSOPHY RE-THINK ESSENTIAL

A new competitive environment will require a regulatory philosophy that supports competition in the same way the FCA does in the UK. This has to be done in an intelligent way, recognising that there are differences between large, systemically significant banks and much smaller banks. The current regulatory environment is heavily skewed in favour of the major banks and there appears to be a tendency from the regulator to nudge all banks into a similar model. Westpac CEO, Brian Hartzer, acknowledged this when he referenced the credit process feedback from **APRA** suggesting that banks are either an outlier, in the middle or too conservative.[299] This signalling tends to drive industry uniformity, which suits the regulator and reinforces the sameness and herding characteristics of the banks. Kay (2015) saw this tendency:

> Regulation is often the enemy of competition. Where regulation prescribes the conduct of business in considerable detail, it is inevitable that all firms will behave similarly: a particular concept of 'best practice' will be shared between regulators and regulatees. (p. 113)

This regulatory tendency for a one-size-fits-all approach was understood centuries earlier by Adam Smith, when he wrote:

> The Man of System ... is apt to be very wise in his own conceit; and is often so enamoured with the supposed beauty of his own ideal plan of government, that he cannot suffer the smallest deviation from any part

---

[299] Eyers, J., 'Banking royal commission: Westpac defective lending controls exposed in review', *Australian Financial Review*, 8 May 2014, p. 40.

of it. He goes on to establish it completely, and in all its parts, without any regard either to the greater interest, or to imagine that he can arrange the different members of society with as much ease as the hand arranges the different pieces upon a chess-board. He does not consider that in the great chess-board of human society, every single piece has a principle of its own, altogether different from that which the legitimate might choose to impress upon it.

The competition problems with a largely one-size-fits-all regulatory environment is that the larger banks are advantaged as they can build economies of scale in managing regulators through the hiring of hundreds of regulatory and compliance staff. Larger banks are also advantaged by the adherence to the deeply flawed determination of RWAs and thus capital. Greater consistency and standardisation of RWA calculations is an important step in reinforcing the integrity of this important determinant of capital. The current approach is anti-competitive but also creates a sense that regulators are taking a 'light touch' to a fundamental tenet of bank regulation. There has long been suspicion about the accuracy of RWAs and the incentive for banks to game the RWA classifications in order to 'optimise' capital requirements. The lower the 'E', the higher the 'R' and the higher the bonus.

Concerns on the role of regulation in stifling competition were raised by Dr Darcy Allen and Dr Chris Berg in their excellent book *Australia's red tape crisis: the causes and costs of over-regulation* (2018). The authors argue that regulators using regulation to prevent new entrants and thus acting as an impediment to greater competition is a legitimate concern. The authors also argue that the absence of the Reserve Bank in the regulatory and political debate as it relates to the function and conduct of banks is an anomaly. The propensity of banks to demonstrate biases towards the housing market has macro-economic implications that are legitimately in the domain of the Reserve Bank, as Jocelyn Pixley convincingly argues in her book *Central banks, democratic states and financial power* (2018).

BROKERS

A healthy and free from conflict broker community is essential to a dynamic market and particularly in promoting competition and getting better consumer outcomes. Brokers have grown to be important actors in the banking market and they are particularly well placed to support smaller banks and non-bank lenders to overcome the disadvantages of not having a branch network the size of the major banks. The Productivity Commission estimated that non-bank lenders and foreign banks rely on the broker market for over 90 per cent of their lending. The Productivity Commission also estimated that each small lender would need to open 118 new branches to generate the equivalent business volumes that they source from brokers. The broker community is going to be even more important to the market in the future, but it must address the perception of conflicting interests, including ownership and other structural ties with individual banks. Brokers should be bank agnostic agents seeking the best outcome for their client. The fact that regulators allow banks to own or have an equity stake in broker aggregators is difficult to comprehend; conflicts aside, it can be a means of blocking new entrants when bank-owned aggregators refuse to deal with them. As a reform, this should be seen as low-hanging fruit.

RISK MANAGEMENT

A bank's business is to take risks and manage them. It succeeds when the risks are commensurate with the bank's resources and competence. Ultimately a bank's quality is defined by the sum of its risk-taking decisions. A risk culture forms the bedrock for risk taking. A bank's strategy in terms of geographical footprint, customers and product must be reflective of its agreed risk appetite as outlined in their **RAS**. The bank's **RAS** should be understood by all executives and all the new business and strategic initiatives should be informed by the **RAS**. Where the business strategy is out of line with the **RAS**, this is a clear sign of a poorly managed bank. Risk management must be restored as a core competency evident at the top of the bank and among board directors. Everyone in a position of responsibility inside a bank must be across credit risk, liquidity risk, operational risk and compliance and regulatory risk. The Three Lines of Defence must have substance with real responsibility and accountability. Employees looking for role models must see professional bankers steeped in the craft and science of banking, where risk management skills are a non-negotiable condition of career progression into senior roles. This is another example of where a credible professional industry accreditation standard is important, such as the Chartered Institute of Bankers, promoted by **FINSIA**.

A risk management culture must become pervasive throughout the bank, not the domain of those who might see their role somewhat arrogantly as 'saving the bank' but are woefully ill-equipped to do so, as recent events documented throughout this book highlight. The **APRA** inquiry into **CBA** and the lending and conduct practices at Westpac and **NAB** highlighted just how weak the Three Lines of Defence and risk culture are across the industry. The **CBA** staff survey referenced in Chapter 6, highlighted just how bureaucratic and sometimes perfunctory much of what passes for risk management has become – bureaucracy like cholesterol has its good and its bad features, the problem is that most banks have far too much bad cholesterol. This is an endemic problem.

What passed for a risk culture at **CBA** is evident in some of the other major banks, based on first-hand experience and from discussing this with numerous bankers working within the major and the smaller banks. In many banks there can be a negative tension between the risk management team and the relationship bankers, or the so-called 'sales' teams. This is not constructive tension, but occasionally deep disrespect for each other, with self-fulfilling outcomes. This alone would indicate to boards and senior executives that the risk culture is weak, if not broken. What passes for a risk culture is often no more than a 'risk regime' that has been allowed to weaken risk management inside banks by centralising it as a specialist and exclusive area. Where risk bureaucracy culture exists, it can become pervasive and counterproductive; like the hydra of Greek mythology, if one head is chopped off, two new ones will grow in its place and the bank will become a very difficult place to provide customer service. This is emphatically not a criticism of risk management specialists, it is a criticism of bank boards for allowing this to happen. Risk specialists are essential to ensure a healthy risk culture, but they cannot hold themselves as being there 'to save the bank', as this undermines risk management as a collective responsibility; this is a core competency and has been a fundamental reason why the Three Lines of Defence exists in theory but not effectively in practice. The core reason for this unsatisfactory state of affairs is the paucity of strong risk credentials at the C-suite level and at the board level of many banks.

Risk management must restore the importance of judgement and common sense to balance, not replace algorithms. Too often the bureaucratic and sterile reliance on models conflicts with sound judgement; a case of AI getting ahead of itself. Senior executives and boards should always be able to step back and see the big picture. The ability to leave the dance floor and go to the balcony to assess patterns of risk is a critical banking skill. Anyone leaving the dance floor of housing market share, house price movements, house prices-to-income, rental yields-to-risk-free rates, etc., would see from the balcony that there is real potential for a correction with significant consequences. Boards have to build the expertise and confidence to say, 'this doesn't feel or look right' and to realise that relying on the comfort of Keyne's wisdom that all banks go down together is not commensurate with stewardship responsibilities and accountabilities. Just as bankers never learn from their predecessors' mistakes, bankers are susceptible to herding. They are also susceptible to over optimism in good times and over pessimism in difficult times. Regulators should avoid that trap; they should ask if the housing risk weightings based on historical measures is such a fail-safe capital cushion in a housing market that carries financial risk without precedent in Australia or elsewhere in the world. Is the past a good guide to the future? Remember that highly credentialed regulators and policy makers in the US and the UK such as Alan Greenspan and Mervyn King did not foresee what happened in their markets. Are Australian regulators really that much smarter than their counterparts in these markets? Maybe, but then maybe not. They are certainly as smart.

No amount of sensitivity and stress test modelling replaces the judgement of an experienced regulator saying, 'there is too much leverage in the households sector and behavioural economics tells us that markets can move in ways that could create "black swan" outcomes'. History informs us that bank boards cannot be relied on to ask and respect such questions. The level of risk embedded in our highly leveraged household sector violates any test of sensible risk management. With the major banks having close to two-thirds of their lending assets in housing and with household leverage at over 100 per cent of GDP and hovering around 200 per cent of household income, the banking system has created a precarious systemic risk for the economy. Adding to this risk is evidence of 'loose lending', with sales targets overriding prudent risk management. None of this is remotely consistent with an industry that claims to have a risk culture. It is the opposite.

SME LENDING AND RISK MANAGEMENT

Rebuilding a credit culture in SME lending, as Handelsbanken has maintained, is a priority for the economy. The craft of credit risk management in the SME sector should be materially judgement based, with an emphasis on the Four C's – character, capacity (cash flow), capital and collateral – and away from an over reliance on the market value of assets offered up as collateral, which is almost always real estate security. This has resulted in SME lending becoming nothing more than an overpriced mortgage in disguise.[300] Society expects well paid bankers to be highly trained and professional and to be able to do better than say 'How much is your house worth?' SMEs, the engine room of the economy, are made to feel by the banks that they suffer from the triple 'U' virus – unloved, unwanted and undervalued – unless they can provide real estate security.

ACCOUNTABILITY: A STEPPED CHANGE IS REQUIRED

The GFC highlighted how distorted incentives can create asset bubbles that eventually burst. As Cassidy (2010, p. 211) observed, 'unfortunately, there is nothing in a typical banker's employment contract that says he should take into account the impact of his actions on the economy as a whole.' This alone is a compelling reason for more active regulatory intervention. The debate over 'light touch' or 'heavy touch' regulation is over; the heavy touch advocates have won and by a big score. This is not to argue for yet more regulation; the current volume of regulation dominates bank board agendas and dulls their senses. It is to argue for

---

300 Roddan, M., 'SMEs "slugged with higher rates"', *The Australian*, 16 March 2013, p. 25.

greater supervision, intervention, direction and real consequence management under existing regulation. The BEAR legislation is long overdue, and it must demonstrate bite not just growl. The 'shocked and embarrassed … worst day of my life' utterances and tweets from CEOs when the bank is found to have broken the law or violated ethical and moral standards, have become so routine that they have lost any currency and are not seen as being authentic, even when the remorse is genuine (as it often is when you are caught).

Societal cynicism runs deep. The hypocrisy and lack of authenticity of such utterances is only underlined in cases where the offending bank has fought hard not to disclose its violation. Society rightly says, 'you get paid enough to manage this, you've failed and should accept accountability'. Instead, in what was a disgraceful year (2018), in addition to numerous scandals, the share prices of the major banks had a significant correction that hurt investors; the consequence for most bankers was to 'lose' $1–2 million from their bonus – that is what punishment feels like when you run a bank; you get a $2 million bonus instead of a $3–4 million bonus. Personal accountability is vital if change is to have any chance of succeeding and boards have to lift their game so that they understand what corporate governance really means and address the concerns Adam Smith espoused in 1776, close to 250 years ago.

There is no history of real accountability in the Australian banking sector, nor is there any, in any meaningful way, in the UK. The societal disquiet with the 'soft' approach taken to offences caused by individuals and banks was summed up by Kay (2015, p. 272):

> If London casinos were even accused of the malpractice to which London banks have admitted – false reporting, misleading customers and unauthorised trading – the individuals responsible would be barred

from the industry and the licences of the institution concerned revoked within hours. The finance sector has experienced actual criminality on a wide scale, from liar loans to LIBOR rate-fixing. Leading firms in the industry have come to regard the payment of billions in fines and compensation as routine. A culture has developed in which any action, no matter how close to the borders of legality, is acceptable if it is profitable.

There is no substitute for the regulator being an active participant in the market it regulates, without being exposed to regulatory capture. This is not a statement on mistrusting banks to self-regulate and do the right thing, but a mature reflection on decades of miscalculations in a sector that has been given many privileges including that of largely acting in its own private interest.[301] It is also reflecting that the major banks are quasi-nationalised firms. The then chairman of HSBC, Douglas Flint, when talking in 2012 about the wave of regulation hitting banks in the UK, candidly acknowledged: 'I think we have lost the right to self-determination … It doesn't really matter whether any of us think it [the new rules] will be our optimal choice as I think we have lost the right to determine ourselves what we think the optimal choice is' (Salz, 2013, p. 77). To his great credit, similar sentiment was expressed by the NAB chairman Phil Chronican, who acknowledged that the banking industry was embroiled in a self-inflicted 'culture and conduct crisis' that made tougher regulation entirely appropriate.[302]

BOARDS

Apart from being able to see the big picture as to the impact of the industry's activities on the economy, boards must be in touch with

---

[301] Danckert, S., 'ASIC attacks bank attitudes to regulation', *Sydney Morning Herald*, 15 March 2019, p. 22.

[302] Yeates, C. & Chrysanthos, N., 'NAB chief blames banks for "culture crisis" and its costs', *Sydney Morning Herald*, 27 March 2019, p. 19.

what is happening in the inner-workings of the banks. Not just in a perfunctory way, but with a finger on the pulse and by encouraging an environment where staff at all levels feel they can access senior management and the board. Boards will learn more about the culture and the problems in a bank by meeting staff close to the coalface than they will by listening to C-suite executives. In the APRA report on culture and governance at CBA, the 6000 survey respondents highlighted this truth in a very powerful way. All major bank boards should commission such a survey on an annual basis for a review that is untainted by management intervention. Regulators should be involved in the design of the survey and be satisfied as to the integrity of the process.

Boards may reflect on their responsibilities as stewards of the bank. The BEAR requirements may act as a catalyst for this and a candid assessment of 'fit for purpose' has merit. Integral to this is a re-examination of capabilities at board level that is more than a quest for diversity. Ideally both can be achieved – expert directors and a diverse board. However, the former should not be sacrificed to achieve the latter. There is also a credible argument that as major banks are quasi-nationalised and the taxpayer provides a guarantee on deposits, as well as a put option on failure, the government or regulator should nominate a director to the board of each major bank. That appointee should in turn chair the remuneration committee of the board.

Boards and management in big banks can be hugely complacent on the risk of new entrants, largely because of the emotional equity they have invested in what is their natural DNA steeped in history and traditions. They can be dismissive and sometimes arrogant to the many advantages that new, start-up firms have; it is hard for them to conceive how 'their' business of a hundred years standing with economies of scale can be 'beaten' by a new entrant, yet they also fear the Eastman Kodak destiny. The 'success is toxic' risk is a reality few banks can comprehend. The risk therefore that something will change the economic model of the industry, just as Uber, Airbnb and Netflix have in other industries, cannot be discounted as remote. For a while there was a sense that blockchain would; others will follow. Bank boards need to make sure that their bank is fit for the future. Part of this is to acknowledge that new entrants may have significant advantages, which can be summarised as the absence of the five legacies: technology, infrastructure assets, business processes, management and board thinking, and culture.

In so many ways, the biggest risk facing many incumbents today is not legacy IT or infrastructure assets (though this is a big issue in banking as it is in retailing), but *legacy thinking* and *culture*.

FINTECHS AND OTHERS

The strategic, digital, operational and cultural challenges facing large firms (banks), argued Harvard professor Clayton Christensen in his excellent book *The innovator's dilemma: when new technologies cause great firms to fail* (1997), is that they want to employ their resources in substantial markets that offer higher profits, play to their comparative advantage and allow them to deploy economies of scale and scope. To expect these same firms (banks) to meaningfully nurture disruptive technologies and to risk significant investment in uncertain outcomes, is akin to flapping one's arms with wings strapped to them to fly. Such expectations, argues Christensen, involve fighting fundamental tendencies about the way big organisations work and how their performance is evaluated. The track record of challenger incubators succeeding within large banks is nowhere near as successful as those same incubators performing outside the 'shackles' of the large banks. Being a fledgling business within a large bank can be a very lonely place to be when the initial enthusiasm wanes and other priorities, often reinforced by short-termism, cause capital and operating expenses to be prioritised on what is counted today – keeping the current business model competitive and short-term earnings in line with market expectations and executive incentive arrangements.

Today, technology is eroding many of the Coasean transaction costs and making it easier for smaller firms, often using a judo strategy (speed and agility to combat the size and strength of incumbents),[303] to challenge the dominance of big banks. It is far too soon to comment on the success of FinTechs and neobanks. Having smart technology and slick apps is one thing, having the management competency to build a profitable, scalable business is something else.

FINAL WORDS

It is important to keep in mind that the criticism of banks is not unique to Australia. Similar sentiment can be found in other markets, as Martin Wolf summed up in commenting on the banking sector a decade after the GFC: 'Today's rent-extracting economy, masquerading as a free market, is after all hugely rewarding to politically influential insiders.'[304] These are confronting words but they strike a chord with many and may help explain the loss of confidence in institutions and in the power of capitalism – though the true spirit of capitalism espoused by Adam Smith has been badly wronged by significant corporate governance and public policy failings. Globally, since the GFC, fines close to US$300 billion have been imposed on banks (King, 2016, p. 100), but for many banks, this is merely a 'cost of doing business' and life is largely allowed to go on. The power of capitalism has also been

---

303 Yoffie, D. & Kwak, M., 'How to compete like a judo strategist', *Harvard Business School*, 16 July 2001, <https://hbswk.hbs.edu>.

304 Wolf, M., 'Why so little has changed since the financial crash', *Financial Times*, 4 September 2018.

badly and unfairly damaged by the demise in competition. This is a tragedy that only government can fix; in the public interest, in the interest of consumer welfare.

A banking system loses much when it is defined by a small group of large banks. A sustainable banking system comprises a variety of players, from large banks to regional banks and to specialist banks. Handelsbanken illustrates how a customer and community focused bank can be both national and local, and in selected foreign markets it can bring these attributes as a hard-to-replicate comparative advantage.

Banking should be a noble and proud profession, one that is central to how society and the economy functions. Professionalism and risk management are core qualities and competencies. Culture matters enormously and cultural capital should be cherished and invested in. Banking should get back to basics, to its social licence; 'banking as it used to be, banking as it should be'. Government policy and the regulatory agencies have a central role to play in addressing the problems that the industry faces. The public humiliation of a number of senior executives following the Royal Commission will soon be forgotten and old habits re-emerge unless the rules of the game are changed. History matters in banking and all ambitious bankers should first and foremost appreciate the history of the industry and learn the lessons that it can teach; they should never, ever, fall into the trap of believing that 'this time is different'. We cannot foresee the future despite what economic forecasts might have us believe, but we can study the past. In banking this matters more than in any other industry, which is another reason that banks, these man-made institutions, are unique and what they do is of legitimate societal interest.

Perhaps it is the profound words of T. S. Eliot in 'Little Gidding' (1942) that captures the journey the banking industry has been on for the last three decades, where it finds itself today and what the future holds:

We shall not cease from exploration
And the end of all our exploring
Will be to arrive where we started
And know the place for the first time.

Banking as it used to be, banking as it should be.

EPILOGUE

IN reading this book, some people may reflect that where I cite publicised events critical of NAB, I was a senior executive there between 2007 and 2014, and thus what role did I play and what responsibility do I take? These are legitimate questions.

During that period, I was on the Group Executive Committee, the Group Risk Management Committee and the Group Asset and Liability Committee of the bank. I ran NAB's largest division, which accounted for 50 per cent of the bank's profits in most of the years I was there.

During most of my time at NAB, I reported to Cameron Clyne, who I consider to be a person of high integrity. I used to compare the NAB executive team in terms of its banking experience with that at ANZ, whom I knew well. There was no comparison. ANZ was headed by Mike Smith, an international banker who had spent much of his career at HSBC, and had within its ranks Phil Chronican, a career banker mainly at Westpac, Bob Edgar, who had been around the senior ranks at ANZ for decades, Shayne Elliott, who had extensive experience at Citibank and ANZ, and Graham Hodges, who was a seasoned banker. NAB lacked that breadth and depth of banking experience after two outstanding banking executives, Peter Thodey and Michael Ullmer, had left the bank. When I looked at the senior ranks at CBA, another bank that is cited much in this book, under the then CEO, Ian Narev, I felt that they were highly talented people, but had limited if any commercial banking experience, particularly outside of CBA.

The lack of substantial and broadly-based banking experience within the senior ranks at NAB did accentuate a problem dating back to 1999 when Don Argus stepped down as CEO. The bank seemed plagued by an inability to get its succession planning at both CEO and board level right. It thankfully dodged a bullet (a nuclear explosion) when it failed to appoint Fred Goodwin as CEO. The debacle in 2004 when the board imploded and six directors including the CEO, Frank Cicutto, resigned, was a huge embarrassment. The fiasco that followed the release of the Royal Commission report in 2019, caused one newspaper commentator sum up the situation: 'Poor judgement and lack of common sense have been prominent features of NAB's public profile over the past year.'[305] He could have added 'indeed, over the past decade if not longer'. The truth is that NAB had, to quote one commentator, 'an unfortunate knack of ensnaring itself in traps of its own making.'[306]

In my time there, a defining moment was when the bank's executive committee met in London in 2010. I openly expressed to my fellow executives how disillusioned I had become over the chronic underperformance that had plagued the bank, particularly since 2007. I felt then that this was only going to get worse given the internal consensus views emerging on strategy, technology platform transformation and other investment priorities. I was concerned that the culture in the bank did not welcome realism and was very weak on accountability. Two events brought this home. First, the hugely embarrassing IT mishap in 2010 when

---

305 Boyd, T., 'NAB governance fails again', *Australian Financial Review*, 8 February 2019, p. 40.
306 Letts, S., 'NAB entrenches itself as Australia's most accident-prone bank as it sets up a mountain', *ABC News*, 7 May 2019.

a corrupt file was loaded into the system, resulting in hundreds of thousands of customer payments being misplaced and causing considerable distress to customers and staff. This event was described as 'one of the biggest failures in Australian banking history.'[307] The accountable senior executive was subsequently promoted into another senior role. The second event related to the senior executive being accountable for the $1.1 billion CDO debacle in 2008; he was then transferred to NAB's UK operations as deputy CEO.

The unwillingness to prioritise areas of chronic weakness contrasted with my time at ANZ. At ANZ, John McFarlane would insist on a discipline that all businesses must first *perform*, then they can *grow* and then they can make major investments in the future (*breakout*). Apart from the well-publicised problems with NAB's UK business, the Retail Banking/Personal Banking division was sucking the economics out of NAB and it needed fixing, before it needed investment. It was a chronic industry underperformer. I had seen at ANZ, first through Elmer Funke Kupper then Brian Hartzer, how top-class management can revitalise a flagging retail banking business. For some time, the market had been sending NAB a strong message on what it thought of its management.

Why then, didn't I leave?

There were several reasons. First, having convinced several talented executives to join the bank, I felt a strong sense of obligation to them. Second, I was concerned that if I left the Business Bank, some of the experimental management thinking that was emerging elsewhere in the bank would filter into the Business Bank and damage it, more than the underinvestment already was. My legacy would therefore be defined by a weaker business than the strong one that others had built and I had inherited. Third, I felt a deep sense of responsibility to the thousands of employees

---

307 Ibid.

who were passionate about looking after the bank's customers and who had enormous pride in the bank's brand. Fourth, I genuinely loved working with the bank's business customers. I saw a strong social purpose in supporting Australia's SME economy and this was something that NAB had excelled at. Fifth, I was hoping that things would change for the better. There was a sixth reason: it is hard to leave a role that can pay up to $3.5 million per annum and be exposed to the thin senior executive banking labour market that exists in Australia – a sense of frustration and disillusionment can, for a while, be tempered by money. I do not feel good about that the sixth reason, but it was a reality.

All that said, I am not distancing myself from criticism levelled at the management team during my time there and the period that followed. Many of the issues that NAB was criticised for by the Royal Commission were evident during the time I was a senior executive at the bank. I deeply regret the decision to offshore the financial analysis of customers to an outsource agent in Jaipur, India. It saved costs but was in essence an underinvestment in core capabilities – focusing on what is *counted* and losing sight of what *counts*. There were other aspects of the operation that, with hindsight, I should have made earlier interventions on.

The chronically underperforming share price that has been a feature of the bank relative to its peers for well over a decade, speaks volumes and requires little further commentary on how the bank has performed.[308] I accept my share of responsibility as a member of the leadership team. I made my fair share of mistakes and miscalculations. Looking back, the major point of self-reflection was my inability to exert more influence. The final irony was a 2014 discussion with the newly appointed CEO in a private room at the Melbourne Crown Towers hotel. Arranged and accompanied by his trusted advisor, Rosemary Rogers, he

---

308 'Those who purchased national Australia bank shares five years ago have a 28% loss to show for it', Simply Wall St, 4 March 2019, <https://simplywall.st/>.

emphasised that his biggest priority as CEO was that of culture and his intention to transform the bank's culture and build a customer centric bank.

The sense of frustration with the prevailing ethos did however inspire me and some others, in particular David Hornery, to establish Judo Bank. While I had other career options, and already in my fifties when most people's risk appetite modifies, I had become convinced in 2015, motivated by a strong sense of purpose, that there was a real opportunity to build a bank that specialises in SME banking. Both David and I had also become convinced, as keen students of and experienced executives in the banking sector, that a fundamental change in culture and operations within the major banks was not going to be possible. The cultural concrete was well and truly set and the protection of the industry structure meant that the pressure to change would wane as it had done so many times in the past. The banks were locked on a path dependent course and had become deeply indoctrinated in the importance of financialisation or productisation – that is that the banks were not there to serve the real economy, but to meet their own private interest needs, notwithstanding the nature of their social licence, the privileges bestowed on them and the quasi-nationalised nature of their risk. The toothpaste would not go back into the tube of the current system.

The industrialisation process evident in the banks (the 'sameness' is uncanny), resulted in a market gap opening in the way that SMEs were being served. When it comes to banking SMEs, a serious market failure had become evident. The banks were largely presenting a 'take it or leave it' one-size-fits-all proposition that took the SME economy for granted. SMEs deserved better. Together with others, building Judo Bank, from the start-up, was driven by a passion in the importance of banking to the success of SMEs and that there was a strong public good in SME banking as it used to be, SME banking as it should be.

ACKNOWLEDGEMENTS

WRITING a serious book on a high profile and topical subject is not an easy undertaking. It is a long and lonely journey, requiring discipline and the support of others. My journey however was made easier by the generosity of others, who took the time to review parts and, in many cases, the whole of the manuscript. The quality of feedback and thoughtfulness that I received from the people who reviewed the manuscript – always a torturous task – helped shape this book. While the views expressed in this book are mine, as are any errors or omissions, I do want to particularly acknowledge the following people: Tim Alexander, Chris Bayliss, Jacqui Colwell, John Dahlsen, Sandra de Castro, Graham Dickens, Milton Harris, Alastair Hawkins, Michael Heath, David Hornery, Kate Keenan, Rick Kennerley, Mandy Jaing, Vimpi Juneja, Arun Nangia, Jeff Price, Jason Maletic, Stephen Mifsud, Denis Novak, George Obeid, Heloise Syme, Meena Thuraisingham, Gulnaz Wahaf, Kris Whitehead and Frank Versace. Many are colleagues at Judo Bank, all are friends and people I hold in the highest of regard. There are others who provided comments but would probably find any reference to their thoughtfulness to be undesirable and unhelpful.

Finally, I would like to record my appreciation to the highly professional team at Ventura Press, in particular Managing Editor, Zoe Hale and Marketing Coordinator, Sophie Hodge. Both have been a delight to work with, consistently providing good advice and skillfully managing the process that allowed this book to be published. The team at Ventura Press are a credit to the craft of book publishing and l recommend them to any writer looking for a first-class publisher.

The usual caveat is particularly important: I made it clear at the outset that the views in this book are strictly personal and should not be read as representing the views of others or of Judo Bank. Equally, none of the organisations or individuals mentioned in the book are implicated in any way with the views expressed in the book. Those views, together with any errors, remain mine.

APPENDIX 1 – WHAT DO BANKS DO?

WHY BANKS ARE IMPORTANT

Information Costs:	• Banks have an incentive to collect information about customers and monitor their actions. The size of banks provides economies of scale in managing and analysing information.
Liquidity and price risk:	• Banks provide financial claims to households and businesses with special liquidity attributes and lower price risk.
Maturity intermediaries & Transformation:	• Banks can better manage the risk of maturity mismatch between assets and liabilities e.g. borrow short, lend long.
Transaction Service:	• Economies of scale give banks an efficiency advantage in transmitting and receiving payments, both domestically and internationally.
International Services:	• International corresponding networks allow banking to assist customers in international trade and payments.
Credit Allocation:	• Banks are often the major (sometimes only) source of financing for households and small businesses. They are an important source as liquidity management for larger businesses.
Transmission of monetary policy:	• Banks are the conduit through which monetary policy actions by the central bank flow through into the broader financial system and economy.
Risk reduction & diversification & imperfect information:	• Banks do this based on economies of scale and dealing with information asymmetry or imperfect information.

APPENDIX II – BANKER RISK ASSESSMENT TEST

BANKER ASSESSMENT TEST

BUSINESS BACKGROUND

Frank Pipedream P/L is an independent boutique firm of lawyers, established by Frank (aged 54) in 1990. The firm specialises in providing high quality legal services to clients in a broad range of industries. There is a diverse client base with no client representing greater than 10% of total fees. Some 80% of clients (70% of fees) have been with the firm for more than five years.

Frank has been a respected lawyer for more than 30 years and is also a collector of vintage cars, having amassed a collection in excess of $14 million that is all in the name of the firm. Currently the ownership of the cars is dealt with via a side agreement which entitles the benefits of ownership to Frank only (despite the cars being shown as assets of the firm on its balance sheet).

Existing partner George Positive (15%) wants to sell his equity stake back to Frank and continue as a salaried partner. This will occur via Frank taking over George's equity loan with the residual payment to be structured as a vendor loan over five years (total payment incl. existing debt $1 million).

Google and credit checks have been completed and there is nothing adverse revealed.

While Frank will revert to be the sole principal in the business, he has a succession plan in place. Two new partners are to be appointed in 2025, in anticipation of an upswing in the demand for legal work linked to SME credit growth. In each case they will acquire equity from Frank valued at $700,000. The percentage of equity this will constitute will be dependent on the profitability at that time to which a multiple will be applied. It is expected to be around 5% to 7% of the equity in each case. In each case it is expected that a guarantee and a general security agreement will be required to support the equity buy-in transaction of the new partners.

Frank is expecting the business to grow, and the aim is within 10 years to be turning over $15 million with partners and shareholders of around six people.

CUSTOMER REQUEST

Customer seeks funding as follows:
- Term debt $1,400,000 to refinance existing debt. The original purpose was for two acquisitions of legal practices in 2010 and 2014. The balance will be used to take out the overdraft, currently a $424,079 debit balance.
- Existing overdraft limit $500,000 of which $400,000 appears hardcore.
- Term debt $800,000 to refinance external equity buy-in loan ($300,000 to Harry (75% shareholder) and $500,000 to Jeff (25% shareholder)). Both debts are held in the respective partner's personal names.
- Term debt $2,100,000 to refinance car loans on the firm's balance sheet.

The firm currently has amortising loans via a mix of 3- and 5-year funding terms, which are creating cash flow issues and the firm is seeking relief via a 10-year amortisation program, which will also assist with allowing the business to self-fund seasonal working capital needs.

ATO RB (ICA) 01/01/2018–28/05/2018 shows an opening balance of $13,730 debit. Regular payments were made to clear this and the closing balance is zero.

Trading account statements for 30/11/2018–08/06/2019 show satisfactory account conduct. Account does not exceed the $500,000 limit but never goes into credit.

Valuation of Practice

6/2018	6/2017	6/2016
$4,903,335	$3,667,501	$5,274,243

Valuation is based on a *multiple of revenue*, a multiple of 2.5 times for wealth recurring income and 1 time for broker income.

6/2018	3/2018	6/2017	6/2016
$4,698,623	$3,523,967	$4,968,792	$5,380,045

Valuation is based on a *multiple of 2.5 times EBITDA* after notional payments to partners. EBITDA used as opposed to EBIT due to the heavy depreciation on the cars.

Valuation based on T/O and EBITDA multiples are not significantly different.

6/2018 are annualised accounts.
3/2018 are managements.
6/2017 and 6/2016 are finals.

Subordination of partners loans
Partners loans (6/2018: $12,785,141) to be subordinated.

Cars
The firm has amassed a substantial vintage car collection that has been independently valued for insurance purposes. Insurance policy from Mean Insurance Brokers confirming insurance on the cars of $6,885,000. The cars are in the name of Frank Pipedream. Estimated value more than $9,500,000.

Frank Pipedream
Frank is insured for Life $5,500,000 and TPD (total and permanent disability) $1,700,000.

Statement of net wealth at 24/05/2019: Net asset position $4,600,000, mainly superannuation and property.

FINANCIAL ANALYSIS
Frank Pipedream & Associates P/L

Profit & Loss	30/06/2018	31/03/2018	30/06/2017	30/06/2016
Revenue	$3,771,796	$2,828,847	$4,057,110	$3,757,556
NPBT	$491,349	$368,512	$620,354	$7,574
EBITDA	$1,013,397	$760,048	$1,072,978	$699,101
Payment to partners	$866,052	$649,539	$914,539	$1,452,917
EBITDA before payment to partners	$1,879,449	$1,409,587	$1,987,517	$2,152,018
Adjusted EBITDA	$1,612,783	$1,209,587	$1,787,517	$1,952,018
Total debt / adjusted EBITDA	2.96	3.94	2.67	2.44

- EBITDA includes HPC due to the asset finance component related to the cars.

- Adjusted EBITDA is EBITDA before payment to partners less notional salary $200,000.
- Total debt is $4,770,000.
- Heavy depreciation due to the cars.

Balance sheet	31/03/2018	30/06/2017	30/06/2016
Debtors	$112,854	$109,869	$122,697
WIP	$975,000	$900,000	$950,000
Creditors	$534,456	$450,767	$397,822
Working capital position	$553,398	$559,102	$674,875
Goodwill	$7,801,783	$7,801,783	$7,801,783
Cars	$14,434,846	$14,643,306	$12,579,497
Loans from directors	$12,121,356	$12,885,585	$11,253,874
Equity	$7,916,588	$7,548,076	$6,927,722
Total equity	$20,037,944	$20,433,661	$18,181,596
Total debt / total equity	23.80%	23.34%	26.24%

- Based on market multiple the practice has a value of $6,174,243 (6/2017).
- Total equity is equity plus loans from partners to be subordinated.

Debtors 15/06/2018
- Debtors listing analysed with no material concentration.

Aged work-in-progress (WIP) 15/06/2018
- Total $694,238 and greater than 120 days $304,431.
- Frank Pipedream & Associates P/L lock-up (sum of WIP and debtors) usually constitutes circa 25% of total turnover. This is considered in line with industry standards. The current lock-up is $1,083,999, which is a bit higher than normal, but not unusual for later in the financial year when such things tend to build up.

APPENDIX II – BANKER RISK ASSESSMENT TEST

Servicing Ratios	30/06/2018	30/06/2017	30/06/2016
Adjusted EBITDA	$1,612,783	$1,787,517	$1,952,018
Repayments (actual)	$881,160	$881,160	$881,160
Repayments (sensitised)	$958,932	$958,932	$958,932
Interest Expense (actual)	$382,462	$382,462	$382,462
Interest Expense (sensitised)	$481,162	$481,162	$481,162
Debt Dervice Cover (actual)	1.83	2.03	2.22
Debt Dervice Cover (sensitised)	1.68	1.86	2.04
Interest Cover (actual)	4.22	4.67	5.10
Interest Cover (sensitised)	3.35	3.72	4.06

QUESTIONS:

1. Discuss the positive and negative features of the transaction.
2. Would you support the transaction as proposed (please feel free to make any assumptions which close any gaps in information – please discuss).
3. If supporting the transaction advise of structure (security, term, etc.). Would you need any further information? If so what?
4. Discuss the potential structure for the future succession plan transactions to the senior staff members. What are some considerations here, how would you structure these transactions?

CREDIT CAPABILITY TESTING

Question	Response
CHARACTER	
How would you assess a business owner's capability and business acumen?	
What are the key management attributes you would look for in assessing management capability?	
How do you challenge the information provided by the customers and/or third parties to ensure their validity and accuracy?	
Explain the relevance of background credit checks in determining customer character. When would you be comfortable to proceed with a transaction where an adverse credit finding existed?	

APPENDIX II – BANKER RISK ASSESSMENT TEST

CAPACITY	
Would you consider supporting a transaction with a Debt Service Cover Ratio of less than 1 time?	
What are the cash flow drivers that you would look at when assessing a customer's working capital requirement?	

Consider the following Balance sheet movements:
 	
                        2017   2018
    Debtors $875k $750k
    Creditors $600k $975k
    Accum. dep'n $300k $375k
    Stock $400k $850k
 	
Assuming all other balance sheet / P&L assess the WC requirement created by the above movements.	

What measures would you take in verifying a customer's personal living expenses when utilising the director's uncommitted personal income for servicing purposes?	

What is the relevance of a customer's tax position in a credit assessment? When would you be comfortable proceeding with a transaction that had tax arrears history?

When would it be inappropriate to add back depreciation when assessing a customer's servicing capacity?

CAPITAL

Why do you think it is appropriate to leverage a standalone Asset Finance transaction more aggressively than a residential property?

When determining the appropriate leverage in an enterprise value lend (i.e. against the goodwill of the business), what factors would you consider?

COLLATERAL

How do you determine the collateral requirement for a transaction?

When would you consider a more aggressive gearing for a property investment transaction than the typical 65–70% threshold of the major banks?

GENERAL

Explain your view on the difference between Debt Risk and Equity Risk?

How do you determine the appropriate covenant/reporting structure for a transaction?

What are some of the early warning signs of a customer in distress (excluding arrears)?

Explain your approach with a customer demonstrating early warning signs of deteriorating credit risk?

What are the key things you would consider in a business acquisition transaction where no additional external property security is being offered?

APPENDIX III – PRINCIPLES OF CREDIT RISK MANAGEMENT

FIFTEEN TIMELESS LESSONS ON CREDIT RISK MANAGEMENT

1. ALWAYS REMEMBER THE FOUR C'S

Character, capacity (cash flow), capital and collateral, in that order. It is important that a banker diligently work through each of the Four C's and be satisfied that the borrowers is strong in at least three and is not weak in the other.

2. QUALITY OF CREDIT SHOULD NEVER BE COMPROMISED TO DRIVE ASSET GROWTH

Anyone can lend money, but it takes skill to get it back.

You cannot charge a high enough interest rate to compensate for loans that are likely never to be repaid. But in times of loan expansion, it is easy to seek to override this rule about credit quality. Such an attitude is just as dangerous as that of the business that sells products without any profit margin or even below cost!

3. EVERY LOAN SHOULD HAVE TWO WAYS OUT

The first way out should be from the cash flows. It will be the successful achievement of cash flows enough to repay the bank from the company's operations that counts. The second way, in the event of failure to generate the necessary cash flows, will be action by the borrower either in realising assets or in drawing on their resources, which would include raising debt or equity by other means in other markets.

Sometimes bankers require borrowers to accept demanding, occasionally unrealistic constraints to make the loan acceptable. If you need to do this in order to feel comfortable, you should question whether to make the loan at all.

4. THE BORROWER'S INTEGRITY MUST BE UNDOUBTED – ALWAYS LOOK AT THE BORROWER NOT THE ASSET OR THE COLLATERAL

The first 'C' is critical. If there any questions as to the integrity, honesty or good intentions of the borrower, you should never lend. You must check on the ethical standing/reputation and style of business before beginning negotiations. Remember that banks who associate with people of less than acceptable character damage their own reputation far beyond the profit obtained on the transaction. Always be very careful with dominant and egotistical business owners/CEOs. Asking questions of others in the industry will also help you assess a company's management quality.

5. IF YOU DO NOT UNDERSTAND THE BUSINESS, DO NOT LEND TO IT

If you do not understand the business model or industry, how can you evaluate the risks?

6. OWN YOUR DECISION AND BE ACCOUNTABLE

Credit decisions are personal. They cannot be made solely based on guidelines or analytic techniques. Each banker must exercise common sense and good judgement. You must also be sure that it is your own independent judgement on each transaction and that you are not unduly influenced by others. It is easy to forget in times of economic growth that the business cycle also has a downswing. These lessons must be kept in mind whatever the phase of the cycle. The cost of loan losses is not just the write-off of the bad debt, it is also the cost involved in managing recovery situations and damage can be done to reputations.

7. THE BUSINESS CYCLE IS INEVITABLE

A banker must always be conscious of the current point in the business cycle so that you can evaluate the risks likely to arise when economic conditions change in the future. Things are always either getting better or getting worse, but sometimes the change is imperceptible. At certain points in the business cycle, lending appears less risky. It has been well said that bad loans are made in good times.

8. LENDING TO NEW CUSTOMERS IS ALWAYS RISKIER THAN LENDING TO EXISTING CUSTOMERS.

This should be obvious as you know existing customers or customers you have done business with in previous banks. Statistics show that banks have a disproportionate level of losses from customers that they have known for less than two years. The ratio can be as high as 2:1 loss from new customers relative to established customers.

9. COLLATERAL SECURITY IS NOT A SUBSTITUTE FOR REPAYMENT

Repayment comes from cash flow; security is taken partly to prevent these assets from being available to other lenders and partly to place the lender in a stronger negotiating position because the assets are usually necessary to operate the business.

When security is valued, there must be no conflict of interest by the valuer. You must also be conscious of differences in market value, liquidation value, and forced sale value.

10. LENDING TO SMALLER BORROWERS IS RISKIER THAN LENDING TO LARGER ONES.

Although the same principles apply to small firms as to large ones, in a small firm managerial resource are fewer as is financial headroom and options.

11. FAST GROWING BUSINESSES ARE RISKIER

Statistics on credit losses consistently show that a disproportionate number of losses are attributable to businesses with high growth rates. Quite often the rate of growth outstrips the management capabilities and financial capital in the business.

12. VALUE ATTENTION TO DETAIL AND SOUND CREDIT ADMINISTRATION

A high proportion of write-offs are associated with sloppy administration or documentation. Never assume that loan agreements will not be relied upon. As fate has it, it is just those that are prepared in a hurry that are most likely to be tested in court!

13. SEE WHERE THE BANK'S MONEY IS GOING TO BE SPENT

If you do not visit the company, you will not get a feel for the atmosphere, corporate style, and other intangible effects. It often pays, especially with smaller companies, to check out what the management tells you. Seek evidence that the borrowed funds are being applied for the purpose they were intended for.

14. THINK FIRST FOR THE BANK – RISK INCREASES WHEN CREDIT PRINCIPLES ARE VIOLATED

Good judgement, experience, and common sense are the marks of the good banker. The principles set out here are not perfect but are broken at your peril. If in doubt, ask yourself: 'Would I lend my own money?'

15. INVOLVE COLLEAGUES FROM RISK EARLY

Building personal credibility with colleagues in risk management is critical to career success. Credibility is built by demonstrating a strong alignment to the bank's risk culture and demonstrating disciplined first line of defence values. Respect for the pivotal role played by risk management as the second line of defence is essential. The ability to work collaboratively with colleagues in risk management is a core value. Good bankers involve colleagues from risk management early in the development of a deal and seek their input and advice on how a transaction might be structured. Poor bankers, on the other hand, look at risk as a hurdle and fail to develop a productive working relationship with colleagues in Risk. Consequently, the banker's own personal effectiveness is diminished and trust within risk management undermined.

The lesson of history is that all too often bankers do not learn the lessons of history.

APPENDIX IV – THE THREE LINES OF DEFENCE FRAMEWORK

THE THREE LINES OF DEFENCE RISK GOVERNANCE MODEL

BOARD	
• Establishes a governance structure (board subcommittees, executive responsibilities and risk management and assurance functions). • Is ultimately responsible for the risk management framework and oversees its operation by management. • Sets the risk appetite within which it expects management to operate and approves the RAS.	• Approves the institution's risk management strategy. • Forms a view of the risk culture in the institution, and the extent to which that culture supports the ability of the institution to operate consistently within its risk appetite, identifies any desirable changes to the risk culture and ensures the institution takes steps to address those changes.
Board Risk Committee	**Board Audit Committee**

THREE LINES OF DEFENCE

While each of the Three Lines of Defence has its own responsibilities, they all have a common approach to risk management.

The **first line** of defence is the business managers, who define and manage processes, people and technology. They take ownership of the risks the units take, including identifying and assessing risk in line with risk appetite.

The **second line** of defence, risk management, supports the first line of defence managers in their ownership of risk and controls by establishing and communicating common risk management policies, risk management practices, assessment methodologies and standards.

The **third line** of defence, external auditors, validates the manager's risk and control assessments, including testing them where appropriate. They also provide the management board and the board with independent assurance of the design and operating effectiveness of the organisation's risk management activities.

The Three Lines of Defence framework is represented as follows:

First Line of Defence Risk Owners	Second Line of Defence Review and Challenge	Third Line of Defence Independent Assurance
BUSINESS MANAGEMENT	RISK	AUDIT
Implementation, ongoing maintenance and enhancement of the Risk Management Framework, including: a. identification and effective management and mitigation of risk; and b. recording, escalation and management of risks as they are identified.	Independent oversight of the risk profile and the Risk Management Framework, including: a. effective challenges to active decisions that materially affect the risk profile of the bank; b. developing, maintaining and enhancing the Risk Management Framework; and c. independent reporting lines to appropriately escalate issues.	Independent assurance that the Risk Management Framework has been complied with and is operating effectively.

Source: APRA, CPG 220 – Risk Management, January 2015, <https://www.apra.gov.au>

APPENDIX V – ROLE SPECIFICATION FOR A BANK DIRECTOR

INDEPENDENT NON-EXECUTIVE DIRECTOR – POSITION SPECIFICATION

THE BOARD

The board is led by the chairman, Malcolm Fearless, and comprises eight independent directors and two executive directors. Appendix X outlines the profiles of each of the directors.

The board is collectively responsible for the long-term success of the company, setting the strategy and overseeing delivery, establishing the culture, values and standards of the bank, monitoring financial performance and ensuring that the bank manages risk effectively. Additionally, the board considers succession planning and determines remuneration policies.

The key matters considered by the board over the last 12 months reflect topics important to the bank:
- Strategy and customer focus.
- The culture of the bank.
- Economic and industry conditions.
- Risk management.
- Contingency planning.

- Capital structure & management.
- Governance and director succession planning.
- Finance, statutory and regulatory requirements.

Last year, a total of 15 board meetings where held, eight of which were scheduled and seven were ad hoc. Over 50% of the board's time was spent on strategy and customer focus, including two biannual sessions of two-day duration to address major strategic issues. There are also regular informal 'deep dives' on topics of particular interest, as determined by the board.

The board aims to maintain an open, collegiate dialogue both inside and outside the formal board meetings – ensuring issues are identified and debated at an early stage and that non-executive directors can contribute constructively to shaping the business as well as providing appropriate independent challenge.

THE ROLE

The bank has set out the primary roles of a non-executive director as follows:
- Help develop and set the bank's strategy.
- Challenge constructively (helping to identify and manage risks).
- Participate actively in the decision-making process of the board.
- Scrutinise the performance of management in meeting agreed goals and objectives.
- Provide entrepreneurial leadership of the bank within a framework of prudent effective controls.
- Satisfy themselves on the integrity of financial information.
- Stay informed on matters effecting the bank's stakeholders.
- Scrutinise management on the quality of the engagement with regulators.
- Challenge management on progress in the development of

the bank's cultural capital.
- Determine appropriate levels of remuneration for the executive directors via the Remuneration Committee.

While non-executive directors are required to devote such time as is necessary for the discharge of their duties, on average this equated to at least 40–45 days per annum (including attendance at committee meetings). Fees for non-executive directors are $100,000 with additional committee membership fees payable at $20,000 for each committee. Non-executive directors are normally members of at least two committees, although free to attend others.

CANDIDATE PROFILE

Candidates must bring significant banking experience, preferably with a strong retail, small business and commercial focus. Expertise in SME banking is highly valued. Individuals will have held senior leadership positions in a large commercial bank or other large and complex financial services group and will bring a good understanding of the overall business and economic model, including customer segmentation, the importance of cultural capital, credit and conduct risk and capital management. An understanding of board governance is important. Prospective directors must complement the cultural dynamics of the board and play an effective role as a team member. The board is transparent, collegiate, thoughtful and commercially focused.

APPENDIX VI – THE ESSENTIALS OF GOOD BANKING

TWENTY ESSENTIALS OF GOOD BANKING

1. Risk management is a core competency.
2. You can't be a banker without first being a risk manager.
3. Uniform and consistent approach to risk-taking is vital.
4. Development of a common risk language is essential.
5. Have a historical perspective on the bank's and the market's risk experience.
6. The bank comes first and ahead of every profit centre/silo.
7. Candour and good communication at all levels.
8. Protect the bank's reputation.
9. Accountability for decisions and actions.
10. Long-term view as well as short-term view.
11. Respect for credit and operational risk management.
12. Reconciliation of market practice with common sense.
13. Use of independent judgement and not the herd instinct.
14. An understanding and respect for the bank's ALCO strategy.
15. Realistic approach to markets and budgeting.
16. Respect for regulators and compliance.
17. Risk appetite defines strategy.
18. Sound value system that will cope with change.
19. Unwavering commitment to the Three Lines of Defence.
20. Be clear on the bank's social licence and purpose.

BIBLIOGRAPHY

APRA, *Prudential inquiry into the Commonwealth Bank of Australia*, 2018, <https://www.apra.gov.au>.

Admati, A. & Hellwig, M., *The bankers' new clothes*, Princeton University Press: Princeton, 2013.

Akerlof, G. A., 'The market for "lemons": quality uncertainty and market mechanism', *Quarterly Journal of Economics*, vol. 84, no. 3, 1970, pp. 488–500.

Akerlog, G. A., & Romer, P. M., *Looting: the economic underworld of bankruptcy for profit*, NBER Working Paper No. R1869, 2004.

Allen, D. & Berg, C., *Australia's red tape crisis – the causes and cost of over-regulation*, Connor Court Publishing, 2018.

Augur, P., *The bank that lived a little*, Allen Lane: London, 2018.

Barney, J. B., 'Organizational culture: can it be a source of sustained competitive advantage?', *Academy of Management Review*, vol. 11, 1986, pp. 656–65.

Berle, A. & Means G., *The modern corporation and private property*, Transaction Publishers, 1932.

Berger, A. N., 'Relationship lending and lines of credit in small firm finance', *Journal of Business*, vol. 68, 1995, pp. 351–81.

Berger, A. N., 'Small business credit availability and relationship lending: the importance of bank organisational structure', *Economic Journal*, vol. 112, 2002, pp. 32–35.

Berger, A. N., 'A more complete conceptual framework for SME finance', *Journal of Banking & Finance*, vol. 30, 2006, pp. 2945–66.

Berger, A. N., Molyneux, P. & Wilson, J. O. (eds), *The Oxford handbook of banking*, Oxford University Press, 2010.

Brevoort, K. P., *An empirical examination of the growth in out-of-market lending: the changing competitive landscape and the role of asymmetric information*, working paper, Federal Reserve Board, 2006.

Browne, J. with Nuttall R. & Stadlen T., *Connect: how companies succeed by engaging radically with society*, W H Allen, 2015.

Carter, C. B. & Lorsch, J. W., *Back to the drawing board: designing corporate boards for a complex world*, Harvard Business School Press, 2003.

Cassidy, J., *How markets fail – the logic of economic calamities*, Penguin: London, 2009.

Cecchetti, S. G. & Kharroubi, E., *Why does credit growth crowd out real economic growth*, NBER Working Paper No. 25079, 2018.

Christensen, C. M., *The innovator's dilemma: when new technologies cause great firms to fail*, Harvard Business Review Press, 1997.

Coase, R. H., *The nature of the firm*, Economica, 1937.

Collier, Paul, (2018). *The future of capitalism*, Allen Lane: London, 2018.

Collins J. & Porras J. I., *Built to last: successful habits of visionary companies*, Collins, 1994.

Collins, J. C., *Good to great: why some companies make the leap ... and others don't*, Collins: New York, 2001.

Connolly, E., La Cava, G. & Read, M., 'Housing prices and entrepreneurship: evidence for the housing collateral channel in Australia', in Moore A. & Simon J. (eds), *Small business conditions and finance, proceedings of a conference*, Reserve Bank of Australia, Sydney, 2015, pp. 115–44.

Connolly, E. & Bank, J., 'Access to small business finance', Reserve Bank of Australia, *Bulletin*, September 2018.

Corrigan, G., 'Are banks special?', annual report, Federal Reserve Bank of Minneapolis, 1982.

Davis, S. I., *Banking in turmoil*, Palgrave Macmillan: London, 2009.

Deloitte, 'Apprehensive millennials: seeking stability and opportunities in an uncertain world', *The Deloitte millennial survey*, 2017, <https://www2.deloitte.com/il/en/pages/about-deloitte/articles/millennialsurvey.html>.

Eccles, R. G. & Crane, D. B., *Doing deals: investment banks at work*, Harvard Business Press: Boston, 1988.

Fraser, I., *Shredded – inside RBS, the bank that broke Britain*, Birlinn: Edinburgh, 2014.

Friedman, M., *Capitalism and freedom*, University of Chicago Press, 1962.

Fotaki, M. & Kenny, K., *Post-disclosure survival strategies: transforming whistleblower experiences*, Wiley, 2018.

Fukuyama, F., 'The coming collapse of America', *Australian Financial Review*, 28 December 2016, pp. 22–27.

Garratt, B., *The fish rots from the head: the crisis in our boardrooms*, HarperCollins Business, 1997.

Gladwell, M., *Blink: the power of thinking without thinking*, Penguin, 2005.

Gladwell, M., *Outliers – the story of success*, Little, Brown & Co., 2008.

Green, S., *Good value – reflections on money, morality and an uncertain world*, Penguin Books: London, 2009.
Hamel, G. & Prahalad, C. K., *Competing for the future*, Harvard Business Press: Boston, 1996.
Hargreaves, D., *Are chief executives overpaid?*, Polity, 2018.
Haskel, J. & Westlake, S., *Capitalism without capital – the rise of the intangible economy*, Princeton University Press, 2018.
Healy, J., *Corporate governance & wealth creation*, Dunmore Press, 2003.
Healy, J., *Chinese firms going global – can they succeed?*, World Scientific, 2018.
Hurley, R. F., Gillespie, N., Ferrin, D. L. & Dietz, G., 'Designing trustworthy organisations', *MIT Sloan Management Review*, 18 June 2013.
Kay, J., *Narrow banking: the reform of banking regulation*, CSFI, 2009, <https://www.csfi.org.uk>.
Kay, J., *Other people's money – masters of the universe or servants of the people?*, Profile Books: London, 2015.
Keynes, J. M., *The consequences to the banks of the collapse of money values*, 1931.
Keynes, J. M., *The general theory of employment, interest and money*, Palgrave Macmillan, 1936.
King, M., *The end of alchemy – money, banking and the future of the global economy*, Little, Brown Books: London, 2016.
Kramer, R., 'Rethinking trust', *Harvard Business Review*, June, 2009.
Kroner, N., *A blueprint for better banking – Svenska Handelsbanken and a proven model for more stable and profitable banking*, Harriman House: London, 2011.
Kwoka, J., *Mergers, merger control and remedies*, MIT Press, 2014.
Jensen, M. C., 'The modern industrial revolution, exit, and the failure of internal control systems', *The Journal of Finance*, July 1993, doi.org/10.1111/j.1540-6261.1993.tb04022.x.
Jorda, O., Schularick, M. & Taylor, A. M., *The great mortgaging: housing finance, crises and business cycles*, NBER Working Paper No. 20501, 2014.
Jorion, P., 'Risk management lessons from the credit crisis', *European Financial Management*, vol. 15, no. 5, 2009, pp. 923–33.
Kingsford-Smith, D., Clarke, T. & Rogers, J., 'Banking and the limits of professionalism', *UNSW Law Journal*, 2017.
Langley, M., *Tearing down the walls*, Simon & Schuster: New York, 2003, pp. 324–25.
Levilee, N. P., 'The role of obedience in society', *Inquiries Journal*, vol. 3, no. 5, 2011, p. 1.
Levitt, T., 'Marketing myopia', *Harvard Business Review*, 1960.
Luttrell, D., Atkinson, T. & Rosenblum, H., 'Assessing the costs and consequences of the 2007–09 financial crisis and its aftermath', *Federal Reserve Bank of Dallas: Economic Letter*, vol. 8, no. 7, 2013, pp. 1–4.

Martin, I., *Making it happen – Fred Goodwin, RBS and the men who blew up the British economy*, Simon & Schuster: New York, 2013.

Mayer, C., 'The future of the corporation: towards humane business', *Journal of the British Academy*, 2018, <https://www.thebritishacademy.ac.uk/publications/journal-british-academy/6s1/the-future-of-the-corporation-towards-humane-business>.

Micklethwait, J. & Wooldridge, A., *The company – a short history of a revolutionary idea*, A Modern Library Chronicles Book, 2003.

Miller M. & Modigliani F., 'The cost of capital, corporations, finance and the theory of investment', *American Finances Review*, vol. 48, no. 3, 1958, pp. 261–97.

Miller M. & Modigliani F., 'Corporate income taxes and the cost of capital: a correction', *American Finances Review*, vol. 53, no. 3, 1963, pp. 443–53.

Minsky, H. P. *Stabilizing an unstable economy*, New Haven: London, 1986, p. 237.

Minsky, H. P., 'A theory of systematic financial fragility', in Altman, E. J. & Sametz, A. W. (eds), *Financial crises: institutions and markets in a fragile environment*, Wiley: New York, 1977.

McKinsey & Company, 'New rules for an old game: banks in the changing world of financial intermediation', McKinsey global banking annual review, 2018.

Moore, C., 'The role of rewards, capabilities, and environment in driving behaviours', in *Transforming culture in financial services*, discussion paper DP18/2, 2018, pp. 60–62, <https://www.fca.org.uk>.

Morrison, J., *The social licence: how to keep your organisation legitimate*, Palgrave MacMillan: London, 2014.

Myers, S.C. & Majluf, N. S., 'Corporate financing and investment decisions when firms have information that investors do not have', *Journal of Financial Economics*, vol. 13, no. 2, 1984, pp. 187–221.

Perman, R. & Darling, A., *Hubris – how HBOS wrecked the best bank in Britain*, Birlinn: Edinburgh, 2013.

Pernell, K., Jung, J. & Dobbin, F., 'The hazards of expert controls: chief risk officers and risky derivatives', *American Sociological Review*, vol. 82, no. 3, 2017, pp. 511–41.

Peters, T., & Waterman, R. H., *In search of excellence: lessons from America's best-run companies*, HarperCollins, 1982.

Pixley, J., *Central banks, democratic states and financial power*, Cambridge University Press: Cambridge, 2018.

Porter, M. E. & Kramer, M. R., *Creating shared value*, Harvard Business Review, 2011.

Productivity Commission, *Competition in the Australian financial system: inquiry report*, No. 89, 29 June 2018.

Reinhart, C. M. & Rogoff, K. S., *This time is different – eight centuries of financial folly*, Princeton University Press, 2009.

Roberts, R., *How Adam Smith can change your life: an unexpected guide to human nature and happiness*, Deckle Edge, 2014.

Royal Commission into misconduct in the banking, superannuation and financial services industry: final report, February 2019, <https://financialservices.royalcommission.gov.au>.

Salz, A., *Salz review: an independent review of Barclays' business practices*, 2013, <https://online.wsj.com/public/resources/documents/SalzReview04032013.pdf>.

Schooner, H. H. & Taylor, M. W., *Global bank regulation – principles and policies*, Academic Press, Elsevier, 2010.

Schumpeter, J. (1942), *Capitalism, socialism and democracy*, 1942.

Selznick, P. 'Focusing organisational research on regulation', in R. Noll, (ed.), *Regulatory policy and the social sciences*, University of California Press: Berkeley, 1985, pp. 363–364.

Shiller, R. J., *Irrational exuberance*, Princeton University Press, 2000.

Smith, A., *The theory of moral sentiments*, 1759.

Smith, A., *The wealth of nations*, 1776.

Steare, R., 'Character, culture and conduct: why good people do bad things in a fear-driven culture', in *Transforming culture in financial services*, discussion paper DP18/2, 2018, pp. 66–67, <https://www.fca.org.uk>.

Stigter, M. & Cooper, C., *Boards that dare – how to future proof today's corporate boards*, Bloomsbury Business, 2018.

Stiroh, K., *Misconduct risk, culture, and supervision*, NY Federal Reserve Bank in *Transforming culture in financial services*, discussion paper DP18/2, 2018, pp. 51–52, <https://www.fca.org.uk>.

Strange, S., *Casino capitalism*, Blackwell: London, 1986.

Taleb, N. N., *Black swan: the impact of the highly improbable*, Random House: New York, 2007.

Taleb, N. N., *Skin in the game – hidden asymmetries in daily life*, Allen Lane: London, 2017.

Tepper, J. & Hearn, D., *The myth of capitalism: monopolies and the death of competition*, Wiley, 2018.

Weeks, J., *Unpopular culture – the ritual of complaint in a British bank*, University of Chicago Press: Chicago, 2004.

Volcker, P. A. with Harper, C., *Keeping at it: the quest for sound money and good government*, PublicAffairs, 2018.

Yoffie, D. B. & Kwak, M., *Judo strategy: turning your competitive strength to your advantage*, Harvard Business Press, 2002.

INDEX

accountability
   in banking 153
   banking executives 147–9, 197–8
   need for stepped change 307–9
   weakness at senior levels 48, 49
Agius, Marcus 48
Alibaba 98
Allco 193
Ant Financial 98
ANZ 45, 151, 194, 195, 225
   Breakout program 225
   culture 234–5, 317
   executives 315
   Smart Choice Super 41
ANZ New Zealand 69
apologies by banks 48–9, 308
Applegarth, Adam 140
Argus, Don 71, 135, 156, 224, 259, 261, 292, 316
ASX Corporate Governance Principles 259
Aussie Home Loans 91
Australian Bankers Association (ABA) 292
   'The Banks Belong to You' campaign 36–7

Australian Competition and Consumer Commission (ACCC) 9
Australian Financial Crisis (AFC) 292–5
Australian Prudential Regulation Authority (APRA) 9, 24, 42
   inquiry into irregular currency option trading at NAB 267–8
   inquiry into CBA (2018) xviii, xix, 42, 153, 196–7, 202, 229, 255, 256, 264–6
Australian Securities and Investment Commission (ASIC) 9, 51
averages, dangers of 81

balance sheet and market risk 188
bank bill swap rate (BBSW) 45
bank market share 59
Bank of England xxiii
Bank of Queensland 70
Bank of Scotland (HBOS) xxiii
bank profits 52
   as share of GDP 26–7
banker risk assessment test 324–34
banking
   dehumanisation 97, 162, 183–4

digital transformation 97–8
dramatic change since 1990s 11–12
essentials of good banking 288, 346
factors fuelling change 12–18
financialisation of 11, 13, 136
fundamentals of 4–8
industrialisation of 164–6, 319
narrow banking xxvi, 145, 296–8
retailisation of 164–6
Banking Act 2009 (UK) 297
Banking and Finance Ethics Panel 146–7
Banking and Finance Oath (BFO) 146–7, 149, 291
Banking Executive Accountability Regime (BEAR) 147–9, 198, 293, 308
banking industry
   case for change 53–4
   crisis of trust in 34–9
Banking Reform Act 2013 (UK) 297
banking system
   averages 81
   Basel 72–4
   brokers 90–2, 303
   challenger banks 100–1, 102
   FinTechs 96–9
   household debt 76–80
   mortgage lending 61–3
   neobanks 99–100, 101
   overview 57–8
   property as financial asset 85–6
   and real estate 86–9
   risk culture 81–5
   risk-weighted assets (RWAs) 64–6
   RWA determination 66, 67–71
   SME banking 92–5
   structural developments 59–61
banks
   importance of 1–2, 323
   as 'retail businesses' 3–4
   role in economy 5, 6
   similarity between 173

'success is toxic' trap 31–4, 294, 310
Bankwest 20, 292, 293
Barclays Bank 24, 46, 48, 49, 239
Barings Bank 14–15
Basel Committee on Banking Supervision (BCBS) 67–8, 72–4
   Basel II 16, 59, 63, 65, 73, 161
   Basel III 21, 65, 72
   Core principles for effective banking supervision 72
   corporate governance principles 262–3
Ben-Artzi, Eric 276
Bernanke, Ben 203–4
Big Bang (1987-2007) xxx–xxxi
big data 180
Bischoff, Win 192–3
'black swan' events 88, 211
'blink' instinct 167, 261
Board Audit Committee 210
Board Risk Committee 210
boards of directors 280
   accessibility 309–10
   banking experience of directors 283
   boardroom information crisis 256–7
   capabilities 261–4
   competing priorities 255–7
   compliance matters 259–60
   core responsibilities 272–3
   corporate governance 249–51
   culture 252–3
   digital expertise 284
   equity stake 279–80, 283
   evaluation of 280–4
   on executive remuneration 273–9
   guiding principles 271–2
   independence and courage of directors 282–3
   responsibilities 309–11
   role specification of directors 343–5
   seeing the big picture 257–61, 305–6

and social licence 253–5
   strategic thinking 258–61, 281
   workload 257–8
bonuses 141, 276–8
Bradley, Graham 112–13
British Bankers Association (BBA) 38–9
British Business Bank 116
brokers 90–2, 303
Brown, Gordon 117
Buffet, Warren 115, 270, 280, 285
business banking 58
Byres, Wayne 69, 144–5, 228, 275

Canadian banks 27
capital
   cost of 75–6
   importance of 23–7
Capital Asset Pricing Model (CAPM) 74, 75
capitalism
   ethical capitalism 127–8, 292
   flaws in 130
   monopoly capitalism 129
   relevance of model 122–3
casino capitalism 15
Centro 193–4
CEO remuneration. *see* executive remuneration
challenger banks 100–1, 102, 311–12
Chartered Institute of Bankers (Scotland) xxiv
Chartered Institute of Bankers (UK) 149
Christensen, Clayton 311
Chronican, Phil 309, 315
Cicutto, Frank 316
Citibank xxv, 155, 172
Citigroup 19, 33, 87–8, 125–6
Cloud Banking 101
Clyne, Cameron 13, 120–1, 155, 315
Coase, Ronald 101
collateral debt obligations (CDOs) 14, 15

Commonwealth Bank of Australia (CBA) xix, 32
   APRA inquiry into culture and governance xviii, xix, 42, 153, 196–7, 202, 229, 255, 256, 264–6
   fees 39–40
   insurance policies 42
   risk culture 196, 202, 208
   sales culture 141–2
   unethical and illegal practices 44–5, 46, 47, 151, 152
competition 49–52, 298–301
Competition in the Australian financial system (2018). *see* Productivity Commission report (2018)
compliance risk 189
Comyn, Matt 121, 230, 241
corporate governance 123. *see also* boards of directors
   Basel principles 262–3
corporate social responsibility (CSR) 107, 114, 127–8
credit default swaps (CDSs) 15
credit risk 188
credit risk culture, key principles 190–3
credit risk management 190
   Four C's of credit 138, 174–6, 179, 212–13
   principles of 335–9
cultural capital 223–4
cultural problems, remuneration 17–18
culture
   in banking 221–3
   board culture 252–3
   cultural problems 246–7
   employee opinion surveys 239–40
   evidence of problems 227–33
   gender diversity 237–8
   as management and board responsibility 232
   meaning of 223–6

Performance Evaluation Framework
  (PEF) 240–3
performance targets 243–4
problems with 48, 132, 222–3
sales culture 140–3
transforming 224–5, 233, 236–7,
  247–8
whistleblowers 245
cyber risk 189

Dahlsen, John 173
Davidson, Louise 277
dehumanisation of banking 97, 162, 183
Deloitte 36
derivative instruments 13–16
Deutsche Bank 24, 33, 104, 276
Dickson, Gordon 209
digitisation 97–8, 105, 180
Dimon, Jamie 225
directors. *see* boards of directors
Dodd-Frank Wall Street Reform and
  Consumer Protection Act 2010 (US)
  113, 297
Drucker, Peter 226, 280–1

economy, financialisation of 11–12
Edgar, Bob 315
Elliott, Shayne 60, 234, 315
employee opinion surveys 239–40
enforceable undertakings 46–7
Enron 2–3
environmental, social and governance
  (ESG) obligations 114
equity capital 188
ethical behaviour, core principles 150–5
ethical capitalism 127–8, 292
ethical leadership 234–7
executive remuneration 17, 22, 63, 67,
  117–18, 124, 273–9
executives, accountability 147–9

Fahour, Amed 13
fairness 151
fees
  income from 52
  for no service 39–40
finance industry 4
finance sector, role in economy 1–2
financial advice, inappropriate advice 40
Financial Conduct Authority (FCA) (UK)
  50
financial crises 295–6. *see also* global
  financial crisis (GFC)
financial services industry 2–3, 5
Financial Services Institute of Australasia
  (FINSIA) 149, 291
Financial Systems Inquiry (2014). *see*
  Murray Inquiry (2014)
financialisation xx–xxi, 11–12, 15, 136
Fink, Larry 114, 119
FinTechs 3, 96–9, 101, 311–12
Flint, Douglas 309
'founder centrism' 225–6
'four-pillars' xix, 50, 59, 109
Friedman, Milton 123, 124, 127, 128,
  129, 132, 294
Friedman Doctrine 29, 49, 123, 125, 126,
  128, 129, 132, 162, 219, 254, 294
Funke Kupper, Elmer 317

Garratt, Bob 252
gender diversity 237–8
General Electric (GE) 33
Gerstner, Lou 226, 248
Gittins, Ross 54
global financial crisis (GFC) 10, 18–23,
  24, 26, 35, 88–9, 200, 292–3, 307
globalisation 16–17
good banking, essentials of 346
Goodwin, Fred xxiv, 199, 224, 316
Greenspan, Alan 18–19, 306
Greenspan Doctrine 18, 116, 117

INDEX

'hard information' 174, 176, 177, 179, 183
Hart, Oliver 125
Hartzer, Brian 13, 301, 317
Harvey-Jones, John xxii, 126
HBOS xxii, xxiii, xxxii, 13, 19, 20, 38, 81, 89, 117, 138, 140–1, 143, 198–201, 203–4, 250–1
Henry, Ken 22, 47, 209
herding behaviour 60, 87, 199, 297
Hester, Stephen 48, 200
Higgins, Benny 138, 201, 232
Hodges, Graham 315
Hornby, Andy 13, 139, 140–1, 199, 201
Hornery, David 319
household debt 103–4
    and bank profits 84
    rise of 76–80
HSBC xxiii

ICI 126
illegal practices 44–9
industrialisation of banking 161–3, 319
instincts, and risk assessment 193–5
institutional memory, and risk culture 205–6
insurance policies 41–2, 43
integrity 150

Jensen, Michael 252
John Lewis Partnership 126
Joss, Bob 225, 248
JP Morgan Chase 225
judgement 152, 180, 305
Judo Bank 96, 100, 106, 118–19, 160, 177, 183, 212, 291, 296–7, 319

Kay, John xxvi, 11, 13, 30–1, 54, 85, 130–1, 162, 296, 299, 301, 308–9
Kelly, Gail 17
Keynes, John Maynard 30, 85, 87

King, Mervyn 211, 306
Kramer, Mark 125

Laker, John 22
leadership
    ethical leadership 234–7
    lack of accountability 228–9, 230
    role in addressing culture 226
Leeson, Nick 14–15
Lehman Brothers 201
'lemon' problem 6
'liar loans' 80, 83, 136, 152, 195, 290
lifelong learning 154
liquidity risk 21, 188
Livingston, Catherine 208–9, 265
Lloyds Bank London xxii–xxiii
loan losses 80
London Interbank Offered Rate (LIBOR) 45–6, 48
'loose lending' 8, 83, 290, 294, 306

macro-prudential policy 87, 105
management consultants 12–13
market failures xxi, 160, 181–2, 184–5, 289
market power, corrupting and anti-capitalism 27–31
Mayer, Colin 133
McFarlane, John 137, 155, 193–4, 225, 248, 287–8, 317
McPhee, Jamie 70–1
Metro Bank (UK) 68, 104
Minsky, Hyman 110, 204
monopolies 129–31, 289
monopoly capitalism 129
Moore, Paul 210
moral hazard risk 110–11, 201, 203, 215–16
Morgan, J. P. 174
Morse, Jeremy xxii–xxiii
mortgage backed securities (MBSs) 14, 15

357

mortgage lending, rise of 61–3
Murray, David xviii
Murray Inquiry (2014) xviii, 69–70, 73

Narev, Ian 13, 18, 47, 121, 202, 241, 316
narrow banking xxvi, 145, 296–8
National Australia Bank (NAB) xix, 32
    APRA inquiry into irregular currency option trading 267–8
    'Break-up' campaign 120–1
    Business Bank 231, 317
    corporate governance 266–9
    cultural problems 222–3, 224, 235, 255, 269, 316–17, 318–19
    disregard for law and regulators 42
    Enterprise Leadership Program (ELP) 155
    executive remuneration 274–5
    experience of executive team 315–16
    fees 39, 40
    insurance policies 41
    Introducer Program 40–1, 42, 195
    leadership profile 13
    market manipulation 45
    risk culture 197, 278
    unethical and illegal practices 47–8, 150, 151–2, 229
neobanks 3, 99–100, 101, 311–12
New Zealand. *see also* Reserve Bank of New Zealand (RBNZ)
    banking industry xix
    banking market xvii, 6, 9
    banking system 57
    economy 12
    regulation of banking 9
Nokia 31
non-bank lending sector 102–3
non-executive directors (NEDs) 249, 254–5
objectivity 151
'obliquity' 162

oligopolies xix, 7, 27, 30, 49, 50, 95, 289
Open Banking 100, 115–16, 293, 299
openness 151–2
operational risk 189
originate-warehouse-distribute (OWD) strategy 15

path dependence xx, 44, 137
Payment Protection Insurance (PPI) 43
Performance Evaluation Framework (PEF) 240–3
performance targets, corrupting nature of 243–4
personal banking 58
Pitman, Brian xxiii, 141, 292
Porter, Michael 125
Prince, Chuck 87
prisoner's dilemmas 60–1, 294
probity 151
product cross-selling 231–2
Productivity Commission report (2018) xviii, 1, 49–52, 129, 170, 298, 300
professional training 149–55
professionalism in banking
    decline of 135–6
    declining standards and accreditation 137–9
    executive accountability regime 147–9
    financialisation and 139–40
    meaning of 143–6
    professional training 149–55
    sales culture and 140–3
    and social licence 291–2
property, as a financial asset 85–6
public interest versus private interest 115–18
public policy, and regulation 289–91
public trust in banking industry 1
purpose of a firm 118–21, 127–8, 130–2

INDEX

RAMS 20
RBS. *see* Royal Bank of Scotland (RBS)
real estate, and banks 86–9
Reed, John 125–6, 172–2, 292
regulation
    importance of 8–10, 25–6, 288
    'light' or 'heavy touch' 307
    need for regulatory policy re-think 301–2
    public policy and 289–91
relationship banking, demise of 171–6, 183–4
remuneration. *see* executive remuneration
rent-seeking behaviour 127, 129, 294
reputation risk 189
Reserve Bank of New Zealand (RBNZ) 9, 69, 211–12
responsibility 152
retail banking 58
retailisation of banking 164–6
return on equity (ROE) 16, 24, 27, 76, 104
risk appetite statement (RAS) 191, 304
risk assessment
    banker risk assessment test 324–34
    big picture 203–5
    credit risk management 335–9
    SME banking 178–80
risk aversion 259
risk management 266
    alternative paradigm 212–13
    demise of 187–90
    Handelsbanken model 212–13
    'head, heart and gut' instincts 193–5
    institutional memory 205–6
    major risks 188–9
    paradox of 214–16
    principles of credit risk culture 190–3
    risk culture 81–5, 104–5, 195–203, 217–19, 303–5
    role of board 210
    RWAs and 211–12
    SME lending and 307
    Three Lines of Defence model xxxiii, 190, 200, 202, 203, 205, 206–9, 266, 304, 305
risk-weighted assets (RWAs) 16, 64–6
    determination of 66
    problems with determination of 67–71, 302
    and risk culture 211–12
Roosevelt, Teddy 113
Royal Bank of Scotland (RBS) xxiii, 24, 25, 33, 48, 89, 112, 200, 203–4, 250–1
Royal Commission into Misconduct in the Banking, Superannuation and Financial Services Industry (2019) xviii, xix, xx, 1, 39–49, 129, 151, 222–3, 293, 298
Rudd Labor government 22–3

sales culture 140–3, 231–2
Sands, Peter 13
scandals 46–9
second-tier banks 6
securitisation 16
securitisation market 14
self-managed superannuation funds (SMSF), debt financed property-based investment 85–6
'shadow banking' 102–3
shared value 125–6, 129
shareholder value 121–4, 129, 130–1, 132–3
SME Bank Trust Index 166
SME banking 92–5, 105, 319
    big data versus judgement 180
    craft of 166–71
    demise of relationship banking 171–6
    demise of SME banking skills 176–8
    industrialisation and 161–3
    retailisation and 164–6
    risk management 178–80

unmet credit demand 181–2, 300
SME lending 65–6, 93, 160, 307
SME sector 160
SME securitisation fund 184–5, 299
Smith, Adam xxiv, 19, 122, 123, 127–8, 129, 190, 301–2, 308
Smith, Mike 17, 315
social licence 1, 5, 35, 90
   boards of directors and 253–5
   concept of xxi, 107, 111–15
   professionalism and 291–2
   public interest versus private interest 115–18
   and purpose 118–21, 287
   relevance to banks 108–11
   and trust 120–1
social responsibility 123–4
'soft information' 174–5, 176, 177, 178, 183
St George Bank 20, 292, 293
State Bank of South Australia 23
State Bank of Victoria 23
Stevens, Glenn 22
Stewart, John 155
strategic risk 189
superannuation, sold by banks 41
Svenska Handelsbanken 178, 183, 212–13
Swan, Wayne 22

Taleb, Nassim Nicholas 88, 211, 219, 279
Taylor, Martin 187
technology risk 189
Thodey, Peter 155, 316
Thorburn, Andrew 121
Three Lines of Defence Risk Management and Assurance Model xxxiii, 190, 200, 202, 203, 206–9, 217–18, 266, 304, 305
   first line of defence 207
   framework 340–2
   second line of defence 207–8

third line of defence 208–9
TJF-EBC 194
training
   in-house programs 154–5
   professional training 149–50
transparency 151–2
trust
   crisis of 34–9, 135, 293–5
   culture and 221–2
   social licence and 120, 121
Turner, David 46
Turner, Jonathan Adair (Baron of Ecchinswell) 11, 24, 69, 79, 254
   household debt and 84

Ullmer, Michael 316
unethical and illegal practices 44–9, 150, 151–2, 229

Vickers report (UK) 296

Walker, David 49, 252, 260
Walker report (UK) 252, 260
Walter, Catherine 266–7
Weill, Sandy 125–6
Wells Fargo 17, 31–2, 36–7, 112, 213, 224–5, 230–1, 236–7, 269–71
Westpac 20, 42, 142, 225
whistleblowers 245
Wriston, Walter 187, 188

Zingales, Luigi 125